D1610829

Edinburgh Law and Society Series

Law, Writing, Meaning

An Essay in Legal Hermeneutics

PATRICK NERHOT

Translated by Ian Fraser

EDINBURGH UNIVERSITY PRESS

For Adrien and Emile

© Patrick Nerhot, 1992
First published in Italian as *Il diritto, lo scritto, il senso:
Saggio di ermeneutica giuridica,* by Corso Editore-Ferrara, 1992.

English edition published by
Edinburgh University Press Ltd
22 George Square, Edinburgh

Typeset in Linotron Plantin
by Koinonia Limited, Bury and
printed in Great Britain
by Redwood Press, Melksham, Wiltshire

A CIP record for this book is available from the British Library.
ISBN 0 7486 0391 3

Contents

1

Introduction

What is the law? How can it be recognised? Can it be recognised by a specific form of reasoning that cannot be reduced to any other type? Or ought we instead to identify it as simply a given object, as if 'the law' were an object 'always already there'? Would it, then, be something specific that reduces itself, identical to itself, down through the centuries? Would knowing it mean in some sort of way recognising it by, as it were, following its traces, which it would be sufficient to read, to describe, in terms of continuity, of novelty, of interrupted or rediscovered tradition? What all these various questions, which we meet up with in one way or another in every essay in the philosophy of law, are pointing clearly to is something that our era of technology, social technology, finds it hard to conceive of: namely that what we call 'the law' remains a set of knowledge that a society expresses at a particular point in its development, the various forms of which, and their modes of interaction, remain to be analysed. We do not know exactly what 'the law' consists of; neither the artifice of formalist definitions nor the theory of sources of law can manage to get rid of this mysterious dimension of law. The philosophy of law is the ever-renewed attempt to penetrate that mystery a little. That amounts to saying that while the questions may sometimes appear somewhat traditional, the answers that the philosophy of law leads to are much less so.

In this essay, we shall seek to take the difficult path leading to an approach towards law where law is seen not as something already given, something always already present, which is as it were offered to the interpreter (observer), who ultimately has nothing more to do than know the code for interpreting it. Thus, to those who think the law can be identified with the trace constituted by a code, or those writings in general – legislative, regulatory or other – which are taken as being 'the law' (this is undoubtedly the way the law itself posits the principle of law), we shall say that they are chasing chimaeras. It is not by declaring the manifestness of the law that we shall solve at a stroke, as if by waving a magic wand, the difficulties bound up with knowing it. All these approaches seeking to posit as obvious what law is proceed only by artifice; they all lay claim to the discovery of something that does not exist, by stubbornly insisting on taking as law what can at most be regarded as a pointer. 'The law' is something that does not exist. The first difficulty, then, consists in identifying what a particular society recognises as law, at a particular point in its history. Putting it another way, we may say that in order to know what a particular society calls 'law' at a particular time, we must refer to the discursive practice through which what is recognised as being law can be stated. That is the first point. The second difficulty for anyone seeking to understand what law is thus turns round this diverse, enormously diverse, knowledge that takes part in the operation of identifying and stating the law. What knowledge is involved? Does it come from a particular area of learned enquiry? Here the methodology is all the more complex because we do not know whether that knowledge is caught up in historical periodisations, which should, if that is the case, be specified.

It is quite clear that not all the problems that might give rise to the difficulties we have just mentioned can be dealt with in this work. All we have sought to do is sketch out some methodological principles, or at least if we have rejected some to have done so deliberately, and also to lay out a few landmarks for studies of epistemology and indicate a few principles of legal hermeneutics. Though our ambition has been clearly stated, namely to break with the tenacious tradition that sees 'the law' as something 'always already there' (thus taking up again what is undoubtedly the major assumption of legal dogmatics, fundamentally influenced as it is by the other great dogmatics of the West, namely religious dogmatics), we cannot arrive at that result through this essay alone. That is because the author may well have come up against his own limitations, but also, and more fundamentally, for theoretical reasons. To imagine that a piece of work can 'break' with a tradition, a previous conception, denotes a view of theoretical work that may be regarded as voluntarist. In order to clarify our thoughts, we should like to take as an example the concept of epistemological break. The idea of an epistemological break, even if it is quite clear that the concept will cover a quite different theoretical area depending on whether one refers for that purpose to Gaston Bachelard or to Michel Foucault, whether it is taken in a strict sense or not, is not in fact sheltered from this voluntarist obstacle. Without wishing in the setting of this foreword to develop a critical study of the concept, which is in any case one we have ourselves widely used, we should like at least to set ourselves off from the idea which it seems to imply, namely that of a before and an after in the way we know things. Certainly, the way our nuclear engineer, our molecular biologist, our cardiac surgeon, etc., knows things is a break with what physical, chemical or organic knowledge once was. But it should be noted that it is only once a process is finally complete that it is possible to speak of a break, that in other words this expression indicates little or nothing about the process of transformation itself. What the concept instead seems to indicate is that we can analyse only 'after the event', that our knowledge is retrospective. For this reason too, the concept came into being with an an idealist conception of 'rationalism'. Georges Canguilhem noted in connection with the concept of reflex in the nineteenth century[1] that 'here we are in the presence of a critical discovery that divides the history of a science into two periods, the one when conjectures accumulate and are juxtaposed, and the one in which experience and its interpretation is coordinated and integrated. But it is only in our days that this break appears clearly.' In our study, instead of speaking of a break, we have preferred to talk about a shift. Perhaps this expression is little more fortunate, if one intends in principle to avoid every idealist or voluntarist danger. It does, however, have one advantage in our eyes, namely that of indicating certain processes where mechanisms of transformation of meaning are at work.[2]

Developing this hypothesis that 'the law' does not exist in the sense of being given as an object, thereby lending itself passively to every kind of study, and thereby making a clean break with the works of legal dogmatics, however abstract they may sometimes be, our study in legal philosophy is primarily interested in reasoning by analogy. What better to lead to that idea of mystery we mentioned earlier in finding what law is than a study on analogy in legal reasoning? Reasoning by analogy, whether in general or in legal science, is a form of knowledge which translates, and that verb is certainly rather strong here, our mode of knowing and recognising things, even though we experience enormous difficulty in giving an account of this principle of analogy as such. However, whatever the difficulty we may experience in explaining the mechanism of analogy, how could our legal dogmatics operate if deprived of that tool? We shall, moreover, see that the attempt to understand this process compels us to bring together what should perhaps never have been sundered; we have in mind studies of an epistemological and a hermeneutic nature. For it is not at all certain that we would gain from denying every relationship between the approaches that attempt to identify the cognitive principle thanks to which a truth can be stated and those which analyse the mechanisms whereby 'the' meaning is extracted, whether of a phrase of some kind or of a piece of writing.

This procedure of analogy has, then, the interesting aspect that it enables the repetitive, unthought (unthinkable?) dimension of a form of knowledge to be located in the place of what nonetheless seems to be obvious, but at the same time setting the path to be followed in order, even if only a little, to raise the mystery surrounding our ways(s) of knowing and recognising things. Studying this procedure can accordingly lead us into thinking about the dogmatic knowledge which, within a corpus, brings together, on the basis of 'resemblance' (but what is resemblance?) or of likeness, things that *a priori* seem very dissimilar. Our thoughts on dogmatics will lead us to proposing a few hypotheses of legal hermeneutics. In doing so, we shall have finished with what we have recognised in hindsight to be the first part.

A quite different piece of work, in the objectives pursued, starts the second part. The hermeneutic question clearly has to lead us to start thinking about Western rationality, so that we come up against medieval exegesis, that great moment in knowledge where hermeneutics and epistemology were mingled (this may, and it is perhaps not its smallest merit, be very useful to those who may occasionally experience some difficulty in reading Foucault's *Words and Things*). In the second part, then, this study becomes much vaster, something for which we shall perhaps be reproached. For how can one claim to study so many things and such different things? Yet our hypothesis ineluctably led us thither. It would have been more negative to refuse the hurdle. In order to face it, we have had to put forward a number of hypothesis which are more or less original, like that of a 'premodern rationality of the Christian West'; we have also had to sketch out some definitions, for instance of the concept of history; and finally, we have had to convert ourselves, and this is something very delicate, into an interpreter of Scripture (discipline that is, alas, somewhat foreign to us). This transformation then condemned us to become interested in philology, which in turn led us to take an interest in certain of the natural sciences, and so on.

It is a long way round, without any doubt, but one of its objectives may perhaps be, more than to convince, to give the philosophy of law an image of diversity; all too infrequently, alas, seen in all the discourse on the 'normative' to which essays in the philosophy of law generally lead.

PART I

2

Logical formalism and analogical inference

Reasoning by analogy, or the type of reasoning traditionally presented as the one in which one moves from one object to another on the idea that there is 'something in common' between them, remains a fairly mysterious type of reasoning. We shall recall in this connection two definitions, from Cornu and Gény.

The former defines analogy as 'the resemblance of conformity of several things among themselves', which may appear to be a minimalist approach, and considers reason by analogy as 'a classic process of rational interpretation forming part of the exegetic method'.[3] The latter, traditionally presented as the decisive opponent of the French exegetic school, nevertheless locates the procedure of analogy at the very heart of what must according to it be a true science of law.[4] There is therefore a sense of mystery about a process of reasoning that is nevertheless common, since we very frequently establish a 'resemblance' between two different objects and use the more accessible of the two to make the other one more comprehensible. There is no need for surprise, then, if this concept has had a 'wretched reputation'[5] and has been regarded as a 'vague, soft, polymorphous, treacherous' concept'.[6] Bachelard and Canguilhem have shown how analogy could in certain cases become an 'epistemological obstacle'. Conversely, the 'analogical imagination', as Bachelard said, could play a constitutive role for a determinate science by helping to split up the area of investigation and suggest images that could each become concepts.[7] Analogy, accordingly, very clearly goes beyond the play of mere metaphors, and can act as an intermediary between already constituted disciplines and a newly constructed reality.[8]

What is the position in legal science? Let us first of all note that everything that has contributed to the lamentable reputation of that concept will be found again here. Through all the definitions proposed for it, it has to be said that it remains 'vague, polymorphous and treacherous'.

Legal analogy is ordinarily conceived on the basis of the notion of general principle of law, or in relation with it, in most work done this century. Thus, we find the question of legal analogy in a section dealing with the general principles of law and equity,[9] but barely sketched out in the turn of a phrase: 'Beyond particular situations, in a process related to the analogy frequently employed to resolve legal questions though going considerably beyond it in breadth, the judge often identifies, with the assistance of legal scholarship, a "spirit of the laws" which he regards as expressing the fundamental principles of the society of which he is a part.' Two elements emerge: analogy is a general principle with slight effects, and analogy is to be conceived of on the basis of the idea of a creative power of judges in the act of dispensing justice.

Analogy has something to do with 'government by judges, which might be not without danger, but is kept within reassuring limits if it confines itself to picking out the essential principles of existing legal organisation, to make these principles into the protectors of a working tool which may be very useful'.[10]

The 'creative power' of judges appears also in the writings of other authors who deal with analogy, but this time on the basis of a legal theory that relates to the idea of 'lacunae in law'. 'Reasoning by analogy' is in this case regarded as the procedure that 'extends the solution dictated by a text for one case to a similar case not provided for by the text, showing that the reason for applying the rule has the same force in both cases'.[11] This comes close to the nub of the mystery that reasoning by analogy carries within it; these theories of 'lacunae' in law contemplate the idea of identity in the form of a *ratio legis*. This conception is very widespread: it can be found in many authors throughout this century. G. Cornu's conception of the 'argument *a pari*'[12] gives us a good illustration: 'reasoning consisting in applying the rule dictated by a text to a case not provided for by the text, since by referring to the reason for the rule's existence (*ratio legis*), it becomes clear that there is better reason for applying the rule to the case not provided for than to the one provided for by the text'.

We may already note, with some interest, that these definitions offered to us of what reasoning by analogy is in legal science all fit the mould of a proposition which (even if only implicit is nonetheless prior), and related to the very definition of what law is. It might perhaps not be wrong in this context to say that the definition offered for this process itself expresses, indirectly, a general conception of law.

Either, for instance, we locate ourselves in an institutionalist perspective and say that, despite the theoretical imperatives of the principle of separation of powers, there is a need to recognise the real power of judges to create law, and the procedure of analogy – in what it has in common with the general principle of law – comes along to supply the proof. Or we locate ourselves in a more systemic view of law and say that, since it is condemned to have lacunae, the law has to forge its own tools to respond to any social needs there may be where 'the law is silent'. This initial statement is however very unsatisfactory, since these two views can, far from being mutually exclusive, be quite compatible with each other.

While the so-called 'exegetic method' (the legal culture dominant in France between 1830–40 and 1880), the idea of a creative power of the judge, is plainly inconceivable, the obligation to deal with a 'case not provided for' nevertheless exists. The technical characteristics of this movement from the 'known to the unknown' were conditioned by this *a priori* position that the judge has no creative power: he was to be regarded as having available a complete 'technical' arsenal (the 'Code') to solve any problem whatever. This brings us back to what Cornu says regarding texts which *themselves* give solutions in the event that legal provisions are absent (*ratio legis*). The incompatibility of the two views can therefore be maintained only on the basis of this hermeneutics; but it was very quickly questioned again (in its rigid form, it lasted barely forty years). The theory of 'lacunae' in law gradually came to prevail, through the identification of other hermeneutic models in which the power of judges was no longer denied, but *limited*. The big question was the nature and characteristic of these limits; and this is a question that we have still not gone beyond. The general problem – which can reconcile our two views – consists in making the principle of separation of powers as traditionally defined for over a century in French doctrine[13] and the principle of the judge's creative power compatible on the basis of a conception of the law as systemic, even though having lacunae.

This is how we must understand what J. Carbonnier says,[14] under the title 'analogy or analogical extension', to the effect that this is a process that is 'more than an interpretation' (and accordingly an explicit reference to a possible creative power of the judge), because the point is to 'extend the law to areas or cases that it has not provided for' (the explicit reference here being to the theory of law a system with lacunae). Thanks to the bibliographical references provided by him, and to the accompanying annotations, we can deduce the nature of this creative power. It claims to maintain intact the idea of the separation of powers and accordingly of the legislature as solely competent to really create law. Analogy is, Carbonnier says, a means 'that interpreters use to extend the law by *imitation*: from the case provided for by the text, the solution is extended to a case that is not provided for but is *similar*. Analogy is generally analysed as a rigorously logical mechanism'.[15] This creation is an 'imitation' of what the legislator has thought and intended; accordingly it is, if not completely passive, at least subject to the legislative power (imitation of the 'similar' case).

This imitation consists in going back to a 'similar' case, this similarity being secured through a rigorously logical approach. Authors refer to a logic that is not argumentative but deontic in nature (bibliographical reference to G.Kalinowski), which means that the interpreter will bring into operation the principles of formal logic – in other words of universal reason – from which all subjectivity is excluded. In this process of analogy, accordingly, the interpreter repeats what the legislator intended for certain cases, in the sense that this repetition, and this is not the least of the paradoxes, is based on what the legislator has never said, deontic logic being there to prevent any straying by the interpreter. We may note here, by the way, that there are two verbs in very strange opposition throughout these last two centuries in legal scholarship, whether in the common-law or civil-law traditions, when it comes to describing the work of the interpreter: invent and create. Initially synonyms (exegesis), these two terms came progressively to be differentiated, one of them being strictly forbidden in the dogmatic vocabulary for describing interpretation, namely to invent, as being too manifestly contradictory with the – mythical – theory of separation of powers,[16] and the other being accepted in very cautious fashion, as the perception of law as a systematic, complete whole came to be less and less defensible.

The first lesson, as we have already pointed out, is, then, that all thinking about analogy in legal science is inseparable from thinking about interpretation. The second lesson is that this thinking about interpretation must be concentrated on this question of creation, as doctrine has conceived it, and in relation to reasoning by analogy. As reasoning of a formal logical type, in making an analogy the interpreter would merely, as it were, have to let himself be guided by those – formal – rules governing the working-out of the identity.[17] Accordingly, this is the question with which we must begin our study, and our reference here will be the bibliography that Norberto Bobbio devoted to the subject.[18]

For Bobbio, it is beyond doubt that analogical inference must have a logical foundation, and only a logical one. Reasoning by analogy would accordingly be logical reasoning where 'formal logic will be more important than the teleological approach'.[19] Bobbio's study is, then, presented in two very distinct parts: one dealing with the logical aspect of analogy (formal logic), the other with analogical inference in legal science.[20]

Analogy in logic consists in linking two terms by a resemblance, with the predicate attributed to the first of them being then attributed to the second. This relationship of resemblance between the two terms leads to a conclusion. In what may this resemblance lie? Here there cannot be a trivial response. There is an analogy between two objects in virtue of *properties* they have *in common*, but these properties already belong to the theoretical order[21]: the examples of the analogy between the earth and the moon, between light and sound, in a classificatory system (cf. Aristotle) or in political rhetoric ('the father is to the son what the State is to the citizen') are examples which show this. Constructing an analogy in the form of logically rigorous reasoning requires the setting of the limits and extension of the 'relationship of resemblance' (which *a priori* risks leaving untouched the question of resemblance as such). This operation is done in two stages. First, one posits that reasoning by analogy, 'broken down into its simple elements', can be reduced to ordinary syllogistic reasoning'.[22] For this reason, the argument will not be regarded by the author as a special type of reasoning but only as 'a particular formulation that may cover any kind of reasoning whatever'.[23] Second, one states that 'between the (major and minor) premises there is always something implied' and that 'the validity of argument is also bound up with the validity of this general proposition'.[24] Bobbio would say that the proof of this can be found in the reality of our discourse through the use of rhetoric, 'where persuasion comes more from an example than from the rigour of a universal law'.[25]

However, this very idea of example, understood in the sense of '*model*', settles nothing, since here too it would be hard to give an exhaustive definition of the concept of model, given that we have many meanings for this term ,all very different. Stressing one particular sense of the term 'model' implies choices relating to the cognitive act that extend not merely to the meaning or the use of models in the sciences (natural or social) but to the very structure of scientific theories, to their explanatory capacity, to their relationships: in other words, with the phenomena they are intended to explain.[26] We can ,moreover, observe this throughout the author's own statements, where the need to discover an 'implied' universal proposition (without which no conclusion would be necessary) leads him to speak of the *validity* of reasoning by analogy, using theoretical elements taken from formal logic. Since, he says, the concept of resemblance is in itself indeterminate and indeterminable in abstract and absolute fashion, the concept must be regarded as relative and as setting its limits in terms of the 'given reference point'. In other words, for an argument from analogy to be valid, 'that is, necessarily conclusive', the relationship of resemblance has to be endowed with '*a definite meaning*'.

'Q is P. S is similar to Q. S is P. The something in common, M, by which Q and S are similar, is at the same time the sufficient reason for P and Q'.[27] *The sufficient reason* is, then, the definite meaning; it is the 'necessary and sufficient condition for the similarity to be a probative postulate'; it is the '*general law of validity* of argument by analogy'.[28] What Bobbio reproached analogical inference with was, according to him, its capacity to lead to arbitrariness, since 'the naked resemblance, while it may have a force of historical persuasion, does not by itself offer a rigour of argument until it has been taken in a sense in conformity with the law of validity'.[29] Analogical inference must, then, be an *argument of certainty*, once taken empirically in the form conforming with the law of validity.

It is, then, formal logic which, according to Norberto Bobbio, enables a certain result to be arrived at: Q is P *because* M; 'because' means: either a relationship of consequentiality (all M – type – are P – predicate) or a relationship of cause and effect (M causes P). The underlying argument in the first case is a piece of deductive reasoning, and in the second an empirical observation (that we observe that the cause of P is M). Let us nevertheless note that there is no *certain result* that follows from these two propositions. In the first case, the idea of resemblance is posited as obvious on the basis, we feel, of an analogical inference internal to the classificatory system.[30] M. Hesse[31] stated that in this type of analogical inference the horizontal relationship may be constituted by one or several resemblances in structures or functions, and each column may contain elements with *no obvious correspondence or resemblance.* The vertical relations in turn may be conceived simply as part of a whole, or be interpreted as causal relationships depending on some theory, or as an interrelation between a part determined either by an evolutionary origin or by an adaptation to the environment. Analogical inference may thus serve either to make predictions or to infer, for instance from the structure of a bird's skeleton, which we know, the missing parts of a fish skeleton. But the most important thing to clarify is once again the *nature of the analogical relationship (in our example, then, this would be a classificatory system expressing a certain state, a certain form of knowledge) before coming to consider the validity of the analogical inference as such.* Bobbio would seem not to have done this. In the second case, finally, the resemblance would be the result of an observational process, but we're told nothing about the actual act of observation.

Similarly, to continue this question of the certainty we are supposed to secure from purely formal logical argumentation, a mathematical proposition would not to any greater extent be the formal process of reasoning thanks to which an analogical inference in legal science might be regarded as certain. This might be an analogical inference of the type: a is to b as c is to d. By contrast with the mathematical proposition, we shall never be able to show the *transitivity* between three pairs of terms as follows:

$$\text{if } \frac{a}{b} \; : : \; \frac{c}{d} \text{ and } \frac{c}{d} \; : : \; \frac{e}{f} \text{ then } \frac{a}{b} \; : : \; \frac{e}{f}.$$

This is simply because the analogical inference is suggested by a criterion of resemblance, which amounts to positing once again the problems relating to relations of resemblance and causality, problems which, I repeat, have to do with the *nature* of the analogical relationship – constituted by mathematical reasoning itself, or in other fields constitutive – and not the validity of the analogical inference. We have seen (note 22) that the validity of an argument of this type was bound up with the validity of a general *implied* proposition. In Bobbio's conception, it is the notion of 'sufficient reason' that must be gone into further; this is the concept that seems to have to determine the nature of the analogical inference. We shall see that here too he does not seem to arrive at the result he hopes for.

'In order for predicate P to able to be transposed in formally valid and substantively certain fashion from situation Q to situation S, it is necessary for Q and S to be similar, not generically, but by having in common M, understood as the sufficient reason for Q and P'.[32] The relationship of resemblance is, accordingly, well expressed by the 'sufficient reason', through an argument of either deductive or inductive type. Deduction will take place where the particular situation provided for by the law that has to be extended to a similar case is understood not as an absolute binding value but as an *example* of a general proposition, i.e. as a *'species representing a genus'*.[33] Induction, for its part, takes place where the validity of the first proposition is based on the empirical finding of a necessary causal network (rather than on the cause of a principle), that is, that 'it refers to the cause of the representation the relevance of which to the case provided for is also noted'.[34]

The 'sufficient reason' is, then, this interpretive principle on the basis of which the continuous 'plot' of a legal order that sometimes appears fragmentary will be 'created' (i.e. *discovered*). Thus, the author says that the function of analogical argument in law consists in filling the lacunae of the positive order. 'The two forms of analogy considered hitherto can be regarded as the typical ways in which the *two typical lacunae* (our emphasis) of any legal order come to be filled: the subjective lacuna (resulting from inadequate legislative regulation) and the objective lacuna (resulting from the new formation of the relationship and of an institution).'[35] However, this 'rigorously logical', this seeing analogical inference as argumentation of formally binding certainty, leads, as the author advances in his ideas, to pushing ever further back the referent of resemblance, to avoiding, in some way, this question, thus leaving oddly disarmed anyone seeking to discover what makes a resemblance be accepted. It is rather as if one had come all this way to get back to the starting point.

In fact, analogical inference to fill a subjective lacuna means in the author's eyes that when the law does not exactly – or partially – express the whole of the doctrinal or case-law elaboration of law, 'thereby bringing about an imbalance between the legislative and the judicial order', then analogical extension is brought about on the basis of general principles set by the case law or worked out by doctrine.[36] Analogical reasoning then takes on the aspect of a deduction, drawing its initial impulse from a specific case governed by the law, *seen as an example*, but basing its validity on the general principles that form a common legal heritage.[37] When instead one has to deal with a new case ('produced by social situations that did not exist when the laws were laid down'), analogical extension proceeds inductively. Identical qualities between the 'new cases and the case regulated by law are noted, and this partial identity is exactly what constitutes the resemblance of the two terms destined to justify the extension. The fact that the resemblance does not refer to a common type is therefore not deducted but merely *noted, that is, inducted from comparative observation.*[38]

In the first case, the 'logical rigour' comes about in the form of a syllogism in which the 'general principle' will be the major premise: let us note, then, that the question of 'certainty' will relate to the inference of this general principle. In the second case, the logical rigour comes from the relationship between theory and observation. But in both cases, we derive the validity of the inference (which may be presented as an argument of formal logical type) from the nature of the analogical inference – which is the real problem. Moreover, the combination of theory and observation would seem today to raise more problems than it solves.[39] If we wish to stay close to a model used in *some* of the natural sciences, the problem will become that of the relation between what constitutes part of theory and what part of observation,[40] as we shall see below.

This long road pursued by Norberto Bobbio has accordingly brought us to the following point: in order for legal analogy to be perfect and the conclusion to be certain, it is necessary for the resemblance established between the case provided for by the legal provision and the one not provided for to consist in the fact that both cases have as common term of reference the 'sufficient reason' of the provision itself. What might the sufficient reason of a legal provision be? What is traditionally called the *ratio legis*, where the *ratio* is identified with the final cause, that is, the object of the law? For Bobbio, the *ratio legis* means the sufficient reason for the law, but this is to have a double sense (which we shall find again later in Betti). The sufficient reason for the law will be *either* the reason for its existence *or* the reason for its truth. Reason for existence means 'reason for existence of a fact', and is identified with the principle of causality. The reason for the truth of a proposition will be identified with the relationship of consequentiality underlying it. Thus, a legal norm will, according to the angle from which one looks at it, be conceived of either as 'a historical fact' the cause of which has to be sought, or as a judgement the basis of which has to be sought.[41]

Analogical deduction can accordingly be made in two ways. The search for the cause of a norm regarded as a historical fact will be done on the basis of the idea that the legal norm is a human fact regarded as a manifestation of intent (or expression of a thought). Accordingly, along with the efficient cause, there will be a final cause to be identified with the reason for the norm.[42] The search for the foundation of the norm will consist in understanding the norm as the consequence of a principle. The norm is no longer seen under the aspect of fact, but under the aspect of a judgement the justification for the truth of which has to be found.[43] *The norm as historical fact has an object; as judgement it has a foundation.* Faced with a situation not provided for, analogical inference may be effected by showing that the two situations have an *identical object* or that they have the *same foundation.*[44]

But once again, all these arguments Bobbio pursues only shift the problem of resemblance, push it further back, without ever approaching it directly. In the generality of cases, in fact, the reason for the law is not explicit; it has to be 'drawn' from a legal provision, and we are almost always faced with either the 'obscurity' or the multiplicity of the object.[45] As for the foundation for the truth of a norm, Bobbio thinks it may derive from a general principle regarded as a dogma by doctrine.[46] The certainty of the object and the validity of the foundation lie outside the argument from analogy; we may even say that they constitute the *presupposition* we do not know the reason for.

Perhaps we can after all find an answer to this question in Bobbio when he opposes the voluntarist conception of law in order to affirm a 'rationalist' conception.[47] The positive system contains a very specific rationality, which will be the foundation for the analogical inference. If the law is rational, and its rationality consists in correspondence with a historical requirement, this will apply in the area of its historical function, but there is no need to attribute to it, through a fiction, a different intent from the one it displays; the point is to draw from it, to extract from it, its 'intimate rationality'.[48] The foundation of the analogical inference will thus be the *'intimate* rationality' of a legal provision, and a hermeneutic will be its introspective technique. Once the foundation of analogy is set in the presumption of legal order and by reason of this presumption, one may then say that the interpreter, when he offers an analogical argument, does not emerge from the legal order but on the contrary remains with it, since ultimately he does no more than 'make the immanent rationality of the system explicit'.[49]

So defined, analogy is effected within stable limits, clearly defined; it departs from any activity of a creative nature. However, the proof remains uncertain, fixed to pillars about which one may have doubts whether they support anything at all. What is ultimately an 'immanent rationality' of law, itself conceived of as a system? How is this rationality recognised, how is it stated? Moreover, the fact that it is expressed through a historicism obliges us to ask about the way this history is constructed. All these questions are left in the dark by Bobbio, which does not however mean that they are not present, since in a certain sense he speaks about them, but only implicitly. All these categories are in fact not starting points for methodological reflection, but end points of an entirely political concern, a construction (reconstruction) on the basis of a historic present. The past (this is where history of law claims its place) is what illuminates the meaning of the present; it is like the foundation of a present position. We shall return to this question at length. Let us here content ourselves with giving the first clues to the plot.

The whole change in traditional systems of interpretation had to be made by way of analogy every time it was necessary to move beyond the scope of legislation, to change the – stuffy air of the codes, to fill up the gaps left by the legislative formulae. It was forgotten that this procedure was very old, and that the novelty consisted merely in assigning a fundamentally empirical meaning and value to it. With romanticism, analogy made a great leap forward, moving progressively away from interpretation of law, with which it has always remained bound previously in law, to end up becoming a synonym of legal creation.

'Analogy has become the typical expedient for remedying the short-comings of legislation, and the justification for all the revolutionary innovations. Analogy opened up the gates to arbitrariness, or at any rate masked the advent of the judges as lawmaker'.[50] Bobbio's essay, which started out intending to locate itself in a logical formalist tradition, thus ends up being shot through with historicism.

3

Legal dogmatics and the question of analogical inference

The conception of law (a system which aims at completeness) expressed by Norberto Bobbio in proposing a definition of legal analogy belongs to a Western legal culture summarised in two cognitive principles that frame the contemporary history of legal practices. The first is the 'rationality of the body of laws', the second is that the 'body of laws' is organised into a 'system'.

The codifiers, whether French or Prussian,[51] could not of course do without these two principles, symbolised by the Code. But if we take an author like Savigny, the master of what is known as the German historical school, who did not really have the conception of law of the French codifiers and clearly not the same conception of 'sources' of law either, the law is seen by him too as a unitary, complete system.[52] The principle of limiting the power of judges implies a legal hermeneutics where the idea of law as forming a system and the idea of law as being complete become two major interpretive arguments. We have never truly emerged from this culture.[53]

The idea of systematicity[54] haunts will work in legal scholarship. The 'history of law' is the history of the point of *origin* of this systematicity, regarded as the point of origin for the modernity of law. With P. Mortari, for instance, we learn that 'the idea of a legislative order as a set of norms linked by logico-juridical relationships was that of the positive, coherent, unitary order ... of the glossators; the thought of the glossators, regarding an internal harmony among the norms constituting the *corpus iuris*, was extended to the whole area of positive law'.[55] G. Lazzaro took up this idea in turn, putting forward the hypothesis that 'at the origin of this idea of coherence and internal harmony among the rules of law, we find the glossators' respect for the *corpus iuris*'.[56] At bottom, the idea of a code as being always already present in any rational legal system makes itself necessary, and is affirmed through one major argument: the unique authority of a source. We may very well continue to cite Lazzaro in his history of law. The origin of a systematic, complete law would accordingly lie in the time of the glossators. The next important historical stage, again for him, comes with the nineteenth century when 'with Savigny we find something more; with the glossators, the idea of coherence referred to the coherence of the goals pursued by the legislator. Now,' the systematicity and coherence of every order comes from the fact that any law whatever is perceived not only as a set of separate rules but as a living organism reflected in the rules.'[57] The retrodictive movement accomplished by Lazzaro moves from a present to reconstruct the truth of a past that gives the understanding of the present, seeking to impose the fixed idea that 'all law by definition constitutes a system',[58] the intimate operations of which are evidently to be brought out.[59]

Let us now turn to an author like Gény, the founder of the 'school of free academic research'; we find the same interpretive principles, even though this author was not, properly speaking, affiliated with the systematising movements. For Gény, the German doctrinal tradition was to be the true way of finally emerging from the interpretive traditions imposed by the school of exegesis. The 'Begriff' was to be central to his approach[60] since, without it, 'the concepts, words, formulas, definitions, divisions or classifications in law would remain deprived of any serious fruitfulness without the judgements in the philosophical sense of the term) and arguments which alone give them their value'.[61]

The arguments will sometimes consist of *inductions*: the principles governing these arguments come from reality itself. Inductions are treated by this author as essential for proving the facts brought before law – but only for that. Otherwise, argument is to consist of *deduction*: the 'jurisconsult' starts from principles (precepts) which he has to develop, the deduction of which (interpretation of these precepts with the aid of general concepts or determination of the facts to be brought under them for decision) appears as the normal procedure.

Setting the Begriff (induction/deduction) at the core of law, however, called for a number of requirements; here we once again find our two cognitive principles, albeit in a particularly idealistic form. The legal construction appears in Gény as an 'effort of thought', dealing with the scattered, isolated material offered by the legal roles recognised either by a formal act of the authority or as a result of independent research in order 'by wise use and adroit handling of concepts, definitions, classifications and arguments to erect a *complete whole* which constrains the institution to decide in logical terms …'.[62]

This approach perhaps allows us, moreover, to understand on the one hand why, contrary to what G. Cornu believes,[63] analogical inference cannot be only a method of argument specific to exegesis, just as it perhaps allows us to understand on the other hand why we are going to find this type of argument in any method whatever. Gény no doubt gives the reason when he considers that 'the division of concepts often comes about in the exposition of law, in order to extend and complete a principal definition by dismembering its object and thus preparing for its methodical development through subordinate definitions. This operation does not assume a truly rational and logical character, does not properly become a classification, unless it starts from the objects themselves which it aims to group according to their common characteristics.'[64]

A systematic law, it clearly emerges from what this author says, places analogical inference *At the very centre of its possibility of existence*, and if the exegetic method, like the method of free academic research, is shot through by utilisation of analogical inference, this is because both methods have something in common, revealed by these two principles we have just mentioned. Analogical inference is, then, a reasoning procedure which is for Gény absolutely central[65]; it is the link between the 'given' and the 'construct', between 'the science' and 'the technique'.[66] Thus, systemism, exegesis and free academic research give major importance to analogy, and this will be still more the case with 'legal hermeneutics' as developed by Betti.[67]

In this work 'Interpretaxione della legge e degli atti giuridici', Betti considers that analogy[68] represents the situation of a very specific problem: that of 'providing for the integration of the legal order through itself, by *assuming an intrinsic coherence* of the system.'[69] The function of analogy consists, then, in the self-integration the legal order, in order to eliminate the inevitable loopholes in legal rulings. The legal order, for Betti, 'constitutes an organic unity, a totality coherent in itself',[70] and the task of case law is to reconstruct the system with the means suggested by juridical experience and with the conceptual tools of dogmatics. This is where the procedure of analogy comes in as the means of self-integration of the system.

Moreover, if the role of interpretation is to 'understand the norm in its intimate coherence', then 'proceeding by analogy is unfailingly, interpretation in normative terms … constituting the necessary method to re-extract the maxims for decision that lead to self-integration of the legal order.'[71] The author goes on to base himself on Bobbio's work published in 1938 and to take up again the ideas of *ratio legis*,[72] of the norm as principle of judgement and as historical fact, ideas on which we must dwell for a few moments. Let us briefly recall Bobbio's position.

For analogical reasoning, two terms linked by a relationship of resemblance must lead to a conclusion. But what is absolutely necessary is for this argument to give an absolute guarantee of certainty.[73] These two conditions, as we have seen, are realised through the *ratio legis*, or 'sufficient reason' of law, which may be understood as either reason for its existence or reason for its truth; in the first case we have to do with the principle of causality and in the second with a consequential relationship of foundation. The legal norm is accordingly either a historical fact (the cause of which is the reason for its existence) or a judgement (the foundation for which is the reason for its truth). That it is a historical fact amounts to saying that the reason for its existence will be entered in its grounds (the norm 'in its historical sense' being nothing other here than a manifestation of intent), knowledge of which will be the result of a teleological interpretation; if it is a judgement, the question arises of its foundation, which refers back to the idea of 'general principle' held as a dogma by doctrine.[74]

Analogy, then, sees two pathways opening up before it: either the search for the grounds, or the justification for the foundation. As for the certainty of reasoning, it will depend on the degree of acceptability of the existence and value of the sufficient reason (existence of grounds, value of the foundation), which amounts to saying – as we have already said – that they are *outside* legal reasoning (and, once again, reducing analogical inference to a merely formal process is insufficient),[75] that they constitute its very prerequisites. We have seen how the author sought to resolve this problem: by positing the law as an act of will (historically given), that is, as a rational act, the rationality of which consists in its correspondence with a 'historical requirement'. The foundation for the analogy will be this intimate rationality of law, interpretation consisting in the explicit extraction of the rationality of the system. That is the point we had reached, and the question for us consisted in asking what the ways were to reach this rationality. This is the problem that Betti was to face.

Betti first of all considered the historical fact as an instrument preordained for a normative end (the notion of finality of the norm) and the judgement as the 'present expression of a perpetual requirement which is incorporated in an ordered whole and calls for compliance'. The *ratio* is given by a 'present foundation which may be either logical (if the norm is represented in the form of a logical judgement) or axiological in connection with a criterion to be applied (if the norm is represented in the form of a comparative evaluation of interests in conflict or as protecting a social function of higher grade).'[76] In this second case, the *ratio* is the conformity of the norm with 'the socially determined historical requirements, evaluated by the legal order in question, *in accordance with its intrinsic logic and its coherence'.* That the *ratio* is recognised on the basis of reflection on the foundation of the norm is conceivable, and that logic be the form through which this reflection takes place is equally so, but that logic as such should reflect what has been called the *ratio* of a legal rule is something rather less obvious.

We have in any case seen how the argument from logic did not enable Bobbio to secure what he wanted absolutely. There remains, then the argument from the axiological foundation for determining the *ratio* of a legal rule; does Betti get us further with this argument that Bobbio had done? For the latter, the foundation of analogical inference lay in the intimate rationality of the legal provision at issue, an intimate rationality which *corresponded* with a 'historical requirement', which led us to say that the 'history' which initially was to appear only in secondary fashion behind the thick curtain of logical formalism reappeared *de facto* in the foreground to occupy the leading role. Be that as it may, the author left us with the problem of this 'correspondence' between the spirit, we might say, of a legal provision and a 'historical requirement'. What does Betti have to say about this? That the *ratio corresponds* to conformity with the norm, to 'social requirements as historically determined'. We do not make progress from this viewpoint, but Betti seeks to set up another angle of approach in order to tackle the question. In him, the idea of the 'completeness' of law regarded as a system finally disappears, being replaced by the term coherence, a term which redefines the principle, still active here again, of the systematicity of law; the second principle, that of the rationality of the body of laws, remains untouched.[77]

Despite this new angle, Betti's hermeneutic approach nevertheless includes a number of traditional positivist methodological elements. For instance, the idea of 'correspondence' we have just mentioned, far from bringing in thinking on the notion of historical 'requirement', is simply reduced to a question of assessing elements that constitute a situation of fact. 'If it emerges from a comparison between the regulated and non-regulated facts of a case that in both the elements of fact particularly decisive for settling the legal case are substantially identical, it may then be concluded that the two situations of fact are similar, or analogous, and that for each of them there is equality of *ratio iuris*, or reason for equal legal treatment.'[78] There is no use coming back to this distinction between law and fact which, far from expressing the relationship between social world, understood as a 'datum', knowledge of which is supposed to be immediate and direct ('the facts') and the world of law which, on contact with our world, acts or reacts, is nothing other than a method of elaboration/construction[79] of the real, a method which ultimately consists in *giving meaning to the legal statement* in question. No break may therefore be seen between an 'independent' reality which comes along to 'rouse' the law, and 'the law'; what has to be understood is that we create reality by stating what the law is.[80]

We will not find a hermeneutic argument of this type in Betti. There, legal interpretation is perceived 'in normative terms'. The interpretation that interests to law, according to him, is an activity aimed at recognising and reconstructing the meaning to be attributed, within the limits of a legal order, to representative forms, 'sources of legal evaluations or of which such evaluations constitute the object'.[81] The sources of legal evaluations are legal norms, along with the precepts subordinate to them, in force because of a normative competence. For Betti, in other words, interpreting consists for the legal sciences in *keeping the needs of a system always in mind* and retaining the efficiency in the life of a society of norms, precepts and normative evaluations aimed at regulating it and acting as guidelines for it.

Interpretation in normative terms, then, would also mean for this author that the interpreter's act is not merely cognitive; the legal interpreter has practical objectives in mind. The interpretive act is not the reproduction of a will but *an enquiry into the interests at stake*. Betti derives two differences from this between normative and cognitive methods: 'as long as the interpretation of pure expressions – works of art or of thought – aims at reconstructing, in aesthetic or logical value, the intuition of thought underlying its artistic or theoretical expression – as historical interpretation of documents or behaviour aims at bringing out meaning *in itself* (our emphasis understood in its autonomy and ordinary coherence – the interpretation that interests law cannot be satisfied with theoretical knowledge, but must go beyond it both to render the precept acceptable to life, assimilable by it, and to subject the fact to juridical diagnosis.'[82]

For Betti, then, in the presence of acts 'regulated by law', one should, starting from the statement made or the behaviour engaged in, find the meaning it has in the social world and 'integrate into it the case in point' (factual situation') by comparing it with the situation of legal fact.[83] But what the author conceals, or analyses poorly, in saying this is that all factual knowledge has a normative source and that while ideally one might imagine two types of situation – one 'proceeding' from the social world, the other from the 'norm' – in practice this separation can never be achieved, since any factual situation can manifestly not be worked up into a 'case in point' except by using tools which are *already* legal. The very 'formalist' view which Betti had of law prevented him, in our view, from identifying the theoretical mechanism that operates in the act of stating the law.[84]

The interpretive act need not be seen as a 'confrontation' between a social situation and a legal situation, supposedly that of the legal norm. The world of law does not exist as such, as 'posited' side-by-side with the social world. Stating the law, once again, is constructing reality; it is unthinkable to have in the raw state, i.e. completely separate in the interpretive act, on the one hand a 'specific fact of a case' and on the other a 'legal fact', in which the first is to 'enter in', or to find the 'relevant features'[85] for a legal treatment, for the quite obvious reason that these 'relevant legal features' are nothing other than a reality affirmed by the person with the competence to do so. And what else could they be, anyway?[86]

Thus, after the logical and formal argument which has on the one hand brought us to the historicism of legal method and on the other led us to treating the interpretive act as the essential preliminary to analogical argument in law, we must go on to consider the question of cognition of reality by legal knowledge. Perhaps we shall in doing so advance along the path to understanding, at least in part, this mystery that pertains to analogical inference in the legal environment.

4

The meaning of a written provision and the question of historicism

Thinking about the elaboration of reality by all these materials that make up what is known as 'law' requires, in particular when it comes to the problem of interpretation, some thought about the notion of time that operates in legal reasoning. The distinction drawn by Betti between cognitive interpretation and normative interpretation was, as we know, rejected at the time by H.G. Gadamer because the attribution of meaning to a legal text and its application to a specific case constitute a single process: the meaning of the law attested in its normative application does not differ in principle from the meaning of the thing asserted in understanding a text.[87] Developing Gadamer's arguments, we have not only concluded that historical and legal hermeneutics can be identified with each other,[88] but have also put forward the hypothesis of *identical methodology* as regards the statement itself, a truth belonging to the past, for both the historical and legal sciences[89] a hypothesis we shall now go into further.

We have seen that for Bobbio and Betti, the legal norm could be *either a historical fact* or a judgment, and that according to the approach chosen, the actual understanding of the norm varied. As a historical fact, a norm was understood in the way any historical event was understood.[90] As a judgement, it was a present of which the foundation had to be sought, and this was ahistorical: 'the present expression of a perpetual experience', said Betti. This distinction seems to us not very pertinent: the legal statement is in fact not either a historical event or a judgement, but, if we wish to keep to this terminology, always both at once. The real question, in our view, is how such and such a rule in the past led to such and such a judgement, or what a judgement reflects at the present moment. Both formulations correspond to the same epistemological problem: actualising a text, in fact, understanding and interpreting it, consists, in our view, in knowing and recognising an 'acceptable' meaning for this text. But in this act, we consider that the jurist's present is inseparable from his past, that his present is also his history.

Accordingly, we must conceive of 'the historic' as a constituent part of law, and not only as was traditionally done, i.e. by accepting the idea that 'the' law is 'historically dated', full stop, without seeking to draw the consequences,[91] but by introducing this historical dimension into the actual act of stating the law.

Let us note that some work has already sought to take this path. For instance, this historical dimension also runs through the work of F. Ewald,[92] who shows that the criteria on the basis of which we speak about law, or do not, fall exclusively within the area of history.[93] The criteria of juridicity, the ways of identifying the law, legal practices, what Ewald calls 'juridical experience', cannot *a priori* define what law is, what are the practices that must be termed such, since this depends on what is though of as being law in the context of a certain juridical experience. For this author, legal experience comes from considering the process of judgement. This means that the legal rule takes its meaning from, through, the rule of judgement; thus, while law can certainly not be reduced to statute (to repeating an article from a code, for instance), this is certainly not for the reasons traditionally adduced on the basis of the question of the sources of law. Judgement is possible at a given moment, in a given society: it expresses a rule which is that by which conduct is judged. What Ewald calls the rule of judgement is the rule commented on, analysed, systematised, by legal doctrine, but cannot be reduced to it. It is never 'formulable as such, but only through a series of successive approximations which, at the same time as they contemplate and grasp it, transform it'.[94]

This rule of judgement, this interpretive principle we might say, is profoundly historical, unformulable as such. It is what Dworkin seeks to identify when he speaks of *principle* on the one hand and *continuum* on the other (Law's Empire). Here too, the past is part of the jurist's daily bread, except that for us this continuum is not related to this work of writers working on the *same novel* (jusnaturalism). If the past is inevitably part of the jurist's daily task, it is as *rewriting* on the basis of the 'present meaning' (meaning *of* the present). If we wish to keep Dworkin's image of the judge/novelist, then we have to say that our novelist does not sit before a blank page to continue what has already been written before him, discovering (stating) these principles, whether visible or hidden, expressing a continuity (or immanence); our novelist can only write a past in order to state his present (the novelist has not one blank page in front of him, but thousands of bescribbled pages, and it matters to him to know which he is to choose, that is, what meaning he is to give to them).

The interpretation of his present, understood as the expression of a principle whether visible or hidden, is the constructive understanding of a past. The statement of a present cannot be made without evoking a past.

This means that in order for Western law to be able to exhort, it was necessary for the category later to be called modern history to exist. 'Modern history' was to be constituted through legal practices: our law needs the idea of history, if a past that creates meaning. Thus, this jurist's present is first and foremost a history, that whereby meaning is elaborated.

Law is stated on the basis of the construction-reconstruction of a set of social experiences which are so many constitutive elements of law, but whose nature remains in a sense always fugitive, in process of becoming, and cannot be recognised until after the event.

Thus, only the positive practice of legal experience enables us to identify the statements recognised as 'the law' in this sense, the method that we recognise for locating constitutive elements of legal experience is positive.

Ipso facto, no doubt, we reject the category of natural law, but perhaps not as ordinarily understood when at the same time the thesis of 'positive law' is advocated. By rejecting the category of natural law, in fact, we do not mean to embrace the thesis of the 'being-in-itself' of positive law, as an expression of a law which denies all foundation outside itself. Neither the positivist theories of the absence of lacunae in law, nor theories of lacunae, are acceptable to us since they both presuppose law as being always already there, always already constituted. They give form to an object whose unity or absence of unity it is claimed to define, in a visible, horizontal coherence which brings together the different juridical terms that exist.

But having said this, we do not consider either that the 'meaning' of law transcends propositions indicated as 'positive law'. By contrast, moreover, with what Hruschka thinks,[95] the positivist thesis does not condemn one to think that the meaning is immanent in the legal act or inherent in it, so that legal propositions would be understood either as a totality of meaning or else as a potentiality of meaning, as vehicles for transmitting relevant meaning. This is undoubtedly, for the reason mentioned above when we cited Ewald, the idea that the meaning of a proposition emerges from legal experience, but also from a 'rule of judgement', if we wish to keep his terminology.

Accepting the positive thesis indubitably means riddling oneself of any traditional or contemporary naturalist idea ('Natur der Sachen'), but with the essential clarification that this positivist order is not immediately given to us, that it is just as much to be constructed as to be found. We have already said that this operation was a historicism. We do not, then, consider that the proposition has an immanent or intrinsic meaning; we say that the determination of the meaning comes about through a process of interpretation of the present, bound up with reconstruction of a past.

While the term 'positive law' (*ius positivum*) was familiar in medieval doctrine, what it indicated was a theory of sources of law, that is, of law as coming from a particular *authority*, a conception that we also find in the modern period (whether the conceptions be 'formalist' or not; we shall shortly be coming back to this point). For our part, when we refer to 'positivism' in recognising legal practices, we do not mean that certain authorities (legally defined) define or determine law, but that particular social experience elaborates what we recognise as law, through (*historical*) *interpretive principles*. The meaning of a text is not a factual or quasi-factual quality of that text,[96] contrary to what is held by the formalists. Putting it differently, the principle of law is not determined in autonomous fashion by the legal texts themselves; the texts, or various legal statements, must instead become the expression of the principle(s) of law which, by definition, is (are) not enclosed within these various texts or acts. This means that legal experiences are not characterised by privileged objects, but by the way in which they *constitute* those objects. In this sense, the law is an interpretive act, and one cannot, at any time whatever, speak about just anything at all! What is called 'history of law' does not have as its chief interest that of teaching us what the law once was, but has in our view the essential merit of telling us how, today, a particular society reflects on itself, understands itself, analyses itself.

Reversing Hruschka,[97] we say that the principle of law is not extrapositive, no more than there exists a 'thing which is law'. Legal hermeneutics is not, in other words, a legal ontology, and by legal hermeneutics it is not (by contrast with what Hruschka believes) the 'law as a thing' that is objectivised, which would be 'the point where a legal text and understanding of that text coincide, the point that would be thought of as objective, i.e. located beyond the text and beyond thought'.[98] The principle of law through which the jurist's present (otherwise called meaning) is elaborated is always to be discovered, which for us means to be constructed. The law is more than the *result* of reasoning of a particular type; it is the whole of such reasoning, that is, all those processes through which a meaning is established. The result is valid only in this reasoning, and cannot in any way express law by itself.

Having established this principle, we must invert the traditional conception we have of legal texts. This is that texts are basically oriented towards future human behaviour ('here is what you must do'), whereas in our view the texts ultimately amount only to saying 'here is how, on the basis of what provisions, you will be judged'. This is neither a retrospective vision of pre-existing, immovable data from the past seen as emerging from legal texts, nor a revelation – 'an anticipatory prospect of the possibilities of practice'[99] – but a retrodiction, that is, *the construction of a past on the basis of a present*. The past takes on meaning only on the basis of an enunciatory strategy of the present, (the famous 'principle' of the 'rule of judgement'), *but the latter can claim to be known or recognised only through this elaboration of the past.* Neither the traditional subjective doctrines prescribing that the person judging should proceed essentially like a historian seeking for the historical background of the law to be interpreted, taking into account, alongside the conscious motives of the legislator, the 'unconscious assumptions', nor the traditional objective doctrines claiming to insert the meaning and scope of law valid 'today' into legal questions debated at a given moment, perceive the problems raised by the principle of law, being incapable of integrating the historical aspect into their own approach. In fact, they take history as an approach foreign to theirs, that is, they do not in any way seek to draw the consequences *for their methodology* of this obvious truth that their subjects are above all historical subjects. It is one thing to say that a legal rule 'depends on history'; it is quite another to integrate that historicism into the very definition given of that rule on the one hand and into its interpretation on the other.

Understanding the elaboration of the meaning of a rule as the construction of a past and the working-out of that past on the basis of this enunciatory strategy, which the attempt to interpret the present is, does not mean rediscovering a vicious circle, if in order to understand that elaboration we keep in mind what we said about the legal rule (in historical science one would be talking about a 'document').[100] We said at the outset that the meaning attributed to a rule was linked to the meaning attributed to 'facts', that is, to the mechanism for establishing reality itself. We went on to say that this mechanism, which did not operate on the basis of the distinction 'world of law/social world', was the process whereby we constructed history (which then goes on to work out the plot of history, with this consideration we are offered by the – historical – principle of law). These two hermeneutic principles allow us to put forward the idea that a legal rule, rather than appearing as a directly accessible, immediately available 'datum', must instead appear as a correlate of certain practices.

It is 'legal experience' (Ewald) that gives rise to what one recognises to be law; not the contrary. Taking as an example the well-known article in the French Civil code on property (movable or immovable), the dominant methodological trend will be to consider that these articles, which have been the basis for diverse, to say the least, case law, have gone through an 'evolution' in that case law. Translating these phenomena in this way already points to the idea of '*a*' law of property, an object which is directly available and systematisable. This statement, the expression of an implicit interpretive method, conceals the heterogeneous nature of the social practices that have developed what jurors recognise as being law. This methodological point has been very well brought out by Veyne,[101] in saying that 'things' are merely objectivisations of particular practices 'the determinations of which have to be brought out, since the conscious mind does not conceive them'. The object is in other words explained by what has been going on at each moment in history, and 'we are wrong to imagine that what is going on, practice, is explained on the basis of what has been done ... The whole trouble comes from our "reifying" the objectivisations into a natural object: we take the outcome for a goal.'[102]

Instead of taking the problem by its true centre – practice – we start from the extremity – the object – in such a way that the successive practice seems to be reactions to one and the same object, 'material' or rational, supposed to be given *a priori*. To paraphrase Veyne, where he speaks of Foucalt's madness,[103] we would say that property does exist, but not as the object 'property'. A practice must be objectivised as 'having to do with property' in order for the prediscursive referent to appear retrospectively as a property matter.[104] Instead of conceiving 'property' as a given object which, as such, has its own evolutionary history and governs practices as such, it is methodologically preferable to conceive of this legal category through its operation of interpretation (elaboration of reality – meaning of a rule), just like any legal act whatever. The history of a concept is not that of its 'progressive refinement, continually growing rationality, its gradient of abstraction, but instead the history of its various fields of constitution and of validity'.[105] Let us now rapidly set forth what is to be the topic of our further considerations.

5

The question of reality and truth in historical and legal sciences

Chronological reconstruction[106] on the one hand elaborated this fiction of a linearity which on the other hand claims to be worthy of reality, and M. de Certeau would consider that modern western history starts with the difference and the break between present and past.[107] This consideration, however stimulating, nevertheless left in darkness the most important point, namely that it was *modern Western law that had the need to create this category of the past in order to state its present*. Before this 'break' was an act necessary to the method of modern history, it was necessary to the method of law.

Through what he calls a 'history of truth', Foucault[108] indicates this phenomenon very well. Enquiry, as it appears as a procedure, is a typical form for the cognition of truth in our society. It appears in political, administrative and legal practice and, from the twelfth century onwards, begins to prevail as the way of seeking truth within the legal order.[109] The enquiry, which appears for the first time in Greece, re-emerges in the eleventh and twelfth centuries in the West; old practices of ordeal were transformed, and certain forms of justice were rediscovered.[110] At the time, this amounted to a *new mode of knowledge*, a rationality in the West that was premodern and Christian.

Justice, as from that period, starts to operate as a power external to the parties at dispute, and to belong to the sovereign.[111] The proof of any act is established by enquiry[112]: persons are brought together who can guarantee that they have seen, that they know, something. It must be established that something *actually* took place; a past must be made a reality. This is the act whereby henceforth law will be stated.[113] The reason why this new way of knowledge came to prevail was that Church organisation ordered the whole of European intellectual life as from the twelfth century. The Church set up the educational frameworks that allowed young people to be trained for the life of the Church, but also for ministering to the needs of the body (medicine) and for administering justice (canon law, civil law). 'Along with the training of lawyers, the presence of clerics in the civil courts (not to mention the ecclesiastical jurisdictions) assured the Church of control over regulations adopted by the judicial apparatus.'[114] It is to this extent that we may say that on the eve of the sixteenth century, in many European states, the clergy was organically linked with the apparatus that did not cease to increase its hold over men and groups: the Monarchy.[115]

The enquiry develops as the *general form of knowledge* in which the 'Renaissance' was to find its place, and the ordeal, the test, tended to disappear from the legal sphere, just as from other spheres of knowledge.[116] The enquiry in Western culture came to be a way of authenticating truth, of 'acquiring things that were to be regarded as true', in other words of making history.[117] Bloch saw the year 1681 – publication of Dom Mabillon's *De Diplomatica* – as 'a great date in the truth of the human spirit', since it was then that criticism of archival documents was finally established. For G. Bourdé and H. Martin,[118] 'the origins of the methodological school of professional historians, often called "positivist", can be illuminated more by turning towards the erudites of the 1700s than by studying the writings of Auguste Comte'. This was the methodological school that inherited 'procedures of textual criticism and the practice of methodical doubt in the examination of evidence';[119] that is, in our view, *this method of identifying truth characteristic of enquiry in legal procedures.*

For historians as for jurists, this meant the cult of original documents, the concern for proper interpretation, for building an exact chronology; in other words, the cult of the 'real fact'. Subsumption and syllogism, forms of legal plot creation, were nothing other than the forms that married proof to truth through the principle of causality. The methods of identifying truth in the historical and the legal sciences are, as we see, similar. The Scottish legal philosopher Neil MacCormic, who in a seminar he gave at the European University Institute the winter of 1988 presented the method of legal science as being: (a) search for the facts, (b) interpretation of the facts, (c) interpretation of the rules and (d) their assessment and incorporation into the legal order regarded as a system, was very close to Taine (1866). The latter, who wanted to be the Claude Bernard of historical science, apart from being the forebear of authors like Langlois and Seignobos (masters of the methodical school), advocated as the method for history: (a) search for the facts and isolate them, (b) classify them, considering each class of facts separately, (c) define the facts, and (d) establish the interdependencies between the various definitions, to see to what extent they form a system.[120] This is a curious resemblance, especially considering the fairly certain hypothesis that Taine (nineteenth century) had not read MacCormick (twentieth), or the scarcely more risky one that MacCormick is not today in the course of proclaiming to us the forthcoming arrival on the continent of 'legal positivism'. We have to understand this methodological similarity; as we shall see in our last section, the endeavour to understand it will take us very far back in time, to the very roots of premodern Western Christian rationality.

This method of identifying the truth makes the jurist state his present, that is, what the law is, on the basis of elaboration of a past. The 'break', the historic cut-off, is the postulate of all interpretation, just as the plot, whether it be legal or historical, consists in the filtering, whether conscious or not, made between what can be 'understood' and what must be forgotten, omitted, in order to secure the representation of a present intelligibility, specifically, the situation one claims to subsume under a rule, the famous 'fact' needed for the act of stating the law or recounting history.

When, through an enquiry, we claim to know what actually happened, we accept that this reconstruction of the past is the sole form of truth possible on the basis of which principles of justice can be established.[121] It is, in other words, one giving of meaning to our present, that is, for jurists, to the legal rule. M. de Certeau saw in the act of writing history a transformation of 'meaning' and 'reality' into the production of 'significant gaps',[122] the position of the particular as 'limit of the thinkable',[123] the composition of a link which sets up, *in the present*, the 'ambivalent figuration of past and future'.[124] If the present meaning is worked out by constructing a past, this is because the latter gives us a way of representing a *difference*.[125] We thereby historicise the present, or, which amounts to the same thing, we *make present a situation lived through, an obligatory act in stating a law*, but we also throw away the elements that shape our future, since we can express what we have in front of us only by a redistribution of the past. Modern law works on its past to prefigure its future, and foreseeability ('control' of the future) is defined on the basis of case law (writing and rewriting of a past). The present – the meaning of the rule – symbolises this limit which makes possible a transcendence, new strategies: this limit is constructed only on a recounting of the past. And it is clear to our mind that there is no difference here between 'common law' and 'continental law' (we shall be returning to this point too in our final section).

We know that in history the boundary (between present and past) is constructed on the basis of the notion of period; this stresses the singularity of each analysis (of each 'case', to use lawyers' language), and where a legal provision 'states the facts', that is, when it places itself outside what it recounts, it is already located in a meaning which it attributes to the rule (historicism).[126] The fact, we have often said, is already the affirmation of a meaning, and this meaning results from the procedures which have allowed the articulation of a mode of understanding in a discourse of 'facts'. Here we find again our concept of 'plot', and if there is a historical function, as de Certeau reminded us, that specifies the incessant confrontation between a past and a present – between what organised life and thought and what today permits us to think about both[127] – there is an indefinite series of 'historical meanings'. The point is fundamental, and is characteristic of our modernity (we shall return to this in Part II).

Accordingly, reality, far from being unambiguous, takes on two forms: on the one hand it is what is known (what the historian studies, 'what happened', in a legal trial, etc.), that is, the *outcome* of the analysis; on the other it will be *implied* in the analysis itself (elaboration of the past through this 'meaning of the present', that is, how the historian studies or how the jurist elaborates a past, on the basis of what forms of knowledge), and will therefore be the *postulate* for the analysis. Both historical science and legal science show this relationship (which the expression 'hermeneutic circle' is intended to qualify). If there is a theoretical possibility of repeating the facts on the basis of which a legal situation was accepted, and therefore if there is the theoretical possibility of an imitation (legal precedent, 'case per case' law, etc.), this is just because 'history' takes the original form of a *limit that constitutes a reality as 'past'*. Foucault's work showed that history was played out along those borders that 'articulate a society with its past and the act of distinguishing itself from that'[128] and that the relationship that organises history is a *changing relationship*.

This point is obviously very important, since the problem is no longer that of 'tradition' (this is the reason why we moved away from H.G. Gadamer's hermeneutics), but of the break and the limit. Barthes noted[129] that through 'established facts' a process of meaning came about ('meaning of history', 'plot'), and deduced from this that the historian gathered not so much facts as signifiers; that he was not recounting facts but *stating meanings*. The historical discourse, that author also told us, does not follow reality; it does no more than signify it, unceasingly repeating 'it happened', without this assertion ever being able to be anything else but the inverse signified by the whole of historical narration. 'It is enough to recall that in the ideology of our time the obsessional reference to the "concrete…" is always armed like an engine of war against meaning.'

We shall see that modern historiography emerged from the way in which Western law identified the principle of knowledge of truth; 'reality' was to become the exclusive reference of the historical narrative, was to be considered as reporting what had 'really happened'. What, then, did it matter if there was 'unfunctionality in a detail, given that it denoted "what took place": the "concrete reality" becomes the sufficient justification for the statement,'[130] which very much amounts to the mechanism of *judicial proof*, where, within the fabric of a life, scattered elements – which did 'take place' – are called upon to state this truth[131] which will justify, legitimate, a judgement.

Summarising on this question, let us reshape the 'historical meaning' (as we have defined it, that is, as the outcome and postulate of analysis), on the basis of which Bobbio developed his study of analogy in legal science. In his work, he addresses the Italian Fascists whom he accuses of subverting the legal order of democratic inspiration, in order to drag that order towards different political and moral conceptions from its original ones, with argument by analogy being the favoured technique for organising this diversion. Thus, for Bobbio, if analogy is to be sure argumentation, if it has to have a 'single logically conclusive meaning' for its relationship of resemblance, this is in order to bar any arbitrariness,[132] in particular the kind 'disguised as legality'.[133] This then raises the idea of an 'immanent' rationality of the legal system, which has to be found (that is, discovered, and especially not invented)[134]; an argument from analogy ought to be regarded, on the basis of its 'intimate logical structure',[135] as 'explication of a legal thought'.[136] Accordingly, this reasoning must be conceived of as an *interpretation that reproduces*, by developing it, the 'very core of the norm',[137] expressed, as we have seen, by its sufficient reason. The author uses the biological metaphor of the legal system as an organism that grows and develops, but always 'by an internal force, never coming out of itself, because it cannot'.[138] The discourse aiming at Fascism is clear; the study on analogical reasoning is, for Bobbio, a political act whereby he denies Fascist legislative action any legitimacy. Who would not support him in this? Thus, if our legal culture is far from being summarised in the (present) act whereby a rule is stated, and if this act is a historicism, it remains true that this historicism, because it always takes form on the basis of a present, expresses a principle of justice on the basis of which a society recognises itself.

6

Rule, meaning, strategy: legal rationality as a coherence of narrative type

The forms of analogy, the utilisation of general and fundamental concepts, the attempts at diversion on the basis of higher-order principles or all the techniques of reasoning on the basis of which we create law, are thus determined by a criterion of justice[139] that guides them. We join J. Esser in saying that the problem of understanding legal texts is not primarily the scholastic form of the methods of interpretation (grammatical, systematic, historical etc.) but seeking the goal of justice in relation to a variety of legal experiences, 'as it (this goal) determines the grounds of judgement, understood as a demonstration of justice'.[140] The pre-understanding of the person applying the law is not homogeneous or unitary, but is constituted by processes of cognition of varying nature; we shall return to this point.

'The law', that is, the understanding we are to have of specific social experiences, has to do with retrospective information coming from the process of applying a particular provision, and the interpreter's responsibility starts with his prior assessment of a situation of fact and reconstruction of the *past* that we call 'the law in force'. For us, however, the interpretive act does not consist in a confrontation between a historico-social 'level of expectation', an anticipatory expectation of the interpretive process. Along with Esser, we accept the idea that the expectations not only of the individual putting forward a legal claim but also of all the other actors potentially concerned with these interests already recognised in anyway whatever, in their condition of conflict with the contrary expectations, form an 'expectation' around the person who 'applies' (states) the law. It represents, as it were, the legal understanding of whole social groups with whom the judge, for instance, in his interpretation, is confronted;[141] but this confrontation does not come along to be added *a posteriori* to the act of identifying the law; on the contrary, it determines its direction and course, it translates the social 'consensus' from which a 'reasonable' decision is recognised.[142]

However, and here we go against Esser, we do not see the anticipation of meaning that guides the comprehension of a text, of a pieced of case law, as being determined by 'tradition'. The question of the admissibility of a particular viewpoint, of particular criteria, for a 'correct' interpretation, is characterised not only through a *possibility of choice* among various means of interpretation, but also by the *contrast* among various interpretations (grammatical, logical, historical, systematic etc.): while one viewpoint requires this means, which is the exact consideration of the literal, grammatical meaning, the other goes deeper into the ideas of 'purpose'; while one viewpoint reconstructs a genesis, the other absolutely requires this approach to be discarded, etc. The choice among criteria of interpretation becomes a purely casual question. The path of individuating law through interpretation is not linear in nature, with a beginning and an end, but is a path of alternatives and hypotheses which must successively be justified on the basis of their plausibility, that is, their capacity to convince. The 'preconceptual' is then, for us, neither an ideal level nor an empirical genesis of abstractions. Instead of designating a level supposed to be at the bottom of history and running right through it, the preconceptual is the 'set of rules that are actually applied',[143] it being moreover quite plainly admitted that 'the law' gives rise to certain organisations of concepts (theories, doctrines) that are each of them strategies[144] (which we also call 'plots').

Once the rigid distinction between the legislative aspect and the applicative aspect of law has been denied, the idea arises that all application is *creative* of law. All the disputes that shook the last century and still persist today between the school of exegesis, the historical school, legal 'enlightenment', the positivist school, the free law school, interest jurisprudence, value jurisprudence, legal realism, the 'critical' schools, systems theory etc., were, are, each of them theories on what law is supposed to be on the basis of origin (its 'sources') and of the powers authorised to create law.[145] We have said that for us the starting point for an interpretation is not a legal text or decision but a 'case', understood as the social problem that the actors seek to resolve in legal form. This means attributing to the case the essential role as initial stimulus to the development of the legal opinion which must be inserted into a (successive and repetitive) order so as to arrive at the concepts of systematicity and of 'continuum'. The interpreter thus only moves from one particular to another, and not from the universal to the particular. Deductive conceptual thought has the function of rendering individual decisions rationally verifiable, and of organising this idea of coherent systematicity of law, since there is no doubt that only the systematic method can allow the new points of lay that emerge from the invention inherent in any topical reasoning to crystallise. At the same time, as G. Zaccaria notes,[146] 'if it is true that jurisdiction is essentially the locating of specific problems which are presented to the judge as cases, and the solutions to these problems, then induction will be recognised as having a primary function, a logical priority in the sequence of the process of finding the law'. The need to state the law in a particular situation implies a series of judgements, experiences, which are not only complex from the logical viewpoint but also include decisive evaluative aspects. Everyone knows that this automatic subsumption in legal reasoning is only apparent. The judge's whole problem, for instance – and this is the basic role of advocates – is not to extract a conclusion from given premises, but to determine the premises.

The logical course (the history of which has still to be written) whereby the judge interprets the legal material, the technical preparation of the characteristics of the 'legal fact' that he will take as the major premise, necessarily passes through the idea of the practical purpose of the norm, which as we have seen corresponds to the historicism of our hermeneutic approach. Just as the legislator's 'thought' is always oriented towards realisation of specific objectives, the thinking of the person applying the law always turns towards a precise objective. *The judge's apparently logical subsumption is nothing but creative reinstatement of an interest and value judgement that was not included 'in nuce' in the norm, but runs through the positivity of law at a given moment.*[147] This is the problem that R. Dworkin is seeking to answer, for instance with his image of the chain novel.

If the dogmatic function is of such great importance in identifying the law, that is because it is what seeks to 'stabilise' and 'reproduce' the law; it is what saves the judge from continually rediscussing everything and from continuing recourse to extradogmatic, axiological assessments for every case brought before him. It is in this necessary work of stabilisation and reproduction that the category of analogy will be unavoidable.[148] It is always 'Rechtsfindung' that remains the truly primary aspect of the jurist's search. While 'Rechtsfindung' is conceptual work on law of a creative nature, the dogmatic function is more closely related to work of a reproductive nature. A court decides specific cases singularly, where a past is recreated in order to state the present; the task of dogmatics is to systematise, that is to say interpret, a set of disparate materials. But at the point where we are, discovering and inventing become indistinguishable.

We have seen [149] that modern history takes the original form of a limit that constitutes a reality as past, that is, as a trace that can be immediately meaningful in constructing other events. This provides us with the theoretical tool that authorises us to repeat facts – acquired in a particular judicial decision, and each of them being meanings – in other judicial processes. The key aspect of judicial decision, the working-out of the premises, is thus an aspect where the analogising function is extremely important. This will clearly also be so for the operation of systematisation, of synthesis, an operation where the analogical category is constitutive of the systematised object. It is in our view wrong to conceive of the judge's decision as a pure application – the well-known version of the interpreter's 'neutrality' via logical subsumption – of a pre-given universal object. The judge's decision is genuine production of law. The content of the norm is not something already thought of, which the interpreter brings to light – we shall return in the last section to this 'hermeneutics of hidden meaning' – but this determination comes from the interpreter himself. This reformulating activity is decisive, but it is only subjectivity; the 'law' absolutely cannot in any 'case' be reduced merely to the subjectivity of the person stating it. This act can be analysed on the basis of what we call the 'narrative coherence' of legal reasoning.[150]

A ceaseless labour of differentiation (events, periods etc.) is in both legal and historical sciences the condition for bringing distinct elements into relation and hence understanding them. This work, as we have said, takes the form of an original limit that constitutes a reality as past. We have rejected the idea of a level of expectation and of a historical tradition, which we find in Gadamer, and we prefer to speak of limits: the limit is that whereby one creates this past on the basis of which a present is stated; the instrument of differentiation, the very principle that makes casuistics possible. How does this mechanism operate?

In legal reasoning, for instance of judicial type but not only that, facts, as forms of apprehension of reality, must be conceived of as *indicators*: through the presentation of the facts and the relations one sets up among them, there comes about a process of signification that always tends to fill out the meaning of this reasoning, of what we have called the plot. We have said, basing ourselves particularly on the work of Roland Barthes, that the jurist (and here we could speak indiscriminately of jurists or of historians) is someone who brings together not so much facts as meanings. This means that a 'statement' of facts corresponds to an elaboration of meaning; in the language of analysis, these 'facts' state 'choices' that are prior to them, so that it is wrong to regard them as the result of a purely observational act of stating (on this, see Chapter 16, 'Direct observation and testimony of nature'). The signifier exists only in terms of a plot, not in relation to a reality; we have accepted the thesis of the epistemological historians that reality consists in the production of 'meaningful differences'. This is the point we have to think about in order to understand the inventive or creative part, all that for us, to repeat ourselves, has meaning, of any legal interpretation.

Any life situation apprehended in one of its aspects by legal observation must be a bearer of meanings, and is therefore constituted as meaningful differences and possesses in the same way the elements that in historical science are said to be constitutive of the historical narrative. But there is more. All these legal 'plots', all these particular cases, are each of them limits; that is, that whereby the present is stated. These are all at the same time an ambivalent representation of past and future. We have already discussed at length, on the basis of various works on epistemology in historical science, the idea that the concept of 'past' was above all the way of representing a difference, of historicising the present (making a situation that has been experienced present). But this historicisation of the present is already the introduction of a future: history is always ambivalent. 'The place it cuts out in the past is also a way of making room for a future.'[151]

While we believe as jurists that we are working only on the present time, we see that in fact the present time tends to dissipate, so that there exists only an ambivalent relation between a past (the limit of the present) and a future. In this sense, all the legal decisions, all the interpretations proposed by doctrine etc. embody a forward-looking dimension. By continually linking up its present to the past, says P. Bourdieu, legal reasoning seeks to link the past to the future by claiming that the latter will be in the image of the former.[152] It is perhaps possible here to go a little further; we shall confine ourselves to what organises the narrative coherence of legal reasoning and argumentation.

We have said that the logical process whereby the judge interprets the legal material was shot through with practical purposes. What can we deduce for the structure of the legal plot? The first constraint on the discourse consists in prescribing as a start, describing as a 'real situation', as an event, what is in reality a point of arrival. Whereas the search for the 'facts of the case' takes place in a present social place and definite institutional apparatus (a court for instance), the account is presented as organisation of chronological order, taking the past as starting point. The narrative, as we have seen, developed in the traditional historiographical mode; 'a time of things as the counterpoint and condition for a discursive time'[153] is posited, and the discourse advances more or less rapidly and extends to more or fewer aspects. Using this referential time, one can condense or extend *one's own time*,[154] produce effects of meaning. Here we come back to what we have already said in connection with elaboration of reality.

'Fact' and 'rule' enter into this relationship that exists between a 'fact' and an 'event' in the construction of historiography, where the point is to relate an 'intelligibility' to 'normativity'. 'The event is what makes the break in order for there to be something intelligible';[155] the fact is what fills up in order for there to be a statement of meaning. The event (the rule) conditions the organisation of the argument; the fact furnishes signifiers which in narrative fashion will constitute a series of meaningful elements. The rule is what has to be assumed in order for an ordered organisation of reality to be possible, and in this sense it allows intelligibility. But here we come to the most formidable challenge that legal science has had to face in the last two centuries.[156] The interpretive act, as we define it, is always the creation of *difference*, and hence in profound contradiction to what was always affirmed through the idea of the 'Code'; this allows us to understand why the two principles we have mentioned[157] have never ceased to be reaffirmed, and why the idea of coherence comes to replace the idea of completeness. Moreover, since by definition it is always stated on the basis of a difference, the interpretive act engenders an infinite diversification of legal experience, whereas one always expects from it an action tending towards unity. This allows us also to understand why reasoning by analogy is an essential category for the construction of the legal order, which constantly has to be begun anew.

This social 'consensus' on the basis of which a 'reasonable' decision is recognised (pp. 35–6 above) rests in the working-out by the judge of what we call the plot (which does not correspond to what is traditionally meant by the expression 'grounds of the decision'). In the structure of the plot, prediction (future) and retrodiction (interpreting the past through a present meaning) are inextricably mixed; a hypothetical from one argument is inferred by arguing from a fact that happened, which amounts to establishing the probability of a past, or retrodiction[158]; but by being said in the present, that hypothetical may also be presented as prediction, a sort of 'extra-lucidity *post eventum*'.[159] This is in fact how we construct the causality in legal argumentation: 'if such and such a (legal) person did this, said that, it is because, *probably* ...', and an argument regarded as the likely cause is inferred. But the construction can equally well be established by deducing the fact that happened, as if at the outset we did not know it and were starting from the hypothetical. The 'because' thus brings about a 'meaningful' break. Consequently, and this is absolutely basic to what we have to say, the analogical inference will on the one hand – and we well understand why – operate without a universal category, and will therefore on the other hand – as the characteristics of the plot teach us – be an inescapable argument.

We feel that P. Bourdieu has well assessed the social issues here: 'the effect of universalisation, which might also be called *effect of normalisation* [our emphasis], acts to reduplicate the effect of the social authority already exercised by the legitimate culture and its bearers, in order to give all its practical effectiveness to legal constraint. Through the ontological promotion that it brings about by transmuting the regularity (what regularly happens) into a rule (what it is the rule to do), normality of fact into normality of law ... the legal institution undoubtedly contributes universally to imposing a representation of normality in relation to which all differing practices tend to appear as deviant.'[160] Through the plot, in fact, this 'ontological promotion' that Bourdieu talks about, which transmutes a normality of fact into normality of law, comes about; the 'reasonable' or 'just measure' of the plot is derived from the category of the 'normal' person (and here we have the 'standard'), and crystallises the sphere of imagination needed in order to elaborate meaning. The category of analogy, with this calibration given by the 'normal', for instance, brings about the synthesis of the differences, organises the principle of coherence.

Theory sometimes loses sight of the banal fact that at the origin there is the social problem and not a normative category; in other words that legal principles are never static elements of a scholastically constructed edifice, but topics, selection criteria of the legal assessment. Through interpretation the principle emerges, with the special feature that legal hermeneutics has a practical purpose. Thus the anticipated representation of the result that the interpreter supposes to be legally relevant before asking any interpretive question at all delimits the scope and direction taken by the interpretive methods: 'between precomprehension as the initial act in legal understanding and location of the deciding maxim that represents its culmination, there is a fine thread of try-outs and anticipations of possible solutions that runs through the dialogical method of questions addressed to the text and allows the normative models of regulation to be consulted in relation to the answers they are likely to offer the given conflict.'[161] In a similar process, the dogmatic plan is ceaselessly interrupted. Understanding of the rule develops in the hermeneutic circle as the relationship between the question asked and the solution pursued, and this circle, far form being closed on itself, is a *continuous creation*, a plot similar to the historiographical model. The legality of a decision, a form of social consensus, refers as much to the capacity the decision has to prove what it alleges as to the capacity of the plot to convince; but the practical consequences of the result secured are far from being a negligible argument!

We have seen that the proof of an allegation is a complex process – the very structure of the plot – where historical method and legal method were not to be distinguished. This point will be dealt with throughout our second part. The choice of the plot itself is just as complex, in part introduced by the operation we have mentioned and in part, too, introduced by the latter operation, which we call the evaluation of practical consequences. The stance taken by the interpreter is without any doubt decisive here, and also has to do with the professional principles that govern the legal world,[162] but it would, once again, be wrong to see this as only an act of purely subjective type. Well before we arrive through the process of application at the understanding of law, we understand ourselves, for instance, in unreflected fashion in the family, the State etc., that is, in a whole set of legal forms that overdetermine our understanding.

The interpreter in this sense belongs to a history as much as he constructs it. It was on this basis that we put forward the historicist hypothesis, and if analogy contains mystery, it is no doubt because it maintains a privileged relationship with it. The provisions inserted in Codes, the various legislative statements, all legal provisions in general, state a legal principle though the application made of it; what we call 'the law' corresponds to the historical space where legal experience is developed and expresses those principles.

Each decision in litigation, for instance, is an aspect of this history, and it is not certain that the idea of 'continuum' gives a proper account of it. A particular case does not, in our view by definition, express the state of law at a given moment, any more than it would be expressed by the sum of *all* cases involving a particular legal question, on the understanding that it is the cases that determine the sum, and not conversely. This brings us back particularly to Ewald,[163] when he posits the concept of the 'rule of judgement' as the basis on which a judgement is made.[164] We have also seen that when one claims to state the law on the basis of the decision in a case, for instance, one in fact presupposes *an overall past state* of the state of the law in question. While in our Codes all the verbs are in the present indicative, that present is nevertheless entered in a representation of a past, which gives it its meaning and is already the outline of a future.

Analogical inference[165] in law is a conclusive procedure in which the determining aspects are not the conclusion – that in other words there is a meaningful 'resemblance' between two cases – but the interpretive mechanisms at work in establishing premises. What is *inferred* from a particular legal whole is a normative proposition that refers to a judgement of consequentialist value according to which, at a particular moment, it is desired that the decisions in that legal whole should generate legal experience for social practices not *a priori* involved in that whole. Let us forget the theories of lacunae in law, of law understood as an organic or historical unity or as an intrinsic rationality, or whatever. Since, as we have said, there is no factual cognition without normative knowledge, positing, say, the hypothesis of the 'situation of fact in search of legality' already means sketching out a situation that bears normative understanding within its structure, which is, in other words, already the end point of understanding as the historical application of an explicit legal provision; it is, as it were, its shadow, its extension in the all-round historical knowledge we have of a legal topic.

A legal experience becomes extended to social practices that were originally foreign to it. This extension thus reflects a *shift in the act of judgement*, of interpreting; and thus corresponds to a creation which it is idle to represent in a minimum sense on the basis of the idea that the legal facts of a case are 'similar in essence', since on the one hand this 'essence' has never been able to be defined, and on the other we have shown that every interpretive act was creative, that is was the working-out of a plot. We may perhaps try, in a very last point, to locate it, very provisionally, in the respective spaces of the creative and the innovative aspects within interpretive reasoning, in other words seek to highlight these 'figures of knowledge' that constitute the relationship of 'resemblance' among things; in short, to take away the mystery of analogy and, to use Michel Foucault's words, of our own 'archives', a little.

7

Elements of historicist hermeneutics

By contrast with H. G. Gadamer, we cannot regard 'tradition' as that
whereby an *authority* becomes anonymous and only that; we have seen
that the mechanisms whereby past is worked out are very substantially the
creators of that past itself. History, the set of processes thanks to which we
lay the basis for our present, very plainly has the function of also
engendering categories such as 'tradition', 'custom', etc., but, since they
institute a present, it would be more appropriate to approach these
categories from the angle of the creative rather than that of the repetitive.
Gadamer insisted, moreover, on 'tradition' not being accomplished
'purely in natural fashion', but on the contrary demanding to be
'affirmed, seized, maintained'.[166] If we refuse to consider that the anticipation of meaning that guides our understanding of a text is not an act of
subjectivity, we do not wish either to conceive of it as something determined 'on the basis of the community that links us with the tradition'
(Gadamer).

It must accordingly not be regarded as a preliminary condition we are
supposed to have been always subject to which overdetermined us, but
more as that whereby one generates and regenerates a present, as something that is not always already constituted, but something constitutive.
This perspective in any case rules out Gadamer's idea of 'merging levels',
since the present, when it is worked out, does not have any historical,
objective truth, always already there, that one would have to recognise.

Let us, however, leave this epistemological question aside for the
moment and act as if every event, however manifest, was not retrodictive;
as if it presented itself 'positively' in all its truth; and let us also assume,
with Bobbio, that the jurists of the old law ('diritto comune') posited
extensive interpretations primary, and regarded analogy, 'or better,
similitude', as he says,[167] as the most appropriate means of legislative
extension. At one time, then, ('dirroto comune'), this 'similitude' was
central to all interpretive doctrine. Having, then, posited an origin,
Bobbio then goes on to present us with his history of analogy, through *a
precomprehension of law in which the two major principles we have already*

mentioned are at work, namely that law is a system in which the constitutive elements – the body of laws – are rational.

Extensio a simili, a method of reasoning antecedent to the period when Bobbio begins his study, is dealt with on a logical basis,[168] regarded as opposed explicitly to the traditional mode of reasoning, namely argument from equity, since henceforth the point will be to organise *into a system* the arguments used by jurists. Here, we are in the sixteenth century; Bobbio analyses the phenomenon, explaining that in order to bring the notion of resemblance under the requirements of legal logic, the specific qualitative element of the legal case in point, the *ratio legis,* has to be identified, and the similitude must thus be understood as an *identitas rationis.*[169] It is mainly through similitude that the *passage from the case provided for to the case not provided for* is accomplished. Referring to the author of the time, J. Hopper, Bobbio posits that in the scholastic interpretation the method of analogy aimed at eliminating the contradictions in a body of law, at making a legal system into a logically linked system. Although slightly in contradiction with what he had said earlier, Bobbio concludes that analogy is not an extensive interpretation but first and foremost a *comparative*[170] one, an understanding which, moreover, seems to us to be in conformity with the archaeological analysis done by Foucault on that period. For Bobbio, the point was to 'grasp the unity of the multiple, *the rational element in the apparent, or actual, logical disorder;* to make a set of laws held together by the illogical logic of history into an authentic legal order, bound by the schemes of formal logic'.[171]

The law, the author points out, is no longer isolated, but confronted with other laws, which explains why comparison is systematic and symptomatic of something: it is no longer an isolated, unrepeatable desire, but the specific moment of a reason in process of development. Let us note that here once again it is more that historical plot itself brought out by Bobbio which makes this causality among events possible than the logical force as such of the elements brought together which forces this conclusion. Thus, at a certain point in the history of law,[172] *the idea of unity of a 'body' of laws* arises, which must of course be linked to the spirit of system (Domat, Vico, Leibniz) that henceforth came to be the driving force of any research programme. The idea of a 'natural law' supplied solid justification for this spirit of system. With Bobbio, however, a continuity is postulated that may perhaps raise a problem. From the uncertain and timid sense of the rationality of the laws (the hermeneutic clue that guided the jurist in reconciling antinomies, on which generations of jurists cut their teeth) to the unitary and complex sense of the laws, over the long period running through the sixteenth, seventeenth and eighteenth centuries, Bobbio wishes in fact to see a simple, gradual passage. This passage, understood as substitution of a comparative interpretation by an

analogia iuris, a substitution that remains for him the expression of one
and the same phenomenon, thus allows him to locate the historical origin
of analogy in an interpretation of comparative type.

The archeological enquiry carried out by Foucault into 'words and
things;' was, as we all know, on the contrary to show two discontinuities
in the episteme of Western culture: one located in the classical period
(more specifically, the mid-seventeenth century) and the other at the start
of our modernism (the nineteenth century). These two discontinuities do
not reflect some sort of improvement in reason, but instead show that '*the
mode of being of things and the order, which by dividing them up offers them to
knowledge, has been profoundly altered*'.[173] The continuity posited by
Bobbio must accordingly appear as suspect, or at any rate not possessed
of an identical logic.

It is in fact resemblance, understood as similitude, a term Bobbio was
right to use, that in large part still guides exegesis and interpretation in the
sixteenth century (we shall soon return to this at length); but the question
Foucault raised was that of *the way this similitude was conceived of*, how it
was able to organise the figures of knowledge. We know his answer; we
know that the four figures of knowledge (conveneutia-aemulatio-analogia-
sympathia) that he identified teach us how the world has to be reflected in
order for things to resemble each other: *the sign is bound up with the
resemblance*. The sign of affinity, what makes it visible, is analogy (for
instance, a nutshell and the human brain), and what constitutes the basis
for the value of the sign is resemblance.[174] A sign signifies to the extent that
there is a resemblance with what it indicates (i.e. similitude), which made
Foucault say that semiology and hermeneutics were superposed in the form
of similitude: seeking meaning meant bringing out what resembled it.

Knowledge must, then, be imagined as an interpretive process consisting in going from the visible mark to what is said through it,[175] but signs
designate the hidden only through a resemblance. 'The specific feature of
knowledge is neither seeing nor showing, but interpreting.' The whole of
thought is shifted into the element of resemblance; analogy can only be
comparative interpretation (cf. Hopper), and belongs to this episteme.
Where Bobbio saw continuity, Foucault discovers discontinuity; soon,
however (at the start of the seventeenth century Foucault tells us),
thought was no longer shifted into the world of resemblance; a break had
come about with what might be called *divinatio*, which revealed a *prior*
language distributed in the world by God. With the seventeenth century,
it is *within knowledge* that the sign begins to signify, and it was from it that
it took its certainty or its probability. *Analysis comes to replace*, rather than
to extend, the analogical hierarchy; for the classical episteme, what
becomes fundamental is the relationship with 'mathesis'.

'Henceforth the relations among beings were to be conceived of in the form of order and measure, with the fundamental imbalance that problems of measure can always be reduced to those of order.'[176] This relationship with mathesis as a general science of order was to bring out a number of empirical areas that had not hitherto existed. *This relationship with order*, unique according to Foucault, was just as essential for the classical age as the relationship with interpretation was for the 'Renaissance' (it would be better here to speak very vaguely of a 'previous' period, as we shall see in our second part). There is a dissociation between sign and resemblance; thought it henceforth to function in strictly binary mode. This is a fundamental feature of the mode of knowledge that brings knowledge of things under the possibility of representing them in a system of norms. Natural history, the new science of the period, assumes the idea of continuity in nature,[177] and has no history except to the extent that it is capable of continuity. *The search for order as the basis and foundation of a general science of nature is posited.* This epistemological disposition, says Foucault, soon begins to appear very plainly in other, more traditional areas: thus, *the idea that all laws are united in a logical system emerges*, and *analogia iuris* becomes established during this period, but in this new form of knowledge. *Analogia iuris was to claim* fundamentally to express the idea that the value of legislation is unitary and rational (Bobbio saw in it, wrongly in my view, the origin and justification of what are today called general principles, drawing on this conception of history as a long continuum in a continuous process of rational improvement).

If 'natural law' becomes a predominant, this is no longer in order to interpret similarities; nature becomes a homogeneous space of identities and differences. *Analogia will henceforth indicate to jurists* no longer the organic connection of laws (proper to an episteme that has disappeared, namely comparative interpretation) but *the truly rational system of law*, which is thus beyond positive statutes and independent of them: the 'system' of natural law. *From the organic connection of statutes it was hoped to extract a system; henceforth it would be a rationality of law, of its systematic nature, that would seek to extract an organic unity.* In classical knowledge, the system expresses the idea that the knowledge of empirical individuals can be acquired through the continuous, ordered universal table of all possible differences. The idea of continuity in nature is central (cf. Chapter 17: 'Sign, sense, proof'). Analogy comes thus to operate in accordance with a radically new feature of the episteme; it comes to express a *continuity in nature through the idea of break* (the naturalist method is founded on this idea of continuity in just the same way); it comes to take on the practical value of a reference point to remedy the deficits of legislation.

In this new arrangement of knowledge, then, we may be able to find the two principles of cognition that guide the statement of the law. First, there is the statement that *all laws are united in a logical system*, which is continuous (and complete). This principle supplements the one from the previous epoch, of the impossibility for the one law to contradict another. Between these two principles one has to see something more than a gradual transition, even if it is quite clear that they can *a posteriori*, on a purely technical approach, appear as complementary. For the view that all laws are united into a logical system means endowing oneself with the possibility of imagining new interpretive principles (for instance, that there are no lacunae in the system) *that would have meant absolutely nothing previously.*

Second, there is this new situation facing the interpreter of having to create informative principles which will be presented as the 'legal spirit'. The analogical principle quite clearly has to do with the first principle, on which it confers its formal, 'logical' aspect. But over and above this formal aspect, we shall find it again in the very structure of our knowledge; this is what Foucault's work shows, and it is plainly the whole 'mysterious' aspect of analogy. *Ratio legis*, for instance, is extracted from the principle of the systematic nature of law; it intends to reflect a unity, but this unity will always be expressed on the basis of a particular structure of know-ledge, the periodicity of which has to be located. In the early nineteenth century, we know that biology came to supplant the 'natural' sciences, providing us with the category of the alive, a special structure of knowl-edge that was pregnant with consequences for the definition of the notion of resemblance. This is where we come to the creative aspect of analogical reasoning, which however still remains rather mysterious.

The representation of reality applied in understanding a text is never a simple copy of the pre-existing reality; it is, as we have said, a *creative imitation*. When rules are perceived as non-contradictory, when social control is bound up only with phenomen of imitation of precedent, legal work consists in identifying the document from which one extracts a premise that will be called normative. Identifying the document, stating a normative premise, consists in creative imitation,and no decision or proposition can ever express a legal truth that would subsequently be recognised systematically and objectively. What may perhaps emerge is not some 'truth of a reality lying outside the rule, which comes along to meet with a preconstructed rule, that is, one with an intrinsic meaning that imposes itself on the interpreter, a meeting that would allegedly give rise to a social code, objective, rational and foreseeable'.[178]

Before and outside its specific application to a case, the law, if you will, exists only as a *possibility*, or potentiality of meaning. It is clear in our view that the fundamental principle of positivist hermeneutics (on the basis of the dogma of legal positivism that serves as its foundation) that we could translate as the 'being in itself' (Hruschka) of positive law (with the consequence that every legal rule totally enclosed the legal 'meaning' is to be rejected. This was the starting point for our thinking, and we shall have to develop it substantially. Since the law exists only as a possibility, a potentiality of meaning, reasoning by analogy is never a 'leap from the known towards the unknown', but on the contrary it is something known that is being repeated. This was our second point. It is a saving. The law being defined as a unitary system (or in a more recent version as coherent), we save the need for continual rediscussion of the nature of its unity (or coherence), this saving recourse to extradogmatic, axiological evaluations showing the nature of that unity. It is undoubtedly the concept of legal order that comes to be the interpretive principle on the basis of which unity is produced, a concept which postulates ('legal positivism') that reality is capable of immediate, direct and univocal description. Here the category of contract, for instance, comes in; it is considered that everything that has been written, decided or judged on the basis of this category expresses something that is common to the whole. This is what we call the reproductive dimension of the legal narrative, and the procedure of analogy is evidently essential here.

This reproduction is at the same time creation, creative imitation, since reality, far from being merely an object that is completely and directly graspable, is so only never through the mediation of narratives, a mediation which remains largely mysterious because what may be said, 'the system that governs the appearance of statements as singular events, the general system of formation and transformation of statements', 'our archives' as Foucault says,[179] cannot be completely described since it is within these rules that we speak.

We must now seek to establish how 'the meaning' has, in the history of the West, been able to be rationally produced. We shall in so doing go through the experience of the historian and his generative limit set by the – necessary – fiction that a distance between a past and a present can bring forth meaning that helps to explain the present. We shall however, at least so we believe, avoid the error of realism by trying to pursue our enquiry into the actual form of knowledge, the knowledge at issue, by seeking to indicate not so much what '*really*' might have been as rather how, on the basis of what, it was thought that truth could be stated. Legal analogy, finally, to conclude this first section, indicates the creative dimension inherent in all interpretation in its reproductive function, even within the legal narrative. The judge's continuous creation must correspond somewhere with a stabilising element that also allows the – largely fictional – history of the principle of the separation of powers to be written, as the principle of the judge's responsibility before the law.

These two principles and their articulation are undoubtedly at the root of the political history of the West. But they also express, or more exactly indicate, something that is equally essential: that the meaning indicated by a piece of writing is bound up more with the reader than the 'author'. A piece of writing is nothing as a system of signs unless a specific culture is developed which is the interpretation of these signs. Legal thought illustrates this. From the day when the concept of law no longer had anything as its sole support but the record that writing constitutes, the whole creative genius of thought has ceaselessly done nothing other than organise meaning, rationally. We wish to see this as the mark of a civilisation, but we shall see that jurists have occupied a fundamental place in it which is common both to the tradition known as common law[180] and to that known as 'civil law'.

PART II

8

'History' and 'origin'

In the first part of this work, we were already able to make a number of incursions into this area of research on the concept of history. But the essential thing remains. The question we must ask ourselves is what this movement of thought developing around a construction limited by an anterior limit, a 'past', and a posterior point, a 'future', means; we must try to understand in part what that brings to play in the very forms of our knowledge. But before seeking to tackle this rather difficult question, we should like to recall a number of traditional and fundamental conceptions of the notion of history.

The view most readily shared by large numbers of historians is to locate *'the origin'* of the modern concept of history in the 'Renaissance'. We do not wish here to drown the reader under a flood of references; we shall merely briefly cite G. Monod[1]: 'History, whether regarded as a branch of literature or as a science, for us dates from the Renaissance'. There follows a distinction between history and chronicle (the account of the past typical of the 'Middle Ages'); we shall return to all this. B. Guénée has written in this connection: 'All theories are at least in agreement in one point: in the Middle Ages there was nothing but naive narrators, "chroniclers" ... because the "medieval mind", according to this tradition, was incapable of conceiving of history: "the sense of the past did not exist".'[2] The great Marc Bloch, under occupation in France in the 1940s, had already set the tone in a very fine work of historical methodology,[3] in considering that 'modern history' began with Mabillon. This general or at least very widespread belief in a serious, scientific history that emerged in the Renaissance is based primarily on an original distinction between the historian and the chronicler, a type of intellectual supposed to have existed throughout a period identified as the 'Middle Ages'.

Who are these intellectuals? People who want to 'conserve for posterity the memory of events they have seen and taken part in, rather than to trace ... a faithful image of bygone times'.[4] This definition is extremely interesting since everything that contributes to the conception of what we call history is present, from the idea of direct testimony to the production of

an oral, indirect account by a spectator whose commitment exists precisely in giving an account of things he has not necessarily witnessed.

Yet we see many reproaches against these chroniclers as poor historians, 'incapable of representing events to themselves and recounting them
in original, personal fashion', at best capable of 'copying their sources',
and most of them motivated by 'religious motives, along with others that
are more of a political than a historical nature'.[5] It is needless to go on: we
can recognise through these accusations the idea that historians today
form of their own work, and far from finding what the social practice of
chroniclers might have been meant to express in a feudal-type society, we
have a brief glimpse of the way certain members of the social group of
historians today intend to define the ideal of their discipline: joined on to
an ontology is the idea of creation conceived of as the expression of a
personal talent,[6] on the basis of scientific methods (theory of sources) and
without political or religious *parti pris*. Thus while this author, once again
taken by way of example, teaches us something of the way the historians
trade is defined today, he does not by contrast tell us much about the
historian's trade yesterday. The attempt to define history also suffers from
another type of very widespread error we must if possible avoid. Guénée's
texts are a good example.[7] The danger lies in regarding history as
something that is always already there, evolving 'down through time' in a
positive direction. We have already criticised this sort of approach in our
first part, but we must now once again return to this very important
methodological point. For Guénée, the 'great age of medieval historiography was the twelfth century',[8] when the historian 'at the same time as
being a historian' was to be a theologian, a canonist, a hagiographer, a
computist, etc. We have this idea of 'history', slowly emerging and
tending steadily towards its perfect point of abstraction. Giovanni Nanni
is for Guénée the ideal discoverer of what history is.[9] With him we are in
the presence of the 'first discourse of historical motion',[10] and 'in the
second half of the sixteenth century', the slow revolution is accomplished.[11]

Yet history, as many before us have already said, is not an object that
pre-exists social practices, but on the contrary is those social practices
themselves, whether these practices do or do not claim a knowledge that
would today be recognised as historical. Thus, to take up the example
cited, 'the historian' was not 'at the same time' a theologian, canonist etc.;
it was the theologian or canonist or computist who were at the basis of
'history' as were many other social practices not explicitly intended to
contribute to it. For that reason, we have to take an interest in these social
practices themselves in order to seek to locate specific forms of knowledge,
instead of making the converse movement of describing social practices
positively or negatively on the basis of an omnipresent conception,

inevitably loaded with dogmas, that we may have of history. This approach, which we condemn, can evidently lead only to the most total confusion, since it wishes absolutely to find a *contemporary* object, namely 'history', in social forms so different from ours that they sometimes do not even have any sort of relationship with what we may be seeking. Thus for some it was nineteenth-century professors who 'brought modern history to the baptismal font'[12]; for others the scholars of the seventeenth century; for still others, sixteenth-century jurists; and finally for others, the 'literary scholars' of the Renaissance. All these definitions, far from expressing the concept of 'history', at most tell us about the specific feature of the historical account laying claim to the definition of the term 'history'.

This concept of history, finally, faces us with a third type of difficulty, quite a major one, which we may seek to illustrate on the basis of the recent work by B. Barret-Kriegel.[13] This author, whose intellectual differences with the previously cited authors is sufficiently clear for it to be unnecessary for us to stress them, nevertheless shares with them – and we might perhaps say here with more or less everyone – the conviction that the Renaissance was the time of a 'great novelty for "history"'. And again, for Barret-Kriegel, in the 'Middle Ages, there are compilers, not historians', and one phrase throws particular light on her philosophy of history: 'It was necessary above all to publish texts, explain points of detail through minute criticism, teach historians to use documents. That was the work of scholars, continued throughout the eighteenth century ... to teach historians to use documents.'[14] Here too, then, we have a continuous time line with a more or less obscure origin (in the 'compilers', defined negatively in comparison with 'historians'), the end point of which is illuminated by the idea of 'scholarship'. Though Barret-Kriegel sees very well, in our view, around what types of knowledge social issues have materialised and developed: 'philosophy, religion, law',[15] she does not, however, offer any very satisfactory analysis.[16] The point is that all the work she has done is guided by a central thesis that inevitably raises problems, that of the 'State', and through it a view of what the 'modern period' is supposed to be is offered us.

We are not here going to rehash all the arguments of these two very scholarly works. We shall mention only a few outstanding points. The fundamental idea is that in the 'sixteenth century, the "monarchical State" steadily imposed itself (quite differently from its German counterpart), and it is law that points us towards the traces that show us the specific features and originality of this phenomenon'.[17] Once again, then, the 'sixteenth century' is an origin starting from which a totality is explained, or from which 'history had become knowledge'.[18] Yet here too, though the author has very broadly accepted a number of Foucault's theses, this idea of a history that was 'always already there', in the sixteenth century, persists. We read, for instance, that 'the search for sources precedes close philological study, history presides over the birth of philology, and the direction of movement is from history to grammar'.[19] Though the author may perhaps refute this,[20] we are still very close to a 'history of ideas'.

The basic error is in our view the desire to uphold absolutely on the one hand this idea of 'origin' (which is there to give an explanation for an enquiry into contemporary society), and on the other a link of direct explanation between a semiology (how, rationally, the Christian West enunciates its principles of truth on the basis of the Scriptures) and what we believe we can recognise as the 'State'. Since this link is posited, a whole work of interpretation will find itself given a final orientation by this. Our hypothesis is not going to be to deny that the idea of territory or financial centre becomes established as a tangible interlocutor on the continent in that period of the sixteenth and seventeenth centuries, but to doubt that we need necessarily use the concept of 'State' to interpret these criss-cross traces represented by theological, legal or philological knowledge[21] even if, as it quite plain to everyone, there is a relationship.

With this link posited in this perspective, Barret-Kriegel was able to incorporate into her position a quotation aimed at proving the justification for her thesis that 'without history, case law is blind' (François Baudoin). As we shall see, however, it is not 'history; that was to furnish the jurist with something fundamental, but on the contrary legal knowledge as the West has conceived it that was to generate the very concept of history. But let us not go too fast, and stay with the extremely interesting and vastly erudite thesis of Barret-Kriegel. The whole of Gallicanism is to be explained on the basis of this distance that jurists were able to create ('awareness') between their discipline and 'history': 'the legal Renaissance measured the distance, became aware of history … the school of historical law took its part in forming the German Nation State; the *mos gallicus* underpinned the constitution of the monarchical State'.[22] Having this 'awareness of history', the Gallican jurists were ultimately able to defend the monarchical state against the pretensions of the Holy See and in so doing to arrive at the 'ambition to reform law … Cujas's work incarnates *the emancipatory eruption of historical method into legal studies.*[23] It is just this thesis that we intend to oppose. As for the rest, it is quite possible, and we would willingly follow this path, that 'the work of the Bourges school exercised an influence not on the reception but on the official relegation of Roman law in France',[24] just as it is equally possible that a new redefinition and reconstitution of the division between public law and private law can be put forward for this period.[25] Yet, if it is true that 'the publications of customary lawyers … replaced codification', let us be careful about seeing this immediately as a 'new form of legitimation'[26] of the State, since what is important, and remains enigmatic, is just this concept of the State. Rather than seek to interpret all these social practices of identification of the truth (and the commonly-shared forms of argumentation aimed at proving it) on the basis of this *a priori* 'State', it would in our view be wiser to show how all these practices (archives, authenticated sources, written documents in general) participate in identifying what we call the 'State'. In this way we might perhaps avoid a history of ideas, something we accuse of poor explanatory and illuminatory capacity.

To do so, once again this link posited by the author between a semiotic and this concept, the 'State', must be broken; this link that makes her say: 'Writing, religion, law (are) three areas with no common frontiers, no regular exchanges'.[27] How utterly wrong! Denouncing this link implies that political, upheaval (emergence of centralised bureaucratic structures with the mission of holding a whole national territory), doubtless important in a political history, is perhaps of very little use when it comes to understanding the constitution, development and interweaving of various types of social knowledge. In this perspective, it is wrong to say that 'the return to charters, the search for documents and investigation of titles, is a general effort of the European *States* [our emphasis]'.[28] This return does not indicate anything much in particular, if one absolutely wishes to interest oneself in the question of the 'State'.

One famous *precedent* shows us that this detour through archives, before being the way of legitimising a particular form of power, had to be a general disposition of the mode of knowing and recognising things, of proving them 'true'. If this detour through archives was once able to impose itself as *evidence* in a legitimising function, this is undoubtedly because the Western way of disposing rationally of things was closely connected with this trace that writing is. Alexander III, King of Scots, died in 1286, without heirs save his infant granddaughter Margaret, the 'Maid of Norway', who died in 1290 in the Orkneys on her way back to take up her crown, frustrating King Edward I of England's plan to marry his son off to her and thereby take over Scotland.[29] Many Scottish claimants engaged in a bitter fight for the succession to the throne, but none was able to do without the assistance of Edward, who now took on the role of *arbiter*. He agreed to support someone in particular, to help to settle the conflict, but on condition that all claimants first formally recognised English sovereignty over Scotland. An amazing pretension? Not at all, since to support his demand Edward I had vast *research* carried out in *archives* and *libraries* of his kingdom, to *prove* the soundness of his claim. This the Scots rebuffed with their own presentation of the history in the 1320 Declaration of Arbroath, the acceptance of which by the Pope was the basis for recognition of Scotland's independence.

We can see, then, that as early as the 'thirteenth' century, everything that Barret-Kriegel regards as fundamental for understanding the radical novelty of the 'sixteenth to seventeenth' century is already present: 'the distance between law and history', 'awareness of history', etc. tell us absolutely nothing special, if we want to talk about this period called the sixteenth century.

Another lesson from the foregoing is that the very idea of a break in the sixteenth century becomes very problematic for the object of our study and from our viewpoint. It is true that far from displaying the superiority of an efficient administration, the archives of the kingdom of England were, as Guénée tells us,[30] in utter disorder: only the papal bulls were properly classified. Even the documents of Edward I's immediate predecessor, Henry III, could not be found. But that is not the essential point. What we have to see here is that some Scottish claimants were willing to accept sovereignty on the battleground of archives. Our English Benedictines (helped by some Augustinians and Cistercians) were to seek to *prove* that the Scots were wrong, by articulating, rationally (a term we shall return to), a number of written traces. This means that there already existed in our Christian West a special form of knowledge on the basis of which what is *true* and the *way of proving it* were to be recognised. For all this, the sixteenth century teaches us absolutely nothing. Once we abandon the basic point, Barret-Kriegel's whole account loses force, and we have to go back to the attempt to explain the link between history and law of what we know as the 'Bourges school'

To understand how 'history became knowledge', we share with Barret-Kriegel the idea that the interrelations among what we call language, faith and law, that is philology, religion and law, had to be understood. However, her account does not satisfy us. It is not in our view true to say that the sixteenth century is marked by the 'introduction of history into legal dispute, of the legal element into historical dispute'.[31] We shall show this below in dealing with earlier legal practice; let us say here merely that the mode of legal thought inherently contains what is to be recognised as 'history', for the sixteenth century just as much as for today. This articulation of time, and we shall return to this point, is an act of legal thought.

It is quite possible that a 'political law', not forged by ancient law, appeared at the time of the Gallican conflict, and that the Bourges lawyers are pointing out something special in that account, but we are no longer speaking about the same problem. The danger here – but can it really be avoided? – is the hindsight the author applies by articulating the whole of the data – by definition a set that can never be either perfect or systematic – around this final point, never admitted but always present of our contemporary 'rule of law' or constitutional state (as, more or less, we understand it). We read, for instance: 'There would have been no constitution of diplomatics in the absence of this great replacement factor that led the powerful to exchange the ancient, feudal settlement of disputes through wars, public or private, for legal negotiation';[32] and again: 'the need for law is the essential motor of diplomatic activity'.[33]

The error here, in our view, is to approach these data from a point of arrival ('the rule of law') instead of from an initial issue (The role of legal thought in Western rational thought). Thus, when Mabillon asks: 'What is a historian?' and replies: 'A judge', instead of interpreting this statement with the idea of the evolution of a State towards ever more law, we ought in our view to apply a question of an epistemological nature to certain forms of knowledge. Only in this way may we perhaps understand why it can be said that 'the historian's first act is to go to the sources',[34] that 'the archives are an instrument of knowledge of the past'[35] and thus put the question of philology[36] in other terms than did this author, in order to interpret the signs – the writing – that unveil the hidden truth.

9

Premodernity and rationality in the Christian West

The reason why we have ceaselessly disputed this date of the sixteenth century as the period, the moment, when a society became transformed in order to lay the first foundations of social organisation of relevance to our modern times is of course that we intend to propose another way of interpreting premodernity. To do so we must venture still further back in the past, raising a tough question of method at the outset. How can one claim to analyse, to understand, major changes in societies that disappeared so long ago? It is clear to us that an explanation or understanding of very remote periods in the past does not claim to say what society 'really' was (and in any case, 'realism' remains an interpretation of things, not the things themselves) but aims more modestly at presenting an interpretation of traces, of particular documents.

In this period called the twelfth century, when a new form of urban life and a new merchant professionalism were imposing themselves, social organisation changed considerably and new forms of legal knowledge spread: *written* codes came into being alongside customary *oral* laws,[37] Roman law cases were rediscovered and taught at Bologna, canon law and the theology of the Christian Church were codified (the Decretum of Gratian of 1140, Peter Lombard's Sententiae, 1150). All these are signs we shall have to seek to interpret, and in doing so we shall as our key of interpretation take the practice of the ordeal.

Around 1050, as P. Brown tells us,[38] it was still possible, in the baptistry of Canterbury Cathedral, in one and the same giant water container, to be at the same time baptised as a Christian by the priest, and, as part of a dispute, be immersed in the water in order to discover the truth of a particular case, as part of an age-old legal procedure. The priest moved from his sacramental to his legal function with no particular problem, just because the ordeal was based on this very possibility of moving easily from the sacred to the profane and conversely. The ordeal, which like any social phenomenon whatever can be given a number of differing if not opposed interpretations, can nevertheless be the object of minimal agreement if we say that it is a sort of 'controlled miracle'[39] aimed at regulating particular social conflicts such as money debts, property, sorcery, imprisonment and murder.

Invoking a 'controlled miracle' through the procedure of ordeal in the context of legal proceedings means 'putting God to the test',[40] that is, abandoning the process of reasoned proof to secure a certainty that men as such were not able to provide. It was God that revealed the truth by this decision making one small social group victorious over another[41] and thereby avoiding a conflict by allowing a solution. The ordeal was a slow, solemn process where accuser and accused were placed outside the group; it was not a judgement by God but referral of a case 'ad iudicium Dei',[42] to the judgement of God. Another basic feature of the ordeal lies in the nature of the proof. The argument brought up to prove truth is changeable, variable, indeterminate, and does not lend itself to a precise hermeneutic. This ambiguity at the very heart of the procedure is certainly anything but innocent. Brown gives us the example of the hand that grips the red-hot iron, which is solemnly bandaged, with the bandages removed before three witnesses several days later.[43] The treatment and the passing of the days meant that the interpretation of the burn was ambiguous; but this ambiguity was desired since it left the possibility of reaching a consensus.

The twelfth century was, then, to see the abandonment, gradual to be sure, of this oral culture: the civilisation of writing took over, reversing the respective spheres of the sacred and the profane. The social consensus that ordeal brought in legal proceedings and among small groups yielded to another form of consensus.[44]

The Lateran Council of 1215 forbade clerics from uttering the liturgical protection on which the structure of the ordeal was held to be based, the reason being that a new social code on the basis of which a truth could be recognised was already in place. A shift came about in the way that subjectivity and objectivity were traditionally defined. While banning clerics from the slightest involvement in practices of the type of the ordeal, the Lateran Council sanctioned the doctrine of substantiation. This was the new line of division we should take, since it was thereafter that Western rational knowledge came to be organised. M. Bloch[45] was right to want to 'eliminate once and for all the notion of a medieval economy "conceived as whole", so as instead to stress the great break of the twelfth century, "*one of the sharpest that ever marked* the evolution of European societies"' (our emphasis).

In doing so, we are taking up the path pointed out by J. Le Goff:[46] 'the long duration of relevance to our history … seems to me to be those long Middle Ages that lasted from the twelfth or thirteenth century of our era, to die slowly under the blows of the Industrial Revolution between the nineteenth century and our own times'. For us too these long Middle

Ages are the opposite of the 'hiatus' that Renaissance humanists and enlightened philosophers wanted to see. We shall seek to show that the emergence of modern society develops throughout the 'Middle Ages', and is still important today in order to understand our modernity through certain forms of knowledge. It would, moreover, be desirable to abandon this term 'Middle Ages'. For it was the 'Renaissance', created to serve theoretical considerations on the development of culture in the West deriving from a definite conception of the role of antiquity, that as a counterweight imposed that gap, that obscurity, the 'Middle Ages'.

Our modest study will seek to show the unfoundedness of these theoretical considerations, the absence of any epistemological break between, let us say, this period of 'theology as the mother of the sciences' and the 'Renaissance'.Undoubtedly this study is difficult of a material nature pointed out in a long essay by Jacques Le Goff:[47]

> using a set of twelfth century texts is a delicate business. The general upsurge in the epoch is reflected in written output. Texts multiply ... many remain unpublished despite the work of scholars as from the sixteenth century and in particular in the nineteenth and twentieth centuries. On top of the expansion come the typical features of the period. To assure a work of success, many writers do not hesitate to attribute it to a famous author. Twelfth-century literature is weighed down by apocryphal ... Moreover, nascent scholasticism produces a multiplicity of texts hard to attribute to a single author (does this word have a meaning?): questiones determinationes, reportationes, often resulting from notes taken by a pupil from a master's lecture. Finally, we rarely possess the original: the manuscripts we have were written later (thirteenth and fourteenth centuries), since what inspired the men of the Middle Ages was the search for eternal truth, not for historical truth.

That is what one of the greatest specialists of the period tells us.

By the very nature of any account – and we shall return to this – by the specific features of the traces one interprets, the explanation and understanding we set forth will, far from claiming to be a 'faithful image of what was', the specific knowledge of the period, seek to understand and explain the arrangement of knowledge in the Christian West in an epistemological perspective aimed at reconstituting the nature of the links between words and things (the paths leading to knowledge) while always bearing in mind the fact that this *reconstruction* is being done today, in other words within an episteme that manifestly determines our 'reading' of the past.

Our attempt will, moreover, let us admit it, be only sometimes based on first-hand documents. P. Chaunu had the courage and honesty to say it forcibly: 'Who can have read everything about the history of four centuries? ... Erasmus has filled the life of more than one scholar ... How many lives have been spent on the corpus reformatorum alone? The complete works of Luther represent over 110 volumes, Calvin 55. In any case, one has to accept writing for the most part at second hand.'[48]

Our intention is to attempt at least in part to reconstitute what we may call the 'premodern' thought of the West. 'Purgatory', which was born around 1170–80,[49] seems to us a very good starting point.

Purgatory, which still bears the stamp of the culture of the ordeal, is a test,[50] and by that token remains essentially marked by legal elements. The variety of judgement that the existence of a Purgatory involves is based on a twofold verdict: the first at the time of death, the second at the end of time,[51] thereby instituting in this interim of the eschatological destiny of each human being a judicial procedure pointing to a new conception of the subjective. The idea of Purgatory in fact presupposes not only the projection of an idea of justice but also an organised, sophisticated penal system that reflects the exemplary limits of good and bad action (introduction of penalties, mitigation of those penalties according to various criteria). The last judgement, being future and general, in fact gives only two possibilities, life or death, and Purgatory depends on a solemn verdict. The elect souls are to be saved through an elaborate judicial procedure, made up for instance of remission of penalty (following the 'suffering' of the living through donations and prayer for the dead), making the likely duration of the penalty depend on both *personal* merits and the intervention of the Church.

Religious thought is accordingly totally impregnated with legal culture just as legal thought is bathed by religious culture. Jacques Le Goff reminds us in this connection that the great initiator of the canonist movement of the twelfth century, Bishop Yves of Chartres, in the prologue to his canonical collection (1094), sets out a theory of dispensation, 'the power of the ecclesiastical authority to permit, in certain cases, the non-application of the rule of law'.[52] To do so, an essential distinction among rules of justice is brought in: the imperative rules, the suggestions and the tolerances, a distinction to be taken up again by Alger of Liège[53] at the very beginning of the twelfth century. The social and the religious order were renewed on the basis of a redefinition of the idea of justice, the very notion of sin being modified, as were the practices of penitence. Henceforth a link was posited between sin and ignorance of it, by seeking the individual's *intention* in his own conduct. Anselm of Canterbury[54] had carefully distinguished voluntary sin from involuntary sin, through ignorance. Henceforth, the whole of spiritual and moral life was to be oriented towards the idea of 'intention': the whole question would consist in establishing the boundary between the voluntary and the involuntary, meaning that the identification of sin, the social order, would come about through a process of interiorisation and personalisation of moral life.

Along this road, new methodological principles were to appear. Vice and sin were to be differentiated, always in order to identify intention, just as were transgression and penalty. Transgression,[55] which leads to damnation, can be wiped out by contrition and confession; the penalty, an expiatory punishment, may be remitted through performance of the penance ordained by the Church. Here we leave the characteristics of the ordeal, *revealed justice*, to enter a different legal culture where the dividing line between the religious and the profane has shifted,[56] a line that can be traced on the basis of all these indices furnished by the new methodological principles that are applied in order to discover truth. To identify the intention of someone who has committed a sin, there is a need for perfect definition of the role of *will* in an offence, so that the individual subject appears as the central point of any idea or principle of justice. With Abelard, for instance, there is a clear proclamation of the primacy of *intentio*, whether in good acts or in sin. In the same way, we see the appearance of a psychological science of the human subject 'which was to take over and organise the spiritual experience accumulated by tradition and recorded by the Fathers' and then by monastic authors.[57] This lets us understand the place of *confession* in this judicial arrangement for seeking hidden truth.

We are on the threshold of the penal universe of punishments fitting the gravity of the sins, aimed at extirpating the evil concealed in the bodies of individuals, and helped in so doing by torture. A hermeneutics is set up. Truth was henceforth to appear as something hidden, something that could be reached if one knew how to read a set of special signs. The first thing was of course that knowledge was possible only through writing (the Scriptures); which provided signs that one had to learn to read. Truth was hidden. Purgatory indicated that truth was to be sought within individuals, the concept of *intentio* being the interpretive principle that was to permit it to be reached. The body was the outside of something, a sort of envelope covering, enclosing, the hidden truth; special features (a look, appearance, size ...) were to be signs that would indicate from the outside the truth that the inside of the body enclosed and hid.

Over and above these new dividing lines pointed out to us by Purgatory between the sacred and the profane, from which new social experiences of subjectivity were to proceed, other discursive practices were also to be transformed or to appear. It is on this that we must most strongly insist. Our case is that the rationality of modern Western knowledge was decisively oriented by this premodern theologico-juridical episteme that emerged between, let us say, the tenth and the twelfth centuries. We are not, for instance, to explain the new theology of law (from Saint Benedict, according to whom transgression of the Rule constituted a fault, to Saint Bernard, for whom certain rules were only lightly binding) by a sort of enlightened dogmatic evolution, but by picking out, firstly, the very deep legal imprint on Christian thought (which still has to be identified as much as understood) and secondly, noting that while this is true for the period we are interested in that theology was the mother of sciences, it could claim to be so only because it was profoundly impregnated by legal methodology. It is this *link between the religious and the legal* that we have to understand more deeply.

Theology was indeed the 'mother of the sciences' because of the new conception theologians had of nature as *external*, present, intelligible reality in which man found his place, himself as nature. There was henceforth to be a dissociation between miracle and the marvellous, that is, the interpretation of the natural interplay of elements that suffice to give an account of the organisation of the world and its creation. It was not the absence of God but, thanks to the identification of natural laws, the revelation of his presence and his actions. Throughout this period we see *systematic search for causes*; Andrew of Saint-Victor states that, before recourse to miracle, one must first exhaust all possibilities offered by 'natural' explanations.[58] We shall soon see how the concept of 'nature' was to be elaborated using the exegesis of Scripture; here we shall note merely that the 'account of creation' in Genesis was to be interpreted according to the natural interplay of the necessary and sufficient factors (principle of rationality), to give an account of the organisation of the world.

This is, as M. D. Chenu tells us, explained through a 'metaphysio-connystic' vision of the world, that of the hierarchy of Denis:[59] the key to understanding the universe and man in the universe is the ordered, dynamic linkage of all beings, the 'theophany' were '*causality and meaning coincide*'.[60] The universe is a perfectly ordered unity; the coherence of beings involves a continuity. Matter has a meaning in this Christian philosophy, and it is man that provides it; he is himself nature within Nature. Order was to be not only the pattern of a religious conviction but was to be proved by method: nature contained sacred values, but was the sphere of profane science. We shall certainly meet with sometimes dense confusion among the descriptions of this physics of the universe, the causal explanations taken, for instance, from the Ancients and the spiritual meanings that may be picked out,[61] yet the essential thing is there: a rational knowledge whose root is the search for causes is affirmed.

The notion of cause, Chenu tells us again,[62] is the most significant case of this rational penetration of notions and principles into the *interior of faith*. This means, and it is an essential point, that the criteria of truth are no longer merely the rule of faith in the revealed datum, but in the *rational coherence of propositions* taken from a philosophy of man and used as premises in arguments. Here lies the unshakeable place of legal knowledge, and the fact that in this episteme theology and law are inseparable. This is the way to understand, for instance, Gregory the Great[63] in referring to '*witnesses*' worthy of faith: it is the *possibility of verifying the truth* of what is stated that is at issue at calling upon testimony. What calling a witness brings into play is the proving that something is true; this is why the principle of the *enquiry* asserts itself. Proving sin in someone is seeking the intimate, *hidden* intention in him, in other words carrying out an enquiry into the voluntary and the involuntary. It would be very hard here to distinguish between the legal and the religious.

Within this set-up, which we have termed the interiorisation and personalisation of moral life brought about through the development of this intermediate world, Purgatory, one single method prevailed as fundamental in Western rationality: the legal method. We mean classification and categorisation[64] but also, or even mainly, new attitudes towards time. Since the penalties are proportionate to be sin, since all sin is fundamentally *personal* in nature, Purgatory brings into eschatology a calculation that is not one of symbolic numbers, but a 'realistic' computation: this computation is that of legal practice, and Purgatory is condemnation not in perpetuity but for a time. The time spent on earth in sin and that spent in Purgatory will be measured proportionately, as will the time of intercession offered for the dead and that of acceleration of liberation from Purgatory. Jacques Le Goff rightly stresses that 'the notion of condemnation for a time is part of a broader mental attitude that leads to a bookkeeping of the hereafter. The fundamental idea (the Fathers, Augustine) is that of a proportionality of penalties, in this case of time spent in Purgatory, according to the severity of the sins'.[65] We shall soon come back to this crucial question of time; let us seek to move forward in this question of the theological and religious aspects proper to the period, first of all locating the scriptural arguments.

Premodern Western civilisation was born in the Church; theology as we have said was the mother of sciences, the supreme science that was to generate new philosophies, methods and disciplines. But theology is above all the science of a book, the book of books, the Bible.[66] All disciplines, scientific or literary, will be built up from basic texts recognised as containing the matter to be worked on. Culture will be made through texts.[67] Philosophy, logic, grammar, the symbolic order of the world, the philosophy of science, will be constituted on the basis of this culture through texts, on the basis of an association between things and concepts.

Once again, this period of the second millennium ought not to be seen as the point of origin of something new. We have taken care to keep Foucault's terminology and speak of an episteme that breaks with the previously dominant forms of knowledge, while, perhaps, *maintaining* particular, essential forms of knowledge. For instance, we know that the knowledge of High Antiquity was based on observation of man and nature and that it was with later Antiquity that the conviction that everything lies in writing took root (meaning specifically that henceforth all discourse would relate only *to a discourse preceding it*). This point of continuity is undoubtedly a major one, but we have been able to put forward the idea that a discontinuity did nevertheless come about between the tenth and twelfth centuries, with Purgatory as an important marker.

Similarly, this premodern thought arising during this period was constituted around the sacred doctrine. Along with this great normative knowledge, the Church had a conceptual instrument – hermeneutics – which, though systematised in the twelfth century by the doctors of the Church, dates at least in essence, as P. Chaunu tell us,[68] 'from the first ages of the Church, from the old patristics with which medieval scholasticism felt itself in reverential relationship of pious affiliation: exegesis of the four meanings of Scripture'. But here too a break was to come: these four meanings were to be the object of a special order that would allow access to the divine revelation hidden in Scripture.

10

The concept of history: fragments 1

Littera gesta docet,
quid credas allegoria,
Moralis quid agas,
quo tendas anagogia.

Scripture is compared to a river, an old inspired image from Scripture itself, on the banks of which stands the Church: this river, Godfrey of Saint-Victor tells us, has four currents running through it.[69] The first meaning, or history, relates to the Old Testament. It is far off in relation to us; the three other meanings concern the New Testament. Such is the method thanks to which one gains access to truth: that of the twofold scriptural foundation. Every truth in the New Testament has an annunciatory passage, a trace, in the Old Testament. Continuing his metaphor of the river, Godfrey shows an army of 'bridge builders' at work; these are the commentators on Scripture. Four among them are distinguished among all by their eminent position: we see them unceasingly passing men from one side to the other, which means from history to the spiritual meaning. This hermeneutics states that the first meaning is history and that there follow in sequence allegory, tropology and anagogy, though the right order is a problem.

The expressions 'leges historiae', 'allegoriae consequentia' and 'rationes anagogicae' date, as we have already said and as H. Lubac reminds us,[70] from the time of the Fathers, but interpretation, that is the relationship of tropology to history and to allegory, must be certain and break every notion of continuity. It is on the determination of this relationship that the new forms of rational knowledge of the Christian West were to be deployed. What was to be at stake around this question of the four meanings was not the authority of the Bible,[71] but only the way of interpreting it.[72]

Scripture is like the world: indecipherable in its fullness and multiplicity of meanings, and the more one engages with it the more one finds that it is impossible to explore to the very end. The more Scripture seems simple and

easy in its words, 'the more profound it is in the majesty of its meanings'.[73]
It can therefore never stop the movement of research. The *De Doctrina
christiana* was a philosophy of science where everything was a *sacramentum,
that is*, technically speaking, the sign of a hidden thing. The hidden meaning
of words and texts was 'sought with willingness',[74] as if the very obscurity
was both a challenge and an attraction of the truth. The symbolism of
Augustine[75] thus took root, and the revelation of the New Testament was to
be all the better imagined as being mysteriously hidden in the old.

From the simplicity of the letter, from the visible creation, we should
let ourselves be guided towards the summit of contemplation, for 'the
surface of the Scriptures and the sensible forms of the world are the two
garments of Christ' that are like two veils hiding the light of truth but
nevertheless containing 'the beauty of truth itself'.[76] Without sin, the
symbol of the world would have sufficed in its unaltered transparency.
Now to decipher it we have need of recourse to Scripture. This Scripture
is considered in its primary simplicity, but in coming down to us this
fecund simplicity 'opens up to the multiplicity it engenders, to gather it
thereafter and hold it within itself'.[77] Thus without losing the primordial
unity it has in the word, Scripture nevertheless conceals for our use a
range of very numerous meanings, in other words an interpretation that is
indefinite.

Revelation is to be deciphered in the visible creation of the world, but
can be gained also from Scripture. The two revelations are organically
linked: Scripture is created by God, like the world, and the world is
written by God, like a book. The whole of this sensible world is like a book
written by the finger of God ... all beings making it up are as so many
figures, not invented by human ingenuity, but instituted by the divine
will, in order to manifest and to signify in some way the hidden attributes
of divinity.'[78] The Scripture is accordingly not only divinely guaranteed, it
is true divinely. The Spirit has not only dictated it: it is wrapped up in it,
it inhabits it. There is accordingly a need for a hermeneutics, a
'hermeneutics of the hidden meaning', since the infinity of meanings of
Scripture does not yet constitute a structure. This is just what we are given
by the traditional theory of the fourfold meaning. This theory is intended
to express the revelation through the Old and New Testaments, and the
most widespread explanations[79] accepted a twofold fullness of times.

The first event had revealed the hidden meaning of the old Scripture:
the second would bring out this meaning in full light. In both cases, the
same mystery was involved: penetrating its significance meant attaining
the mystical or spiritual meaning. We will then have two formulas to
express this authentic doctrine.[80] Father Alberto Vaccari and Father C.
Spicq tell us in connection with the twelfth-century exegetes that 'some,
following Origen and Jerome, took the trichotomy of history, morals or

tropology, mystery or allegory: others were to explore the fourfold distinction of Cassian and Augustine, taken up by Bede: history, allegory, tropology, anagogy'. The interest of the distinction lies not only in the numerical difference; what really matters is the *order* in which the three or four meanings are distributed. More exactly, it is the respective place occupied in the one and in the other by tropology and allegory.

Many authors[81] distinguish among 'history, morality and mystery', or 'history, tropology, allegory and anagogy'; others on the contrary[82] place allegory, the *'science through riddle'*, in second place. This is the direction habitually taken by most great scholastics, and was also to be that of Nicholas of Lyra, Occam or Wyclif. Let us cite the very interesting letter from Adam of Perseigne (after ca 1221)) to the Archbishop of Rouen, Robert Poulain:[83]

> Sacrae etiam lectionis quadriformis est intelligentia. Prima est historia, quae est rerum estarum narratio. Secunda est allegoria, quae est earundem rerum gestarum spiritualis significatio. Tertia est tropologia, quae pertinent ad rationem morum. Quarta est anagoge, quae sursum animum ducit.

The difference between one formula and the other is of basic importance as reflecting mental conceptions and orientations that do not entirely have the same provenance. Depending on whether it precedes or follows the allegorical meaning, that is to say, whether it is unrelated to it or is dependent on it, the 'moral' meaning may be something very different.

Thus, for H. de Lubac,[84] only the second of the two orders, that which places allegory immediately after history, expresses the authentic doctrine of the faith in its fullness and in its purity. It alone is adequate to the Christian mystery.' This formula was to be regarded as the *doctrinal* theological formula.[85] Summarising, there is a threefold non-literal meaning that must be sought behind the letter of the history. Cassian perfectly points out the doctrinal issue we would do well to bear in mind in our endeavour to sketch this episteme of Western Christian premodernity:

> Certain texts have no need of any more sublime interpretation than an immediate literal meaning (for instance: the Lord thy God is one); certain others must be understood in an entirely allegorical sense ('let your loins be girded about, and your lights burning'); some are to be taken simultaneously literally and allegorically ('whosoever shall smite thee on thy right cheek, turn to him the other also'); others, finally, in the simplicity of the story, help less able readers, each according to position and capacity, to gain strength in their beginners' labour.[86]

Once this literal meaning – that is, the 'story' – is accepted as primary, two different orders are counterposed: the sequence history-moral-allegory, which is Cassian's and was already Origen's, and the sequence history, allegory, tropology, anagogy which is Saint Augustine's and especially Saint Gregory's. Access to the mystery is based on an interpretation of the signs that the Scriptures are, based on the fundamental distinction between 'letter' and 'spirit'.[87] The book of the Scriptures is written 'externally' according to the letter, 'internally' according to the spirit, and one must move from one to the other in order to understand. From the word deposited in the Bible, one must derive spiritual understanding; this understanding, 'higher, deeper, more absolute' than the letter, far from being an *invention*, has a structure that *imposes itself* on us. The distinction between letter and spirit ought in other words not to be a separation, since it is only the letter that leads to the spirit.[88]

The decisive aspect, stressed by Karl Barth,[89] is that: 'while the Old Testament never knows any present except in reference to the future, the New for its part knows a real present that nothing could question ... The new covenant is not repeated; it is concluded once and for all.' What is definitive here is the new relation that a society posits in the understanding/explanation of itself. The 'present' becomes the category through which the natural signs – nature, man – take on meaning, but by introducing this new category, reforged by Western rationality, namely the past. Barth is right to say that the Old Testament never knows a present except by reference to the future, but it is also necessary to note that that knowledge, the present, comes about only through knowledge of the past.

This hermeneutics of the letter and of the spirit is in fact based on a special conception of time that institutes a *linear* link between a past and a future that will enable all these natural signs that make up the sensible world, whose meaning is hidden from us, to be interpreted. This conception of time, and we shall return to this, at the same time brings out a circular pattern of rational explanation where, as we have seen in our first part, prediction and hindsight ceaselessly refer to each other. The past will henceforth serve as a key for understanding the present, while transforming itself into an allegory that points out the future to us. The present, as constitutive of meaning, thus tends to disappear; the truth is not only in the letter or record but in the spirit, that is, in its interpretation.

The Christian allegory thus bears an essential significance in the exegetic tradition. This term allegory may, as H. de Lubac tells us, quoting Cicero,[90] have been coined around 60 BC by the grammarian Pheidomenes of Gadara to designate the figure of grammar or style that consists in 'saying one thing in order to make another understood'.[91] It would perhaps be erroneous to bring the whole of Christian allegory into an 'essential relationship of origin and nature with the doctrines of intellectual paganism that allegorise the myths';[92] this would amount to regarding all Christian interpretation of the Scriptures as a colony of Greek allegorisation on Christian territory. For H. de Lubac, adopting a widely accepted conception, Christian allegory comes from Saint Paul. This point of paternity is certainly fundamental, since in Saint Paul's theology the noted events in the Bible are, by contrast with myths, regarded as 'sure facts of history', which have in other words their truth 'according to the letter'[93] though the need remains to reach their allegorical meaning.

Allegory becomes a synonym of 'spiritual meaning', which comes along to complement the 'literal meaning', that is, the historical one.

The 'spiritual meaning', sometimes replaced by the term allegory, has a second replacement term, namely mystery. More than allegory, this involves a strongly objective nuance, more specifically objective than 'spirit'. The mystical meaning is the sense relating to the mystery, *which is a reality*, hidden in God and then revealed to man. It will accordingly be the meaning that 'contains the fullness of doctrine'.[94] The literal meaning is inseparable from the mystical meaning because the literal meaning becomes the *sacramentum*, the external element, the envelope, the sign or the *letter as bearer of signs*. It is the sacrum rather than the arcanum.[95] The mystery for its part is that arcanum itself. It is accordingly the internal element, the reality hidden behind the letter and signified by the sign, the *truth indicated by the figure*. In the relationships between the two Testaments, the *sacramentum* has to do more with the Old and the *mysterium* with the New (present time). The whole New Testament is a great mystery hidden within the sacrament, or signified by the sacrament, that is the Old. Following Origen, we have behind the letter sought 'quid mysticum': Richard of Saint Victor distinguishes the narration of facts (to speak in today's terms), the 'juxta historian', and their interpretation 'juxta intellectum mysticum'.

There is therefore not only a twofold meaning in Scripture: one consisting 'in history' and the other called spiritual or allegorical, or mystical. The tripartite division,[96] or the quadripartite one, expresses a dimension not so much exegetic as doctrinal: a morals aimed at systematically organising social life. This division also has a close relationship with legal practice. If the question of tripartite or quadripartite division arises, this is in our view because the dividing line between the sacred and the profane sometimes remains too subtle, with the quadripartite distinction perhaps offering an easier principle of separation to apply, as tending directly to express the new boundary between the 'subjective' and the 'objective', the human and the divine. The historiae and the tropologia in fact are intended to express life here below; and allegoria and anagogia relationships with God.

The historiae and tropologia feed new legal practices, since these concepts enable law to be stated in a new way.[97] Let us here merely briefly note that the tropologies, heterogeneous in Christian exegesis (see de Lubac), have a considerable pedagogical advantage that is fully taken advantage of by preachers. It is here that tropology developed, taking up the figure of the '*exemplum*', something in which the new legal practices had something to do. If just this relationship between tropology and allegory is so fundamental, this is because quite clearly it is a Christian legal doctrine that is at issue. To place tropology, as we have said (and we shall return to its link with exempla), before allegoria means putting 'morals' before the Christian mystery, and hence not subjecting it to the latter; in other words, to 'marginalising' Christian theology and morals. The reason why problems relating to the tripartite order appear thus from the thirteenth century onward was not considerations of a pedagogical[98] or psychological nature, but more likely because socially increasingly sharp conflicts were opposing the institutional Church to lay powers.

H. de Lubac, in an analysis both erudite and astute, seeks to show[99] that at bottom it was normal for the doctrine of the quadruple meaning to prevail, since 'implicitly' it was already in the Fathers on the one hand, and on the other this formula has the advantage of being able to be brought under the two fundamental meanings of letter and spirit. But instead of seeing a 'single good answer' between these two doctrines, in our view one should forget the scriptural issue as such, to relocate the conflict between these two doctrines in what was at stake institutionally. The fact that the doctrine of four meanings ended up prevailing means that an equilibrium was set up between the lay and religious powers and that, perhaps, morals would risk being more lay than Christian (tropologia, as we have seen, precedes allegoria and anagogia).

But another fight was proclaimed, which would again see the jurists at the centre. For Origen,[100] 'there is no reason for superstition in names provided that one knows how to look at things'. For Clement of Alexandria, equally,[101] 'the seeker of the truth must find his expressions without premeditating them nor worrying over them; let him endeavour merely to name what he means as he ought; since things escape him who is too attached to words and devotes too much time to them'. Thomas Aquinas thought the same thing, and felt that when the basis of things was clear all verbal dispute was idle. Words were nothing; it was the spiritual meaning, the anagogy, that must prevail. Saint Gregory of Nyssa[102] said: 'This anagogical contemplation (of Scripture), or this tropology, or this allegory, or whatever name one wishes to call it, we shall not argue about the way of saying it as long as through it we arrive at useful thoughts. For the great Apostle, in saying that the law is spiritual, meant by that name also the historical accounts ... In all these names that designate the spiritual intelligence, Scripture teaches us at bottom only one thing: that one must

absolutely not stop at the letter ... but move on to immaterial contemplation ... as it is written: the letter killeth, but the spirit giveth live.'
Grammar was thus to be a major discipline for theologians and its rules to
be the first interpretative instrument they were to use in the criticism of
the sacred texts and the working out of the revealed datum, but understanding thoroughly that the act of knowledge is *divinatio*, which presupposes signs as already given, with the task of 'finding a prior language
distributed by God in the world'.[103] Words resemble things; only Scripture holds truth.

'Moving to contemplation, as it is written'; it is by this hermeneutic
procedure that we gain access to the symbolic mentality specific to that
period. As we have already said, one of the great spiritual figures of that
hermeneutic was Saint Augustine. His *De Doctrina christiana* set out the
principles of his sacred hermeneutics on the basis of a philosophy of signs.
Everything is *sacramentum*, that is, a sign of something hidden; the
translatio verborum is, then an operation necessary to the understanding of
the sacred text, the latter containing not only 'signa propria' (words) but
also 'signa translata' ('figurative' meaning).[104] Recourse to allegory is
therefore regular: the hidden meaning of words and texts is sought
readily, as if the very obscurity were both a challenge and an attraction of
truth. Metaphor is not a literary procedure used to evoke a spiritual
reality, but a hermeneutic principle tending to signify the internal content
of things; the discernment in the density of beings of their *profound, secret*
truth. It introduces two worlds: the second, in depth, becoming accessible
through a metaphor of the first. The symbolic transfer is the means that
we have in order on the other side of the shell to attain the kernel of
truth.[105]

The doctrine of the four meanings of Scripture reflects belief in this
truth of the world. The Sacra Doctrina organises the interpretation of the
Bible, as we have seen, through hermeneutics of the literal meaning (the
'surface', one might say), and the hidden meaning, or literal meaning;
that is, the first world, or the history of men, is posited as the basis for a
continual transposition to suprahistorical realities (second world) which
terrene events prefigure. The very nature of the Judaeo-Christian revelation calls for the progressive continuity that is the basis for this
hermeneutics, and we again find the creation of a linear time regarded as
linking the 'origin' of the world and the 'end of time'. Here once again we
find this parallelism, methodically pursued, between the Old and the New
Testaments. The least details, indeed the least words, are transposed in
continuing allegorisation. M. D. Chenu points out that the literature of
'Distinctiones', or biblico-theological dictionaries, is the typical fruit of
such work.[106]

It is just here that we shall find analogy, as it still questions us even today. The Greek word indeed comes to take on a special technical meaning that well records what we have just said, since in fact it reflects a 'transfer of the spirit, rooted in sensible forms, in order to perceive spiritual realities'.[107] Symbolism, the 'natural form of poetics', is thus the major access to knowledge of the mystery of things, divine or human. This symbolic hierarchy of the two worlds is reflected in theology by the anagogic meaning: anagogy is a radical necessity for the true understanding of things, since things are true in their being only through their ontological reference to God. It is in sacred knowledge, 'initiation', that one knows them, and symbolism is consubstantial with the mystical experience. Chenu teaches us that 'the Augustinian sign is conceived according to the resources of the psychology of knowledge as the instrument of a spiritual experience that coves the whole field of language and the various words of figurative expression'.[108] This is just what is radically new in the conception of subjectivity: the knowing subject becomes the principle and rule of this epistemology.

It is the knowing subject that 'confers value on the sign, over and above an objectivism founded on the nature of things'.[109] Signs are constructed on a psychological analysis: it is the theory of *res* and *sacramentum*, the basis of the theology of the twelfth and thirteenth centuries. The sign provides knowledge, the mysterious tends towards visibility. Saint Augustine,[110] finally, gives the materials and methods to feed a symbolism that can be a means for rationally constructing a (Christian) temporality: the events, linked from the past to the present and the future (according to the stages of the Old and New Testaments) not only prepare but *prefigure the future* in the present. The events, the *res*, beyond the account, the *verba*, signify.

While this philosophy of the sign took part in this new episteme that defined the age of premodern rationality, this does not mean that it found its 'origin' in this period. Moreover, this concept of 'origin' is very closely linked to a Christian philosophy of history. Scriptural allegorisation had already long been presented in the West as the application of symbolism on a literary or scientific basis: stones, colours, animals had meanings suggested by their forms, properties, etc. Bede is regularly presented here as the obligatory reference. The Augustinian influence on the venerable monk needs no stressing; let us merely point out for the sake of the anecdote that this Augustinian sign, conceived of according to the resources of psychology of knowledge, was to lead Bede to be the first English author faithfully to describe the external appearance of people, to say 'what they resembled'.[111] What the premodern period was not to accept in Bede's theological doctrine was his allegorical meaning, and it is interesting to know why.

We know, for long having said it, that for discerning truth to be identified and obstacles to be met with, allegory constitutes a major piece: it is in fact the typological procedure applied, beyond the letter of the text, 'the symbolic value of the historical realities preparing and prefiguring at a distance the various contents of the Kingdom of God, its beliefs (mystery, allegorical meaning), its morals (tropological meaning), its final accomplishment (anagogical meaning)'.[112] It is this 'application' of the literal meaning to the spiritual meaning that revels the specific forms of knowledge, and from Bede to Hugh of Saint Victor a radically different apparatus of knowledge was set up. The Didascalion of Hugh of Saint Victor is not only a reminder of the laws of Scriptural exegesis but primarily, as Chenu tells us,[113] a *methodology of the sciences* (sacred and profane), an organised, constructed theology. In it there is applied, and defined in accordance with certain principles, the very special truth contained in Scripture, namely the *past.*

Scripture has a twofold meaning: the words are the instruments of meaning, but also the things expressed by these words. The construction of meaning through the episteme of the premodern period was to pick out the form of knowledge we will later recognise as 'history', but for this the *allegorical meaning was to go through a very considerable shift.* With Hugh of Saint Victor, symbolism was perceived as forming an integral part of Scripture and of the Doctrina Sacra that emerged from it. It is in other words a constructive principle emanating from the surplus of meaning that the text, of divine essence, furnishes. But at the same time, and now everything becomes suddenly different, this essential symbolism relates to all of the texts according to the stages. This whole set is coherent, continuous; it is a *true story.*

So much for Bede.[114] His knowledge was exercised through those forms of knowledge today called theology, hagiography, geography, chronology and, finally, what I for my part would call legal knowledge and is wrongly called 'history', which relates to the way of *proving the truth on the basis of those historical records, the 'archives'* (which are found essentially in monasteries). Chronology involves a number of pieces of scientific knowledge, such as the computed tables for calculating the date of Easter. Hagiography is a type of knowledge that should not be neglected either, since it is a form of accounts of lives of saints that serve as 'exempla', that is, they are intended to express *typical actions capable of being the effective rule, through their actual content, for human actions.* This has never been sufficiently stressed, yet it is very important.[115]

Coming to speak of historiography in Bede, we have to say that it was to take the form of an account of events, involving simultaneously legal knowledge,[116] closely bound up with geography[117] and chronology[118] but also hagiography, an account of events that allowed a *preponderant* place for the irrational and the miraculous.[119] The premodern episteme tends to marginalise the place of the miraculous through a reasoning of rational type speaking in terms of causes and effects (we would recall what we said regarding the ordeal). Chronology as such does not in fact necessarily posit a causal link among the various events reported. With Hugh, one seeks to authenticate the *truth of past events* before doing any allegorico-theological construction and arranging them in the form of an *evolution of coherent periods*. Henceforth it is the truth and nothing but the truth that is to be told, and the borderline between hagiography and knowledge of the real past tends to become increasingly clear.

11

The concept of history: fragments 2

It is no doubt needful to give a few very brief reminders here of the various forms of historiography we find before the period that concerns us, in order to avoid a twofold ambiguity. The first is one that might imply that nothing before this period could claim to be a form of knowledge with a close relationship with what we today recognise as 'history'. This ambiguity would, in other words, present our period as 'an origin'. The second ambiguity might imply that, in a past before our period, what we today recognise as history already existed. As we have already said, the origin is a myth, but it serves to draw a boundary thanks to which the concept of history was developed (see the previous chapter).

Thus, in past times before the period we are interested in, we can find a number of special types of knowledge which, in one form or another, were later to belong to 'historical science' (to be constitutive of it). Take the work of Herodotus. The very word *historia* is a homage paid to him, Momigliano tells us, since it was he who invented a new literary genre.[120] With Herodotus, history is an enquiry, that is, a specific research into past events that actually occurred. However, the role of *visual witness* remains absolutely preponderant in him for the collation of past events, which means that direct visual observation is the accepted form of authentic testimony, in other words that oral culture remains preponderant. The most suitable way of knowing an event is to be there, to be a witness of its occurrence; the accounts coming from 'trustworthy' witnesses (as one would say later; see above); information from those not directly present take second place. Written evidence is not a suitable proof. A fundamental point here is clearly the secondary place given to writing, even though this term *historia* aims at knowledge that provides a sure transmission of the past. Momigliano further notes the weakness of the Greeks in their method of working with documents and in that of collecting data,[121] and the very weak impression of contemporary art on historical accounts.[122]

Herodotus insisted on the importance of reporting what *one had oneself seen and heard*, and Thucydides made *direct experience* into the foremost qualification for a historian worthy of the name. The object of enquiry was *change* within a society, recorded through the testimony of contemporaries. Classical history was the expression of the change, and the lesson to be drawn from history related to the way of coping with change.[123] The reception of all these testimonies was thus taken as a justification for action, and traditional modes of behaviour were thus reported and proposed for emulation in the literature of *exempla* which we find here again (the Homeric poems, for instance, are very rich in exemplary anecdotes).

Momigliano tells us that orators suggested precedents and that 'compilers' (cf. Ephorus) prescribed them in historical works and in oral tradition.[124] In Cicero, the tradition seeing history as the *narration of true facts*, of political events that actually occurred and the truthfulness of which is verified, remains vigorous. The whole problem was clearly to know how to distinguish perfectly the true from the imaginary, in other words, to create truth. Herodotus had the reputation of being a liar for having attempted to recount the Median wars that had taken place a generation before him. To develop his account, he had travelled in the Orient (where he had essentially found written records he was unable to decipher) and had employed 'his eyes, his judgement, his talent as enquirer'.[125] Thucydides doubted Herodotus's method and maintained that a serious history related only to events of which one was a contemporary. How, said Thucydides, could Herodotus have recounted so many things about events he had not seen, of people whose language he did not know, of countries he had visited briefly or not at all? 'Either he had concealed his sources, which is plagiarism, or else he had invented the facts, and was a liar'.[126] For classical Greek historiography, only the contemporary moment could be the object of a discourse of truth, which means that the historian dealt only with '*present time*'. Herodotus, for his part, sought by his sort of historiography to bring in a 'history of testimony'.

Accordingly, with Herodotus, we have certain forms of knowledge that we shall again find in our premodern Western period: the written document as witness in an enquiry seeking to recount the truth of a 'past time' of which no direct witnesses an longer exist. Similarly, the exempla[127] are central to historiography and utilised as models of social integration. But all these forms of knowledge belong to an episteme too different from that of our own time for us to be able to posit the least continuity between them. Momigliano illustrates this in pointing out that for the historiography of the later Empire, the notion of truth is troublesome, giving us by way of illustration the invitation from Sozomenes to Theodosius II for the latter to add or omit what he wants from his history. This was nothing other than a request to Theodosius to approve a history book officially, since 'no-one could raise objection to what you, O

Emperor, have approved'.[128] Here truth is secured through authentication, by the powers that be, of written records.

It would here no doubt be needful to ask very precisely about the various forms of knowledge that were to be art of 'history' in the period of Eusebius. His 'ecclesiastical history' in fact opens a new literary genre where written documents are abundant and persecutions and *heresies* (a new concept) are recounted. The history of Eusebius was founded on an *authority*, no longer on free judgement, and recounted the truth of a time that had existed *very far* from the contemporary period, a truth that emerged from numerous doctrinal controversies.[129] The civilisation of writing was coming to prevail, and thus to upset the concepts of reality and truth. The proof of each was to be established on the basis of completely new 'testimony',[130] and the very concept of 'time' to be transformed too.[131] It was these new forms of knowledge that were to generate what would one day, much later, be called 'history'.

Let us start by saying here, or rather saying again, that henceforth *truth had to do with the civilisation of writing*, which was to engender the development of new forms of knowledge to establish the truth of the document itself (notions of authority, authenticity, apocrypha which we shall meet again soon), and a philosophy of the sign in which, as we have said, biblical hermeneutics was a central figure.[132] Hugh of Saint Victor represents this thought well. The term 'historia' appears in him in the part devoted to sacred disciplines: the religion of Christ is at the basis not only of logic but also of events recorded in a history that had to be 'read' (the medieval *lectio*) according to an appropriate method (and here we again find the four meanings of Scripture). This, as Chenu stresses,[133] is all the more noteworthy since in the profane disciplines historia existed too, but in moving to the *lectio* of the Bible we change object and method, since *historia* was to designate the content and method of the new scientific discipline.

With Hugh, the Sacra Doctria became articulated in two parts: the lectio historiae and the construction of allegoria. History was simultaneously the literal *content* of the account and the *structure* of this account (which embraced allegory). The account was a *succession of events*[134] expressed in a '*series narrationis*'. This expression is systematic in Hugh; it is a series, that is an *articulated continuity*, the links in which have a meaning, which is that of 'history'. Time is transformed, since it is no longer a cosmic time but a succession of actual events whose meaning reflects God's initiatives in the time of men. This systematic research for causes that took up in the start of this part to understand the mode of thought of the period is found fully again in this *lectio* of the Scriptures: the sense of continuity is accompanied by the identifying of constant causes (in the determinism of natural or social phenomena). The religion of

Christ does not have a basis of logic but of events recorded in a history, which once again must be 'read'. The 'historia' was to be simultaneously that sequence of actual events and their reading, with Hugh positing an indissoluble link between these two approaches to texts, positing the fundamental reality of the historia before any theological construction (just as he was to seek to oppose the invasion of theology by speculation when the quaestiones and their product, the Summa, claimed to emancipate themselves from the lectio of the sacred texts).

Biblical exegesis thus fixes his belief in a historical meaning. The series narrationis fixes the feature of a human history in opposition to the logical connection of abstract disciplines; this series is an organised sequence the links in which constitute the meaning and are the object of the intelligibility of history (and here we have the introduction of the concepts of time and place). With Hugh, a temporal realism comes in, being opposed to, for instance, the theology of Abelard,[135] for whom the unity of the faith required the identity of its content through the ages (and he drew support from the Nominalists to put forward the logical identity of propositions stating temporary different actions). The important thing to note here is that through theology of the type put forward by Hugh there began to be a careful distinction between the knowledge of the real which aimed to be true and invention of the literary type (fabula). This theology in fact brought to the fore the wish to find the lessons supplied by the real past.

Medievalists agree on saying that the 'historians' of the Middle Ages refrained from stating the causes of the events they noted, a definitive proof of the absence at the time of what was one day to be actual history. To prove this statement, they give us the case of the 'Annals' (events are recorded as they become known, annually), the 'chronicles' (chronological reconstruction of a past, not a causal chronology) and even of 'history', whose priority is given to an account, but mixes the true and the invented. The error is here is that these medievalists, rather than seeking *forms of knowledge* that can be said to be constitutive of history, seek *social forms* of such knowledge (the individual historian), and a form of organisation of labour (the function of the historian in a society, stating that their ideal type is the historian as he appears in Western Europe in the nineteenth century). Very well, then, this ideal type, for the period we are interested in, does not exist, cannot be found. However, the forms of knowledge that organise the reconstruction of past events in the way our society even today conceives of such reconstruction were definitely present. This biblical exegesis in fact sought to recount *true* events, the articulation between them being of *causal* type, whose truth was to be *rationally proved*.[136] Among these forms of knowledge that were constitutive of what was one day to be recognised as 'historical science', we have in particular legal knowledge, and it occupies an absolutely central position.

We know that in order to defend their powers (we might also say their rights), the monasteries, as from the tenth century, compiled *cartularies*. These were documents of a legal nature which had no other aim than to set forth a situation regarding heritable property, but were around the twelfth century to take on a different significance. Thus Peregrinus,[137] Cistercian abbot of Fontaine-les-Blanches, wrote a two-volume series narrationis of his monastery, giving in the first volume an account of its foundation and in the second a list of its privileges and possessions. Here we find the classical juridical link between the history of a house and the catalogue of its goods and possessions, between a genealogy and a cartulary. A competent abbot had both the cartulary and the genealogy of his monastery written down as written records that utilised the same archives and aimed at the same objective: to prove title from texts.

The abbot cum jurist had to know local history well (chronology, names of abbots, bishops of the diocese, genealogy of donors etc.), but his legal knowledge had also to be impressive, since one had to be an able, trained palaeographer in order to read Merovingian, Anglo-Saxon or other documents. Let us further note that the verb 'compilare' became a key word in the twelfth century, an exact synonym, as B Guénée tells us,[138] for 'excerpere'. While losing the original taint it had in antiquity (to despoil, pillage), henceforth it was to be the compilator, an able palaeographer, that could translate, analyse, indeed give a 'diplomatic critique'[139] of, documents, to supplement the study of texts by the epigraphical study of accessible documents; this compilator also took care to transcribe in his cartulary 'the lists of popes, bishops, abbots and kings, a geographical nomenclature, statistical data and local information',[140] all in order correctly to locate *in time, space* and *reason* his documents.[141]

Working on a cartulary meant mastering genealogy and heraldry. Very soon too, in great families, genealogical concerns were to become affairs of State. But once again, what should be noted is the specific legal feature of all these types of knowledge – where an account of the past of a house was inseparable from a catalogue, an inventory, of its possessions. *The form of the account meets the manner of proving truth of possession*; notaries (particular Italian ones) *wrote the account of the past the same way as they wrote their contracts*.[142] Guénée[143] reminds us that as early as the end of the eleventh century, the *Historia monsterii Figiavensis* was a sort of judicial memoir in favour of the Abbey of Figeac against that of Cargues. Nor was it entirely by chance that the flourishing of 'true accounts of the past' in the years 1090–1130 in England was located at a time when the great monasteries had after the Conquest to defend their powers (their 'rights') and privileges.

Still better, the very structure of the – argumentative – legal discourse was already in place, and was to reserve a precise locus in the apparatus of truth to the argument from the past: to defend their rights against the archbishop, the argument from the past as a *true event or 'precedent'*[144] was definitively accepted.[145] Our jurist monk, apart from having to be, as we have said, palaeographer and archivist (chronology, catalogue, etc.), had also to be capable of synthesis, that is, of integrating that knowledge into a causal apparatus. In doing so, he had to state the epistemological principles that enabled him to demonstrate the superiority of his documents (here we have the question of falsification, authenticity and apocrypha, as we shall very soon see). This is what we are told by the ups and downs, irksome one might say, of our famous king of England before our poor Scottish barons: this was henceforth to be the way to show truth; the past emerged from these records that writing is, and only from it would it be disputed.

We again come to our problem of enquiry: it is part of an apparatus of knowledge that articulates reality and truth within a culture where writing has definitively come to prevail over the oral. What the witness most easily and most faithfully reports at least one assumes in a culture of oral tradition (and hence with more assurance and more detail), is what he has seen with his own eyes, what he has been an eyewitness to, fide oculata. The gospel according to Saint John, moreover, reminds Christians of the superiority of those who have seen (21:24): 'This is the disciple which testified of these things, and wrote these things: and we know that his testimony is true'. We may say in this sense that reality (naive observation of things) and truth are here on the same level. This is, moreover, a link with Greek historiography, as we have seen, but there was to be a very clear break here that distinguished 'present' time (the truth of which could always be stated by an eyewitness still alive, and thus by a form of oral culture) from 'ancient' time (where a statement of the truth could by definition not be the object of such a process).

The problem would henceforth be to be able to state these new forms of truth in the absence of eyewitnesses, and it is here that the legal knowledge that extracts the truth from written depositions is intimately linked with theology, since the sole method henceforth available for distinguishing the true from the false was to be based on the records provided by Scripture. Let us further note this special feature of Western knowledge lying in what we often regard as a poverty (or a confusion, as far as the common language goes) in vocabulary between history as the account of a sequence of events and the story as the event making up that sequence. We shall find this again in legal reasoning, in the very structure of this account: an event is alleged only for a particular claim, the latter is absolutely inseparable from this event; it institutes the meaning of which that event is the sign.[146]

In principle, the only testimony henceforth accepted was to be that which links up what is regarded as establishing the account; and in the event of disagreement in testimony, the actual quality of the witnesses had to be assessed. Thus testimony comes, with the culture of writing, to be assessed using the concept of authority. The fundamental criterion on the basis of which the jurist theologians of our period established the truth of texts was through a hierarchy of 'sources', that is, through the concept of 'authenticity'.[147] Authentic means firstly a document or a person full of authority, authority in which *one must believe,* 'worthy of faith'. The ultimate sanction comes from *one* special authority, determined by the Sacra Doctrina. Since by definition one authority has more weight than another (from pope to emperor, from bishop to abbot, etc.), some texts will be more authentic than others. Thus, henceforth, the concept of authenticity was to develop in parallel with publicist doctrines (until one day we have the definition of authentic as that which has been guaranteed and approved by the public authority).

At the same time as this definition of truth through authenticity, theologians put forward the term 'apocrypha' to describe the false; apocryphal became in fact the contrary of authentic or approved. An apocryphal text has no authority.[148] The search for truth was thus to favour the testimony to the detriment of the witness; it consisted in better disclosing the error contained in an authentic account, or better recovering the truth hidden in an apocryphal text. Documents were henceforth to be put to the question,[149] taking up Bacon's *mot.* But as soon as we no longer intend purely and simply to record what our witnesses say, as soon as we force them to speak, be it against their will, a questionnaire is essential. A statement has no right to be produced except on condition of being verifiable. The jurist comes to share the theologian's concern, just as our theologian shares the jurist's concerns.

Throughout our period, the majority of false diplomas, false pontifical decrees and false capitularies, then forged in such great numbers, were made out of interest. Assuring an abbey of a disputed property, supporting the authority of the Roman See, defending bishops against metropolitans, etc., were all written records whose truth or falsehood had to be proved (on the basis of an event or the account of that event). Legal knowledge was therefore increasingly inseparable from Christian religious science. The practice of exempla equally took on a quite different meaning in this alliance. Here too, there is for us no question of speaking within terms of 'origin'. We know[150] that for the Greeks the traditional modes of behaviour were listed and offered for imitation in the very abundant literature of exempla. The Romans too showed a keenness to follow this practice of exemplary models; one may see a connection between this and the first Christian hagiographies. For Cicero, knowledge of the past was fundamental, since it was 'magistra vitae', the possibility of bringing up examples to imitate, a conception that was maintained in Western Christian tradition[151] and was to flourish through the sermons of preachers in churches. Here too, exempla were to emerge from saintly history in the strict sense and take up a place in the life of men.

Since Isidore of Seville, ecclesiastical law had been the 'rule of good conduct', or 'canon law'. Everyday morality was certainly to stake a claim; but still more essentially in our view, exempla were to become part of argumentation with a completely new structure, given rhythm by Christian time. Christian linear time, where the present, such a hard time, was eliminated in order to set up a direct relationship between 'a' past and 'the' future, required exempla to be truth of the past for a morality of the future, or, what amounts to the same thing, a morality of the past for a future truth. The exempla ought in effect to extract from the confusion of past times a clear representation of the destiny of men.

One must of course bear in mind what we have already said about the Sacra Doctrina (temporality, causality) in order properly to understand that this genere of exempla was henceforth to belong to a form of account of the world that tells the truth as much as the quality of things here below. Putting it differently, exempla, within this premodern Western episteme, became a 'precedent'. As exempla, they kept its characteristics (model of conduct); as precedents, they became a new form of statement of law in a Christian figure of time (linearity), in a rational reading of the world (causality). This period we are interested in is a 'renaissance'[152] that sees humanity finally triumphant, that is, sees men gaining their capacity of judging others and themselves when they perform what is their primary duty, the creation of law.

Our period is a great period for legal thought, a decisive moment for our civilisation. Peter Grassus, jurist of Ravenna, wrote a memoir 'In defence of King Henry' (1084) which for the first time used Roman legal texts for public interests, those of King Henry against the Pope, the latter being supported by ecclesiastical law (we shall come back to this). Here we have a typical form of legal thought. In support of an assertion, events are put forward that are claimed to express the truth of the past (proof of this statement); proof through texts, where the sense of the text becomes the account of an event and where it is rather difficult to distinguish between a 'certain' event and an 'interesting' event. This form of reasoning was to become just that of a historical account, as it was also to be that of preachers and mendicants.[153]

Knowledge of the past came from an account of past events that had to be true, but these events were henceforth set in a series narrationis articulated through causes. This was why the first writing about the past in England was also done by Benedictine monks. They had the science of the Scriptures,[154] the hermeneutic through which 'evidence' (records)[155] was produced so as to prove the truth of the past. But once again, let us not here seek to see 'historians'; they were jurist monks seeking through records to prove their rights (powers). They sought to collect all documents existing, they arranged charters, transcribed the different documents attesting rights, sought to reclassify them chronologically just as to locate them topographically, and they interested themselves also in the various inscriptions on the walls of buildings, and assembled biographical texts, etc. It is not by doing this that one becomes a historian; one becomes a Benedictine scholar-monk, perfectly understanding how to 'make documents speak'.[156]

When he tells us that '850 years before J. H. Round' William of Malmesbury had discovered 'how to use charters like a historian',[157] R. W. Southern in his judgement gives proof of great lucidity, but only *post eventum*. Whatever may be his genius, in fact, William did not in a moment of transcendent intelligence accede to a form of knowledge that was to be equalled only eight-and-a-half centuries of civilisation later. His merit, assuredly considerable, consisted in expressing in a very beautiful way the scientific truth of his own times:

(1) every charter was read as the *sign* of something hidden;
(2) every charter was an account, a *narrative series*, not only of acquisitions and losses through the centuries, but also a rational series within whichever king or bishop was animated by *goals* and *will*;
(3) the *witnesses* were the authenticity of the account and the *chronology* of bishops and abbots;
(4) the archaeological remains – traces – were put forward as witnesses to prove certain aspects of the account;
(5) just as tombs, inscriptions, crosses, reliquaries etc. were used for this end.[158]

The 'evidence', this qualified record, called on to prove an argument is the expression of this understanding of the world, a 'hermeneutics of hidden meaning'; it is the rational form of Western premodernity, the form of knowledge we find on each side of the Channel. *An epistemology of Anglo-Saxon legal practices is identical to an epistemology of continental legal practices.*[159] While this knowledge Benedictine monks had of the English past may be interesting, it is not so because of something very special about it by comparison with the way of knowing things on the continent, in the history of forms of knowledge in the West (nor very advanced); it is interesting, on the contrary, for what is very general about it, what it expresses so well about our Western knowledge.

William of Malmesbury did violence to the rhetorical tradition and was equally irreverential towards accounts such as Bede was still able to write, since the point was thenceforth to make the texts tell a truth whose causality was earthly, rational and human. Thus, for William, the fundamental thing became the associational links that made the most trivial objects or events a part of the life of the community, made them memorable events; any object, any piece of ground, any act of daily life, was located in a causal pattern. This science of the jurist-theologian in this account of knowledge of the past was at the same time the only possibility of understanding the present; it was very much from texts that one could discover and prove to a community its present identity.[160] In parallel, in legal discourse, every record henceforth becomes the potential support for an argument, the potential proof of an underlying truth. The causal, explanatory account unfolded along a time axis where the present was unveiled to incredulous eyes on the basis of the elaboration of a past, becoming nothing more or less than the meaning to give to a present situation.[161]

12

Christian time 1

'For sacred books the Christians have history books, and their liturgies commemorate, along with the episodes of the earthly life of one place, the annals of the Church and the saints. Christianity is historical in another way too: located between the Fall and the Judgement, the destiny of humanity appears in our eyes as a long adventure which each individual fate, or "pilgrimage", in turn reflects; it is in duration and accordingly in history that the central axis of all Christian meditation, the great drama of sin and redemption, unfolds.[162] We have cited Marc Bloch at such length because he covers well the historical dimensions of the Christian religion here. The Scriptures are in fact in part accounts of true past events and in part they announce something to come, divined on the basis of a certain past.

"From the creation to the Christ, the whole history of the past, as related to us in the Old Testament, is already part of the history of salvation", O. Cullmann tells us.[163] This time, as we have already said, is a *linear* time, tending towards a goal, towards God. With Hugh of Saint Victor, as we have seen, theology is articulated in two parts (lectio historiae and the construction of allegoria), thus organising the discovery of reality *in time* into the form of a series narration is, a causal sequel of events. 'It is not the classical tradition but the biblical message that has opened our eyes to the future as the time of a future consummation ... In consequence of the historical expectation of salvation, we have a modern, futurist, historical awareness which is just as Christianly motivated as it is Christianly and even anti-Christianly oriented ... Our modern conception of universal history springs from the faith in an event of salvation, while escaping it.'[164]

Time is no longer merely a cosmic duration, but a historical succession of events (Hugh, once again, was to reject Augustine's hierarchical conception of the six days – a hierarchical classification of different natures – in favour of a temporal realism.[165] This succession of events raises the question of the nature of the bond that links them, and we have seen that this bond was to be conceived of as a relationship of causality consisting in a move towards the universal,[166] reflecting the sense of continuity. In a Christian society, it is undoubtedly the case that the future has first and foremost an eschatological meaning, but this is flanked by a chronological meaning: this world and the hereafter are united as events in the same plot. Temporal structures were now completely reconsidered as part of these segments of linear time to which a meaning applied. For J. Le Goff, these temporal structures have to do with a new application of individual and collective memory,[167] and we shall see the establishment of a special chronology, namely the grand genealogy, but what is more important for us here is that this successive time is above all the *time of narrative.*

This narrative account completes its perfect development through the scientific aspect of legal practice where enquiry is made into whether the events alleged are true (problem of proving them, of the quality of witnesses) and where the whole of the account has a meaning (leaving a very slight portion to the miraculous) secured by bringing the various details of the 'plot' into relation with each other. Historia est rerum gestarum narratio, says Hugh of Saint Victor; that is, the account of true events organised into an articulated continuity in which the links have an (explanatory) meaning, which is the understanding of history. Knowledge of the past conserves the memory of past times, memoria temporum, recounts a past event, gest temporum, gives the description of the times, description temporum, presents anew the order of times, series temporum, and establishes the certainty of time, temporum certitudo.[168] Chronology becomes a constant, permanent concern: henceforth time is rationalised (and we soon come to have clock time), and is measured.

Here too, our period is not at the 'origin' of measuring time. The requirements of the liturgy introduced into the monasteries a broadening of culture, since the establishment of an Easter table raised enormous problems, requiring the creation of a discipline, the computus. Chronology takes a central place in Bede. Similarly, the adoption of a Christian era required exact knowledge of when Christ was born (comparison between the Scriptures and the calendar), thus raising the question of the certainty of the date. Chronology, dating, was the major rational form for knowing the truth of things, but took on its whole importance only once oriented by the episteme of our premodern period, as we are shown by the work we have already cited at length by Jacques Le Goff on Purgatory.

We have seen that the souls in Purgatory were subject to a complex judicial procedure (remission of penalty, early release thanks to 'Suffragia'), which reflects a new criminalisation of deviant social practices and brings the time of the penalty and the merit of each into relation with each other. As Le Goff tells us, 'with Purgatory there appear new attitudes towards numbers, since it brought into eschatology a calculation that was not that of symbolic numbers or the abolition of measurement in eternity, but on the contrary a realistic computation'.[169] This counting is that of legal practice, which makes Purgatory a hell not in perpetuity but for a time. The creation of Purgatory comes about thanks to an arithmetical logic: the time spent on earth in sin is calculated, as is that spent in Purgatory, since the intention (Augustine) is to make the penalty proportionate to the gravity of the sin. The thirteenth century is the century of calculation, of accounting and of the first budgets; time was the rational measure of things, and the great genealogies of our aristocratic families appear, as we have already said.

Theologico-juridical knowledge definitively imposed the conception of a variable, measurable and manipulable time (proportion between sin and penalty); the exempla took on narrative form in the preacher's sermon, with the example of good conduct finding its reward in the securing of paradise and that of bad conduct unfolding throughout a judicial plot enumerating the actual actions (to which some could testify) that had taken place in the past (on such and such a date, in such and such a place), and had by their gravity justified a penalty of so and so many days (with the benefit of a remission of penalty if the bereaved yet on earth were sufficiently generous to the Church).

13

Allegory: Christian time 2

This chapter is intended to relate to Scripture and the capacity which it has, and it alone, to reveal the truth of men and things. In so doing, we shall be taking up a number of indications and conclusions supplied by Foucault in 'Les Mots et les Choses' in the sections on 'Signatures', 'The Limits of the World', 'The Writing of Things' and 'The Being of Language'.[170] On all these points, however, Foucault continually speaks of the 'Renaissance', the sixteenth century. This is in our view a limit that absolutely must be given up, since on the question we are interested in it says absolutely nothing specific. In the 'archaeology of the human sciences' pursued by Foucault, we must in fact abandon the idea that the Renaissance was a privileged moment in the 'writing' of things.[171]

If we wished to retain this concern for periodisation, then the great moment of Western rationality would as we have already repeatedly pointed out have to be located as from the end of the eleventh century and the epistemological arrangement made in the whole course of the twelfth century, and regard there as being a perceptual shift in the order of knowledge with what Foucault calls the classical period. As to the 'history of the sciences of nature', it should in our view be based on this modelling. Foucault was indeed right to stress, after so many others, the absolute privilege of writing, and to see this phenomenon as one of the greatest 'events' of Western culture,[172] and also right to state that writing alone would henceforth be the truth, and that accordingly the specific feature of knowledge was to interpret; but the illustrious philosopher was in our view very wrong, in saying or resaying all that, to talk to us about the Renaissance and the sixteenth century. Back, then, to our Holy Scriptures at the start of the second Christian millennium.

We have already discussed at length the hermeneutics of the Scriptures, through the doctrine known as that of the four meanings, and we have seen that a dividing line is introduced between a meaning supposed to be on – in – the letter (the sign) and a meaning supposed to be outside the letter, determining the two interpretative techniques of historia and allegoria.[173] Here, however, we should be wary not to bring in a *contemporary positivist* conception of this 'literal' meaning ('historiae')! The relation, for instance, between etymology and 'exposition' should put us on our guard against that. Recourse to the etymology of a word was to be practised once it came to be considered that the best way of grasping the meaning of words was to reconstitute their *origin*, to give their *derivation*. Etymology, then, sought to give the 'true meaning' in that way.

However, as B. Guénée notes,[174] as early as the ninth century the term etymology was sometimes applied to the analysis of a word by explanation. By the twelfth century, everything was played out: derivations were submerged by explanations and even confused with them. Etymology was a form of knowledge that determined a meaning by a 'literal grammar' – we shall return to this question with Lorenzo Valla – whereas in understanding the Scriptures, historia *prefigures* allegoria. If 'exposition' predominated, that was because knowledge of things was arrived at using the approach of similitude (here we again find Foucault), where hidden truths are signalled at the surface of things. Historia came to be the visible mark of invisible analogies, and resemblance at once what is most manifest and best hidden. The literal meaning, which, in order to avoid all ambiguity, it is best to call 'historia', taken together with the allegorical meaning, sets up a semiology, that is, 'that knowledge which enables signs to be distinguished, that which sets them up assigns to be defined, their interrelations and the laws of their linkage to be known'.[175]

In the twelfth century, once again not in the sixteenth, the relationship between semiology and hermeneutics gave a fundamental place to similitude, with the meaning of things being secured from comparisons among things that resembled each other, and exegesis cutting across analogy. With expositio we reach the depth of things, since the space of immediate resemblances becomes a sort of great open book. Theology is indeed the mother of the sciences; there is no difference between the marks that are the physical world, the surface of the earth and the words of Holy Writ. The relationship to texts is of the same nature as the relationship to things; knowing is interpreting, and no distinction can be drawn between what one sees and what one reads. Historia gathers together into a single form of knowledge all that has been seen and heard, all that has been recounted by nature or by man. Grammar is therefore a very complex exegesis,[176] granted a major place within the theological science. Our contemporary world, crushed by 'positivism', has huge difficulties in thinking of this: that words are nothing, no more than are things, apart from the particular knowledge within which they have meaning.

The unity of enunciables (the theory of the semantic unity of the word, known as nominalism) expresses the unity of the faith, since if the word enunciates the action in its substance (doing, praying) through a time (past, future, present), this time changes neither the reality nor the truth of the action concerned. The proposition, when it is true, is always true. The 'literal' meaning, then, of Holy Writ is recognised by nominalist theory, in conferring on the grammatical categories sort of abstract objectivity, in a verbal realism; so that we can understand how our theologians – in search of timelessness for the divine science – were able to imagine they had found a solution to their problem there. It is in this relationship that reality encloses, conceals, a truth. In 1121, to decide the question whether it was indeed Dionysius the Areopagite who had founded the abbey of St Denis, Abelard applied to the texts he had collected the principles of his 'Sic et non', that is, of logic. Grammatic structure and logical truth met, implying each other like the two facets of a single problem.[177] Grammar and dialectics are thus reconciled.

However, this exegesis was to be unceasingly disputed. We have already seen this with Hugh of Saint Victor, for whom events and things had meaning, but as contents, as substances. This was also Thomas's criticism of the theory of the semantic unity of grammatical categories;[178] he said that since substance was liable subsequently to become the subject of contrary attributes and since denominations and statements referred to substance, these therefore had to adjust to these variations. In other words, nouns and verbs had to be treated as pure grammatical values, that is, abstraction made of their value as meaning in order to be able to accept the nominals. Unfortunately, the voces (words) are voces significativae (signs),and there could be no parity between the laws of logic and those of grammar, with the first going well beyond the second, whatever the 'modi significandi' of Bernard of Chartres may have been able to claim (the modi significandi supposedly changed a word in its grammatical structure 'only from outside').

Verbum significat tempus: a proposition whose verb, expressing the action, constitutes the pivot is necessarily bound up with the tense of that verb in both its logical structure and its truth-value. The laws of truth are not established solely on the basis of reality or of the various realities; the specific feature of knowledge is neither to show nor to demonstrate, but to interpret. This is the whole point of the commentary, 'entirely turned towards the enigmatic, whispered part hidden within the wording commented on',[179] which gives birth, in the margin of the Scriptures, to another writing, more fundamental and more 'primary', which the compiler takes it as his task to restore. Knowing consists in causing to speak, in putting to the question, that is, in giving birth, alongside these marks that are the Scriptures but are seen as supplementing them in order to arrive at hidden truth, to commentary.

Voces are voces significativae, and the theologians taught that Christian allegory, quite distinctly from Greek allegory since it was presumed to be a true story,[180] encloses a mysterious – mystical – meaning which is reality 'hidden firstly in God, then revealed to men in and at the same time realised through Jesus Christ'.[181] The *sacramentum* was as it were the envelope, the external element, the letter as bearer of sign: rerum signa sunt in sacramentis. The sign is the sacrum rather than the arcanum, and the mystery is the arcanum itself; it is the internal element, the reality hidden behind the letter and meant by the sign, the truth pointed to by the figure. The allegorical (or mystical or spiritual) meaning is not dissociated from the 'literal' (historical) meaning. The way they fit together is, on the contrary, fundamental. Christian hermeneutics was to locate allegoria before tropologia; Christian morals could not only depend on the Christian mystery, not anticipate it. This is the way we have to understand the sentence: 'he who has a care for truth will not encumber himself with questions of words'[182] since the important thing is not the care for the letter as such but for the word as trace or, in other words, to know how to look at things.[183]

Historia – littera gesta docet – is the consideration of the external, perceptible aspect of things apart from their mystical or hidden meaning, and is henceforth to be counterpoised to poetic fictions, to 'fables'. It is all records that are read or which one can see that must be made to speak; but all of these records must be proved, authenticated; they must appear as indisputable. History is the account of these records which are to be authenticated, and if history can make the claim to truth, it is because of this operation of authentication. Scripture supplies events, a series of real events[184] to the obtaining of and the conserving of the testimony to which one must apply oneself. Hermeneutics and semiology are once again superposed: the letter is only a record, whose meaning is not simply its reading, but arises only on the basis of the record. Allegory precedes tripology: the Christian mystery is transformed into civic morals, into 'excellent lessons of prudence',[185] where the life of forebears serves as a model for successors. But allegory comes first, since it alone can know the final causes that events as such could not supply, which lend retrospective illumination to their whole course.

Overall explanation belongs only to the mother of sciences, theology, since only the Christian faith surely anticipates the truth. The doctrine of the four meanings, the hermeneutics of the hidden meaning, seeks to establish the objective meaning of the world's destiny, as the destiny *thanks to which* one may lay claim to true knowledge of the things of the past. The former is extracted from the latter, but through understanding the mystery. Allegory – the core of hermeneutics – lies in these realities the texts speak of and is therefore located not at the level of the account, but within the events themselves; it belongs to the account only insofar as it relates a real event. The text therefore serves only as a means of access to the truths of the past, but at the same time prophecy is inscribed in it. The present disappears completely, or more exactly it is the mysterium, in the Christian sense of the word. Only the Scriptures contain truth: 'they transmit the memory of allegorical events whose reality they divinely guarantee'.[186] This truth is inscribed in a figure of time where the present is mystery, where knowledge of the past (the Old Testament) prefigures the future, which is however nothing but an allegory of that past (the New Testament), the mystery of our present. The object of allegory in relation to the events reported by the Old Testament is a reality to come; not that it ignores the dimension of the present, but because it is a knowledge that distinguishes the relevant signs – from its capacity to know final causes – among the traces of the past.

The Christian mystery is a very special event which knowledge of the past does not suffice to state. This knowledge of the past is a sign of something that is internal to the sign, contained within it, but at the same time the reality of this sign is deeper than the sign itself; in other words this knowledge is not a passive knowledge of existing, preconstituted objects, but itself constitutive of these signs. Hugh of Saint Victor conceives the object of the allegory, that is the New Testament, as a facta mystica.[187] It is first of all facts that one must know how to recognise, which, moreover, enclose a message and which, finally, are saving, absolute and definitive. But this view is possibly only because allegory's relation to the past is a relation of after to before, which alone allows the distinction and constitution of these 'remarkable' signs.[188] It is through this institutive reading that a hermeneutics develops.

We have already seen at length how henceforth, through the principle of enquiry that emerged from Greek historiography, even that of Herodotus, knowledge of the past was arrived at and proved; what the new interpretative principles were that were to come to apply. The episteme of the period we have termed premodern, rational, in the Christian West thus sets up a specific relationship between a semiology that institutes the signs and a hermeneutics that interprets them and posits a new relationship to time.[189] If theology occupies a fundamental place, that is because our theologians wished to construct 'the edifice of faith', [190] or knowledge of Christ, through allegory, the 'hidden' object (inward and spiritual). This knowledge escapes carnal eyes: the secret must, as it were, be wrested, and allegory may present itself as a doctrine (the doctrinal meaning understandable only to a few) that will make the allegorical meaning of Scripture into a 'Catholic' meaning.[191] An order of levels of knowledge is thus clearly posited, reflecting the ever-renewed links among those aspects of knowledge that make signs speak (and disclose their meaning) and those that discern these signs (and constitute them as such). This was, as we shall see, to be the way we would one day speak of philology.[192]

This is the perceptible relationship among 'the law, the faith, the word', to take up B. Barret-Kriegel's expression: the articulation between this hermeneutics of the hidden meaning and semiology that reflects a special arrangement of the order of knowledge. This sort of definition is always moving, arousing, as Foucault in particular has shown us, shifts within the order of knowledge. These shifts are fundamental because they institute forms of knowledge that are at the basis of another conception of truth; but the term 'epistemological break' used by the philosopher to describe these shifts is perhaps rather too radical. This concept of break, conceived of as the epistemological critique of a philosophy of continuity and progress of reason, is presumably essential because it well indicates the constituted states of knowledge, the differences – or breaks – in the way of knowing and interpreting things. But the term is nonetheless, in our view, too exclusive since it inevitably also suggests the idea that there was a 'before' and that there is an 'after',[193] two completely different worlds that no longer communicates, so that ultimately knowing one does not count much for knowing the other, except in negative terms (in terms of break). This is where we may come up against another problem.

Certainly, the episteme of Western premodernity is very considerably different from that of modernity. The theologico-juridical pattern and its critique, philology, were, we are taught, succeeded by 'mathesis'; however, we assert, a whole set of knowledge identified with modernity cannot be understood except specifically using the theologico-juridical episteme. We shall seek to illustrate this observation using the book by F. Dagognet[194] on the natural sciences as practised in the eighteenth century. Perhaps this book may enable us to show the influence that legal knowledge, already very old, and methods of scriptural interpretation may have been able to have on knowledge of botany at the time.

Botany, like biology in general, on the one hand postulates a *secret* logic of living things, a logic 'hidden' from us; and on the other imposes a systematicus, a logic of the classification of plants, in the dictionaries in which the eighteenth century was to abound. How are the semiology and that hermeneutics structured? The name no longer represents the plant but replaces it;[195] what is henceforth important is to name the plant, that is, to abbreviate it, to reduce it to a few essential signs. Here we still have the view of the exegete who knows how to extract from an event an initial truth, draw a 'natural truth' from a sign. Since writing comes to replace the plant itself, the methodological question comes to be of a lexicographical order, and the legal influence is fundamental here. 'Natural families' are created, 'characters' are posited,[196] and structured into reasoning by analogy ('the great hope of substitution', as Dagognet says), positing that a species cannot belong to a family without possessing its essential qualities (and conversely).

A lexicography, a hermeneutics (ontology), a systematics; here we have all the ingredients of a legal knowledge. To name is to classify: it is the linguistic card index that authorises the deductive reasoning. By naming, one undoubtedly announces more than one states, that is, one engages in theoretical and alphabetical exercises, so dear to lawyers, consisting in the last instance in imagining all possible situations. In this exercise the ploy pursued is to *change the indexes* (of the 'factual situation', as one would say in today's legal language) and to imagine the most elliptical formulae; in other words, one engages in a 'systematics'. And this is the episteme we find from Dagognet's pen when he presents Linnaeus's work to us. Botany becomes a dictionary, a sort of Ariadne's clew for the botanist. 'The Linnaean science of plants implies only a glossology (or the art of arrangement and disposition). Linnaeus is a taxonomy and a linguistics'.[197] The 'civil status' of the lawyer acts as a guide: a plant is recognised – (is) – by its name and surname (without any need to mention its provenances or relationships).[198]

The scientific problem for the botanist like Linnaeus is, ever and anon, to articulate this hermeneutics and this semiology; for Linnaeus, a single 'character' has to govern the systematic arrangement:[199] the seed condenses the plant, and an index, an external apparatus, announces it. It is this relationship between a sign and its 'deep meaning' that Dagognet reproaches Linnaeus for: 'Linnaeus wants to read or decipher, whereas one must *first*[200] analyse and discover cleavages, relationships, groups. Being guided by an index leads to artifice.'[201] Dagognet's critique is undoubtedly interesting for well pointing to the locus of the problem: the articulation between what the analysis proves and what the index shows. It is, though, perhaps over-quick, since we know very well, as medieval exegesis amply illustrates, that there cannot be any sign whatever unless there is simultaneously a particular knowledge that institutes it. Accordingly, one has shown nothing in saying: 'to be guided by an index leads to artifice'. Dagognet, moreover, shows this himself in presenting Adanson, who abandons 'forms' for the 'living thing' (thus another semiology), and must hence invent other determining indices.[202]

The status of Western rationality lies, as we know, in the constitution of this link, and perhaps here the modes of knowledge of the theologico-juridical episteme have not entirely disappeared. When, for instance, Dagognet presents De Jussieu,[203] he does so similarly on the basis of criticism of the sign (De Jussieu was in fact to accept the idea of the multiple, not unifiable, plant), but always on the basis of a 'hermeneutics of the hidden meaning',[204] concerned to discover 'sympathies' (affinities), in other words the hidden relations among substances. At the same time, and very significantly, he was to posit as a problem for solution, following the acceptance of a multiplicity of signs, a problem we have already met with on the basis of this hypothesis, that is, the discovery of an invariant. De Jussieu thus sought the constant factor in the composites of a body, where understanding of the body 'ought no longer to be founded on fluctuating appearances, but on assemblages or linkages among many'.[205] The point is to arrive at constant structures within phenomena that are themselves variable.

At bottom, in order to be able to speak of an epistemological break, one would have to be able to show that there is no one single form of knowledge, specific to a given period, that might be evoked in speaking of another period. But this is absolutely impossible. It therefore seems to us wiser to speak of 'shifts' than of a break. No doubt the example we have given of the sign and its reading by the botanist are no longer either the sign or the reading that a biblical exegis was pursuing and developing, but what remains in common and undoubtedly reflects the legal aspect and the reading of signs in the botanist's method is that the truth of botany, the result of rational knowledge, emerges, just like the truth of Scripture, from a semiology. At the same time, the shifts have the same effects as those that can be shown through the concept of break, that is, they become new ways of looking that recognise things differently. This point is important, since it allows a more specific understanding of how, why, these shifts take place, and perhaps also enables a rewriting of the history of the types of knowledge that have chiefly organised these shifts, to qualify these shifts. In doing so, we shall perhaps be led to raise again problems today regarded as solved, in particular that of the distinction from the viewpoint of rational proof between the truth in history and in natural science. We shall return to this; but let us for the moment remain with Western legal knowledge, still during our premodern period, and particularly in England. Written culture definitively supplants oral culture and therefore, here too, the law will henceforth be written (in French), and the writ will henceforth characterise English law.[206] The order of classification of these writs is very much common to the period, since it takes up the principle of annals: the yearbooks (entries of legal decisions and disputes, under the year they were handed down), with a special feature we should point out right away. The books do not give the whole of a decision, a 'judgement', but only fragments of it, which are 'indices'.[207] The point was thus, through these legal yearbooks, to train lawyers to read signs pointing to deeper truths (and therefore able to bring about effects in law). This institutive reading can clearly not do without a hermeneutics, since henceforth it was to be necessary to 'seek the indices' (in ordinary French legal language, the 'évidences') that contain legal effects, that are the sign of a hidden legal truth.

It is important here to recall what we have already said, starting with the absolute predominance of writing: the relationship with texts is the

same as the relationship to things, to know is to interpret, and there is no
way of distinguishing between what one sees and what one reads.[208]
Everything we said about the culture of the text that our lawyer monks
had,[209] or our lawyers, can clearly be repeated here;[210] we must stop
talking about English law as radically different from other legal systems,
and supposedly nothing but 'procedures' based on 'empirical' knowledge. The knowledge is far from being empirical, and is organised on the
basis of a certain reading of things (as on the continent), a semiology. As
to the term procedure, it is hard to see what it is meant to mean;[211] our
English lawyer, often a Benedictine, knew how to read and analyse charts
and cartularies, and was thus an archivist, a palaeographer, a 'diplomatist', accustomed, moreover, to tracing the lines of affinity among the
various signs that had managed to produce effects of law (the notion of
'case', where the legal principle and its index are intimately mixed) and
setting up a continuity in time (giving to it a linear structure where the
present could always be stated through a reading of the writings – the
truth principle – of the past).

Yearbooks and writs[212] constituted the state of law, a written truth, as
well as a lexicography; in other words an account (legal statement) that
points to signs and a reading that aids in piercing the secrets of those signs.
There is nothing specifically English here; quite the contrary, we are at the
very core of the premodern rationality of the Christian West. The statute,
the third type of written document with legal value – 'authentic source' –
only confirms this. The statutes have to do with political history, expressing the legislative function of king and parliament (Redbook, Liber, Great
Roll), and from the Statuta Antiqua to the Statuta Nova we find everything we already said on testimony of the past, the account of it and the
status of truth. Far from the historiography of Herodotean type, we have,
for instance, the 'Statut Comme Hugh le Dispenser'[213] which is[214] the
official version of the troublous times preceding Edward III's coming to
the throne. The text is particularly interesting for being a historical
account within a constitutional history (bringing us back to our Greek
tradition) but with the notion of truth shifted by Christianity (the eyewitness has been replaced by the 'authentic' witness, and therefore oral
tradition by written tradition). In its Greek aspect, this charter has as its
peculiarity that of seeking to be a succession of true, essential events for
English political life (exempla), and in its Christian aspect that of being an
authenticated history, an official version (as such constituting a precedent). Magna Carta is another example. Sir Edward Coke sought in the
seventeenth century to see it as the formalisation of an immemorial
natural law, which teaches us more about the methodological concerns of
the seventeenth century in Europe[215] than about premodern European
historiography. This charter was intended to recognise powers – once

more stressing the predominance of writing – and to be part of the knowledge whose truth, and proof, we have already largely discussed – through texts. The special feature perhaps of this charter is that it can refer to a past that it claims to be true as to an ideal past.

Throughout this Western premodernity, English legal culture appears similar to continental legal culture; it is this knowledge which, through texts, recounts a significant past – for the present – where rational causality takes first place. This is what the collection of statutes is. It is only in the sixteenth century[216] that lexicography, as we have defined it for this period, was to take the form of 'abridgements', where naming would, in other words, consist in arranging (bringing us again to our linguistic card index authorising deductive reasoning),[217] which does not at any rate refer to some epistemology supposedly purely English. But before this, just like any Italian notary writing down the past as he wrote down contracts, our English lawyer created knowledge of the past by the method he applied to law[218] and through a hermeneutics of Christian inspiration.[219] Here we have the same epistemology:[220] knowledge of the past is arrived at through biblical exegesis and proof through texts. Thus the writ – which institutes the sign – brings in the conflict, presented in the forms of tales, a causal account of past events that remains succinct ('history'). The fight beings, and for the defendant the point is to show – that is to prove, reading and hearing being the same hermeneutics – the absence of correspondence between the signs mentioned and the manifestation of a hidden truth, between the words of the account, which institute a reality, and the meaning of the legal statement that encloses a truth, mysterious and hidden, that resounds from the mouth of the judge.

We are thus sometimes told, no doubt to show his specificity, that the English lawyer had particular tastes for poetry and theatre. Apart from the fact that these tastes were certainly not peculiar to the social group of English lawyers, or lawyers in general, far from pointing to a special feature of English legal knowledge, these tastes certainly point more to the fact that poetry and theatre are *useful* to legal knowledge in general. The poet is he who finds the 'lost relationships of things',[221] the resemblances between signs and things. 'By the established signs and despite them, he intends another, deeper discourse',[222] which teaches that 'the word shine in a universal resemblance of things'.[223] Poetry recalls this hermeneutics of the hidden meaning. We find theatre, in a very real way, in the moots set up by those big initiated into legal knowledge, parodies of trials that stressed the importance of lexicography to all legal knowledge: 'natural families' and 'characters', we said for eighteenth-century botany; classification-categorisation and 'legal nature', we shall say here. Systematics meant learning to recognise analogies, to work out a factual locus, a scene, where the knowledge that makes science speak corresponds totally and unambiguously, finally, to the knowledge that institutes them. This is not yet the perfect mirror game, but more a shift into fiction as a means of identifying reality where one speaks not of the object of enquiry – how to make the signs speak – but of knowledge, of the characters that seize that nature – what these signs are. Fiction thus maintains an inverse relationship with madness as Foucault defines it for us.[224] In the unceasing work of reason that links similitude and signs, 'the madman, understood as constituted, maintained deviance, becomes the man of savage experience. This personage is the one alienated in analogy. He is the disordered player of the Same and the Other.'

14

Theology, humanism, language

The sacra doctrina consisted, we said, in a hermeneutics where symbolism was an integral part of Scripture, where it was a constructive principle, expressing most directly this surplus of meaning special to that text of divine essence. Thus allegory (see p. 91 ff.) is not the order of recounting events but is *inscribed within* these events themselves, which actually took place. This means that the text is a means of access to the past, to the extent that one can manage to recognise a prophecy *inscribed* in it. The rationality of premodern Western, Christian, thought thus consists in a halfway house, in the gap between a science that interprets the signs (hermeneutics) and a science that institutes them (semiology). The Scriptures contain the truth because they transmit the memory of allegorical events whose reality they divinely guarantee.

Christianity, as we have also seen, posits a radically different relationship with time: the present is mystery, the future is constitutive of these signs that institute the reality of past events, and the act of knowing the past comes to consist in a retrodiction in which the present unveils part of its mystery through its knowledge of the past. Here we have the structure of Christian time that we shall find throughout the centuries to come – which determines the birth of a science of politics as from the late fourteenth century, the founding act of which is that of knowledge of the past.

Allegory is a sign that points to the *relevant* events that have actually taken place; it institutes them itself as records containing a truth. These records of the past are therefore nothing, in the sense that they are visible but could not be read without knowing the Christian message. Thus the relation between faith, law and language – which B. Barret-Kriegel treats as mysterious – was to become the axis from which strategies in the area of knowledge and in the practices of power were to be developed.

Perhaps Wyclif was among the first to join battle against the authority of the Church, the authority of Holy Writ (1378). The Commentary, the authority of the Church, comes to be dissociated from the *primary meaning* of Scripture: finding this meaning under the dense commentary becomes the means of struggle against the Roman Church. We are not yet at the point of developing political science, that is 'history', in the sixteenth century. Truth is still to be discovered in texts, and exegesis is still the science whereby one arrives at it. Finding the 'real meaning' under the commentary means chiefly condemning a dogmatic development in order to reaffirm the unique referent of Revelation, Scripture.

We are half a century before Lorenzo Valla, and Wyclif speaks of betrayal of Holy Writ: 'Woe to the adulterous generation that believes more in the testimony of Pope Innocent than in the meaning of the Gospel; it is the Roman Church that has invented this lie'.[225] That was, as we know, the period of the Great Schism, and the effort being made was to prove rationally the authority of Scripture, heralding the Reformation, which was in the sixteenth century to culminate in reformed Europe, where the proofs of the authority of Scripture were to be the great question of knowledge. Calvin said: 'there are proofs, as certain as human reason can furnish, to render Scripture indubitable'.Before them, 'textual' criticism had taken giant steps: John Huss (Wyclif's contemporary) did not content himself with citing Scripture to emphasise the gap between it and the Church as institution, but *opposed* Scripture to the institution, condemning the latter in the name of the former. The reformed movement was to remember this: in the dogmatic chain of transmission of revelation, a short circuit had been introduced: recourse to the authority of Holy Writ *against* the Roman institution.

What was the major pattern of knowledge in the period? It was the one we have identified in the tenth to twelfth centuries as premodern Western rationality, theologico-juridical knowledge. Wyclif, born around 1324, one of the most brilliant canonists of his time, was from 1365 to 1375 in the service of the English monarchy, which employed his legal skills in the financial conflict between it and the Avignon papacy.[226] A lawyer,[227] possessed all the knowledge we have identified to prove the truth of titles on the basis of diverse written records, in particular the 'legal bases' – as we would say today – of the authority of the Roman central power. This knowledge of writings, of which legal practice was as much the implementation as the formalisation, allowed the interpretative scheme utilised for lay texts to be applied to Scripture. And it was in terms of 'reserved' or 'delegated' justice that Wyclif enquired after the legal basis of Roman central power. He considered that God the creator could not deprive himself of his Dominium, so that God's justice could not be other than reserved. Man has no dominium; the law of the gospel is enough, in a state of grace. Temporal government and civil law are consequences of the state of sin,[228] so that the priest could not assert any delegated power, meaning that only the nascent lay States legitimately held the temporal, exclusive power of legislation.

No separation can be found between proof of the authority of a religious institution (its temporal legitimacy, if you will) and that of the authority of Scripture. When thanks to the latter a truth is established, it applies immediately to the other.

The shift that was to come about in the hierarchy of knowledge is quite basic: it consisted in submitting the interpretation of Scripture to a theory of language that no longer had as keystone the theory of the four meanings and was no longer dominated by the 'allegorical' meaning. The world was explained by the Bible; henceforth the Bible was to be explained by a new philosophy of the world.[229] Lorenzo Valla[230] opposed the Aristotelian cum scholastic tradition that maintained the distinction between logic (the rational 'technique' of discourse) and the rhetoric (the 'art' of persuasive discourse), in order to abandon the greater distinction between the sphere of science and the art of language. Valla identified the whole science of language with rhetoric, which is no longer to be treated as any technique of persuasion whatever, but as a science and an art of discourse.[231] All disciplines were to be brought under it: grammar, philosophy in general, theoretical and moral philosophy, and of course theology.

Taking up Quintilian's scheme,[232] the reading of the original text of a classical author was to consist in a critical analysis of the 'form' and 'content', the 'judicium', where primacy was to be given to grammar and the primary element in it was to be language.[233] A semantics of terms criticised scholastic semantics and then the interpretation of fundamental texts done by the Scholastics.[234] The theory known as 'nominalist', a theory of philosophical grammarians, affirmed a verbal realism, conferring on the grammatical categories an abstract objectivity. In reference to Boethius, for instance, Saint Thomas was to refute the theory of the semantic unity of grammatical categories, noting that 'substance' was likely to become successively the subject of contrary attributes.[235] The rules of grammar were accordingly the foremost instrument used by theologians in criticism of the sacred texts to recognise the revealed datum. With Boethius,[236] the 'ration significativa' was specified in accordance with various 'modi significandi' that constituted just as many species: noun, pronoun, verb, adverb. It was just by grasping these modes of being that interpretation conferred upon words their own mudus significandi. While the verb led one to interpretation of an action, the noun opened up interpretation constituted by a twofold element: substance and quality. All reality could thus be broken down into 'quod est', designating the subject itself (quality) and 'quo est', designating that whereby the subject is (substance).

Legal conceptualisation regained all its rights when Valla disputed with the scholastics the interpretation of certain neutral (verum, bonum) and abstract (veritas, bonitas) terms as indicating some thing in itself, while all adjectives are merely the expression of a quality, never of a substance. These terms were reducible to a qualification, never indicating an object as such. To qualify a thing, an event, any object whatever, meant to recross the space we have mentioned so often between the articulation of a hermeneutics and of a semiology.[237] Valla refused to consider that the logical formalisation of language corresponds to 'real' language,[238] and drew a distinction between culture and formalism. For the humanist, a translation was valid only so far as it rationalised the meanings that words have in an equation in which language was regarded on the one hand as an autonomous, coherent whole, and on the other as a record of a culture.[239] In theology, for instance, but also in philology, he regarded as unfounded the transposition without philological verification of words and expressions from the Greek and Latin languages.[240]

In the enunciation of truth, something decisive was in motion. Christian universalism was splitting up: philologists began to post cultural relativism, a distance between words and their meanings, that was different from what had been brought in by the doctrine of the four meanings on the basis of the idea of a literal meaning and an allegorical meaning.[241] We have seen that exposition had, with this doctrine, submerged etymology; from this moment on that was no longer to be true.[242] For instance, to translate the term fides, faith, Valla used the term persuasio, which according to him best expressed what Christians *understand* as faith; and he posited a close relationship between probatio and persuasio.[243] The opposition to scholasticism is clear: the semantics of terms seeks to oblige theologians not to restrict their theological demonstrations to a logical deductive structure based on necessary conditions, while inducing them to use various forms and instruments of rhetoric. The theologian should become a philologian of Scripture, which has to be submitted to scientific methods and to the rational criteria of grammar.[244]

The lectio of an imprecise original text (in orthography, punctuation or otherwise), like its emendatio, should be capable of revealing the '*authenticity of an authority*', literary or historical, and this knowledge has obsolutely to be used to determine the authenticity of Holy Writ as a literary manifestation of the word of God.[245] The text (emendata lectio) became the object of analysis for its content and as such, as did the vocabulary used in it and the composition of its sentences. A text thus appeared to the philologist's eyes as a 'mosaic of words and phrases',[246] which was studied in its constituent elements, however small they might be, before being taken up as a whole. The truth contained in the text was no longer masked by the words themselves, as in the doctrine of the four meanings; it was to be reconstructed on the basis of this code making up the sentence and its parts. The truth lay in the reconstruction of the text, and this method was to be applied to Holy Scripture. The break with scholasticism was achieved. Here, exegesis (as against the exegesis of Hugh of Saint-Victor) was established by the technique of division of the whole text in order, only at the end, to arrive at the 'local' meaning, sentences and words.[247] A relationship was established between lectio and quaestio, the famous dialectic between reading and problem, where the predominant concern was for conceptual development of the content of the text within which grammar was to find its place.

The humanist certainly echoed Hugh of Saint-Victor's concerns for the literal meaning or 'historia', but abandoning the allegorical meaning: language was definitively in a sort of 'sole sovereignty', using Foucault's expression. One of Valla's greatest difficulties related[248] to the structural and semantic differences between the Greek and Latin languages, an essential consideration particularly in respect of demystifying the onto-logical language of scholastic philosophy and theology.[249] In sole sover-eignty, language is only language whose truth is to be secured the way legal truth is established using causal chronology. The authority of a text is proved by identifying and proving its authenticity, in a very complex legal science, as we have seen, where the actual *iter* of the document was reconstructed; the authenticity and authority of a term, a phrase (the meaning) referred only to terms, to phrases, but proof of their truth was to be established by derivation, that is, by reconstructing a true iter within a Christian structure of time recognising the past as the interpretative key to understanding the present.[250] A point of origin is sought (often very difficult to find – and the difficulty was got round by the concept of 'usage', a sort of origin whose record is lost but is presupposed, which logically existed, with usage as testimony to it),[251] and from this point, inductively, the meaning of a term is derived. The etymology is the reconstruction of this iter, making the chronology it provides a bearer of meaning.

The mark of the legal is essential, and well indicates the semantic conviction of the philologists: language reproduces the configuration of the real, and against scholastic abstraction which spoke for example of 'true', Valla spoke of 'true things', just as he rejected terms of the type 'entity', 'identity'. Valla rejected this metaphysics, speaking only of 'things'. Reality was directly accessible through language,[252] it was only to words that importance was to be attached,[253] a textual interpretation was to be interested only in the letter of the text and the 'literal meaning' became the 'meaning of the words'. An epistemology was asserted claim-ing that to an objective reality made entirely of observable, manifest things there should directly correspond a categorisation and classification of subjective realities, a correspondence allowing access to truth. The philo-logists formed part of this legal tradition that recognised the truth of the past in the act of reading documents as witnesses to true acts that had happened, but in a radical exegesis where grammar alone gave meaning to reality and every cognitive act was possible only through the conventions of language.

These conventions can be recognised only from knowledge of the past. They are what men knew through them, and logic could not be enough to define them. Legal knowledge remained very much present, as far as the very definition of the convention. It was in fact said that the rules of grammar came from usage more than from logic, 'not from reason but from example',[254] not from a law of discourse but from *observation*.[255] The – artificial – rules coming from logic were rejected in favour of usage, evaluated in the same way as truth of a written document was. The properties, the meaning, the interpretation, of Latin terms was arrived at from recourse to the authority of ancient writers, the meaning attributed to words by these being used as a precedent (true example). Legal knowledge was, finally, a great help in seeking to prove the meaning of terms by an argument from authority, authority of the author; doctrine and lexicography were thus able to be in close relationship. Philology came to establish a new similitude between writing and reality, through the word and its meaning, excluding all allegory. A literal interpretation was to become a 'historical' interpretation, understood as a 'grammatical literalism', since this meaning was to exclude all idea of mystery and to be worked out rationally.

The truth of a text is obtained from the words alone: they are the signs which, to the exclusion of everything else, indicate a meaning. Etymology was knowledge that posits an origin (through the authority of an author), a chronology (to which a meaning could be given) and a present truth (the definition). When the etymology is false the definition is false. We have said that with the second Christian millennium the civilisation of writing became established: henceforth no power could legitimately be imposed save by showing written documents, by archives. Changing the truth principle of texts could not help but have considerable repercussions on the powers that were. Philology disputed biblical hermeneutics by demonstrating the importance of Greek influence and positing the priority of literal grammar over allegory. Roman law, or more exactly the use made of the Digest, was reinterpreted on the basis of these philological acquisitions in a search to restore 'authentic truth'.[256] Canon law too went through the test of this method – the influence of which was to be essential in religious disputes and in the development of the Gallican tradition – in particular with Lorenzo Valla's *Treatise on the Donation of Constantine*.[257] The importance of this philological critique compels us to say a few words about it, albeit briefly.[258]

The *Donation of Constantine*, probably written shortly after the middle of the eight century (and widely known from its incorporation into the

Decretals of the Pseudo-Isidore, the parts of which were included in most
medieval collections of canon law),[259] was the document that was the
basis for papal authority in the West. The object of the document was in
fact to reproduce a document having the value of law in which the
Emperor Constantine the Great, in consequence of baptism and a cure
from leprosy at the hands of Pope Sylvester, made the latter the head of
the Western church;[260] and the document ended by condemning to
hellfire whoever ventured to doubt its authenticity. The document was,
then, particularly fundamental for the church; Lorenzo Valla criticised it
from top to bottom, proving that it was a fake. The approach is strictly
legal: to recognise the truth on the basis of written records and prove it,
and the critique follows a twofold strategy. The first part is to dispute the
very concept of 'donation'; using 'usages', the second establishes the gap
between the text's claims and the actual terms it uses, proving its 'non-
truth'.

There can be no 'donation', says Valla, since a donation of this type is
a public matter, organised through feudal links, a procedure that puts the
stress particularly on the – highly ostentatious – acceptance by the
beneficiary. But as Valla observes with fierce humour,[261] we cannot find
any record of this acceptance anywhere. Nothing can prove this acceptance, no witness to this ceremony is presented, nor is there any written
testimony, not even the slightest inscription.[262] This sort of donation
breaks with all the usages for the transmission of public and private
powers, making it highly suspect; a grammatical study will definitively
show that it is a fake.

Valla's first attack relates to the *authority* the text may claim (once more
a determinant of its authenticity),[263] breaking any possible link with the
Decretum of Gratian, from a systematic reading of it.[264] The second
related to the *validity of the testimony*, the name of the witness being
unknown:[265] if the witness is unknown, the testimony does not express any
'evidence' and cannot claim to be an 'irrefutable' proof. The tradition
cannot be invoked here in any way,[266] since it cannot furnish the name of
the writer of the history of Sylvester, nevertheless presented as the sole
witness. There is a shift here from a knowledge being reproduced by
compilation[267] – which was the foundation of the idea of tradition – and a
knowledge in search of its primary sources, which makes etymology
prevail over 'tradition'.[268]

Usage, the third attack, was that every agreement of this type should be
engraved, should be written. Usage is thus invoked as a *precedent*,[269] in the
legal sense of the term; that is, it is given exemplary truth value, and if a
usage is to be disputed, this can only be by invoking another usage, one
precedent against another. But in this case the donation conflicts with all
usages, all precedents; accordingly, its truth must be rejected. This

rejection was further reinforced by the grammatical analysis as such, where usage and language were brought together, and words invoked to prove the truth of things. Thus, Valla notes that some usual expressions are wrong,[270] that the names of countries change, that there are 'barbarisms of language'.[271] In short, everything shows that the text is apocryphal. The definitive attack, a perfect example of the Roman philologist's epistemology, is proved by the semantic analysis of the term emperor, a terminological truth that expresses the observable truth of any exercise of power: an emperor can only expand his empire, he can never atrophy it, this being shown into the bargain by the term Augustus, which comes from 'augere' (to increase).[272]

We now have all the factors that enable us to understand why today such importance is attached to the Renaissance in 'dating' the modern concept of history. Philology proves the truth of an event as the written exposition of a reality (the legal act par excellence),[273] by a literal grammatical method that confers upon language the exclusive bearing of meaning. Language refers to language: the meaning of a term is the conventional acceptance a social group has of it. This semantics of terms, as we have said, posits etymology as a science of origin of words, from which the present meaning has come. This movement is retrodictive:[274] it sets up a temporal gap to give meaning to the present by constructing an 'original' past, exactly reproducing the structure of Christian time as the interpretation of Holy Writ had forged it; the search for the origin means more than ever the ultimate foundation of all truth, but this origin henceforth has accounts to render to philological knowledge.[275] Theology, philology and law remained inextricably mixed, and religious controversy, the Reformation and the methods of the school of Bourges referred to the same epistemology, where the question of origin is the condition of all truth.

15

Direct testimony and the observation of nature

We have seen throughout the tenth to twelfth centuries, theologico-juridical knowledge had been at the root of knowledge, of the statement of truth. The authenticity of a text, from which truth was derived, was secured by evaluating its authority, its author. To decide every controversy, Christians had recourse to the authority of predecessors: Fathers, Councils, Popes. This technique of proof merely reproduced the legal knowledge applied in order to determine the authenticity of a document attributing any power whatever to any particular authority. The authenticity and authority of a text were thus subjected to a political authority: the person of the witness. It was very exactly this link between authenticity and authority that philological knowledge was to change and denature. Religious controversy shows this well. Philology posited as principle of all truth knowledge of the origin: instead of the anthologies, chains, Summas and commentaries on sentences, what was needed was to go back to the 'sources', to the Bible and the Founding Fathers. To the logical method was to be preferred the critical method (Erasmus was profoundly influenced by Valla, as was Luther, not only by John Huss). This critical method invented, one might say, another world, that of the origin, that is, a 'past as it really was'. The authentic thus became the origin. The Protestant principle was to overturn completely the authority of the patristic argument (Luther admitted as theological proof only arguments based on Scripture and therefore philological): the doctrines of the Fathers were henceforth to be checked against the doctrine of Scripture. This overturn was indeed fundamental to Western culture; it is at the very root of what we today recognise as modern historiography (the 'birth' of modern history).

In their opposition to Rome, as Pontien Polman shows,[276] the Swiss reformers applied the philological method[277] with more breadth and, in general, more erudition than the Lutherans. Zwingli followed Luther in seeing in *disclosure* of the 'literal meaning' the true aim of exegesis, but by contrast with him, he considered that this study was possible only through a study of the Bible in its *original*.[278] This grammatical study was to be augmented by study of the literary genre and 'study of original usages', one might say.[279] Exegesis of the four meanings of Scripture was rejected, as was scholastic interpretation. It was against exegesis of the four meanings that Calvin put forward the clarity and sufficiency of Holy Writ alone, against the allegorical meaning, in other words; which would as we have seen generate a Catholic doctrine through the link posited between authentic interpretation and the authority of the witness cum interpreter. Calvin opposed this Catholic thesis whereby the Church was above the Bible, so that it could impose an authentic interpretation, positing the exclusiveness of the text and a mode of interpretation deriving from philological knowledge.[280]

The proof of truth was henceforth to come from grammatical knowledge, the only kind capable of finding the primary truth from which present truth is derived. A Scriptural argument was to *precede* a truth of the Church, which was to be called 'history of the Church'. The relationship between philological knowledge and histories of institutions and doctrines for the knowledge of truth was posited. Heresy was to be defined as innovation against the truth *originally and authentically* (everything lies in this relationship) attested by the Church. The question or origin is its appendage, enabling a separation of the authentic from the false, purity from deviationism. Through this reorientation in recognition of truth (an apocryphal document would henceforth always be a fake, and could thus no longer ever be 'authentic'), new witnesses were to appear, manifestations of new developments of knowledge. Bullinger[281] launched himself into a search for the origin of the institutions and doctrines of Rome, in order to prove that the Roman Church never ceased to depart from gospel truth. The question of origin in a search for truth is given impetus by an explanation of the *origin of errors*, which is ultimately the way a society *politically* interprets its present.[282]

The place assigned to legal knowledge in establishing the legitimacy of power on the basis of a written record remains intact. The hypotheses that established the divine right of primacy of the bishop of Rome were carefully philologically checked (Valla had not wasted his time): was the Lord supposed to have appointed Saint Peter head of the Apostles, a primacy transmitted to his successors in the see of Rome? Let this be rationally verified, let the words addressed by the Lord to the Prince of the Apostles be examined very closely, let the historicity of Saint Peter's stay in Rome be checked (some strove to prove that the chronology of the New Testament ruled out the possibility of a stay of twenty-five years by Saint Peter in Rome).[283] Do the canonical texts prove the legitimacy of the Roman Church? Let the philological criticism of these writings be developed, let their authenticity be proved, that is, the truth of these texts, by a return to their origin, the sole rationally acceptable authority. The change in the authority of testimony, separating it from the institutional authority of the witness, was to reject the 'tradition'. For Luther, for instance, the sole reason for the existence of collections of canon law was to antedate the testimony in favour of the divine right of primacy, since 'all these canons, claimed to be ancient, date only from the modern epoch when laws and rights began to increase'.[284]

Theologico-juridical knowledge, excluding all enunciation of truth, was thus disputed by this set of knowledge that redefined the status of grammar, and new and rational principles of truth indicated by these records (or indices) constituted by writing in general. The whole set of such knowledge, grouped under the term philology, was certainly not imposed holus bolus: far from it. It was first disputed, quite obviously, by the Catholics, who took up the arguments coming from scholasticism (the 'formal' insufficiency of the Bible, which could not by itself specify the canon of sacred books) and of the old exegesis of sacra doctrina (the 'material' insufficiency of the Bible, since a number of truths forming part of the law had not been consigned to it). This set of knowledge was also questioned by all the jurists who worked on the definition of legitimacy. The main point, however, is contained in the research being increasingly concentrated on the notion of 'historical meaning' that textual criticism was to supply. As Erasmus had ventured some eight years earlier for the New Testament, Budé was to claim to restore the authentic doctrine of Roman law by textual criticism and, like Erasmus, regard philological knowledge as a true science.[285]

We have seen how such knowledge is structured. Philology, by developing the concept of origin as the root of all truth, allowed probative rational demonstration ending in disclosing an 'origin of error', in other words a 'primary untruth'. In this the movement was undoubtedly retrodictive, but very importantly, *the grammatical meaning was henceforth the pattern of knowledge that could claim to rational understanding of the present*. This was the issue in what we call the 'school of Bourges'. What was it actually that interested Budé in 'Roman' law? Surely not the discovery of a legitimating authority, as theologians were doing with Scripture, but the conviction that this written record allowed access to a past as it really was, to a true reconstruction of Antiquity, that is, the recreation of an identifiable space and time thanks to all these signs, all these directly observable records which bore their own meanings. Understanding this space became the primary condition for any attempt to explain the present time.

Budé[286] picks up the challenge exactly where Lorenzo Valla (grammatical literalism, origin and original usage of terms, etymology and causal chronological derivation) and Angelo Poliziano (textual exegesis on the basis of palaeography, thanks to which access could be secured to what could scarcely be made out any more) had thrown it down. The truth was established from the authenticity of the text as we have defined it through the religious controversy: shifts in vocabulary, archaisms and neologisms, were pursued because they were the proof of changes in the social world, and thus a backdating, because what a term expressed (cf. Valla) was a social act. The practice of emendatio brought a historical measure, since it was henceforth accepted that a given society was to be interpreted on the basis of its own terms – and of the usage it made of them. There nevertheless remained a problem that grammatical literalism had trouble solving and was to be the great problem of modernity. In hindsight it is easy to perceive, particularly after the nineteenth and twentieth centuries.

'Usage', the discourse on origins, was as it were the limiting point from which a meaning was created inductively. Semantics developed in parallel with the working-out of a context, and in connection with Valla we have even said that this context was the proof, the 'evidence' of that semantics. Henceforth the problem was to consist in establishing this *context*, and only scholarship, as a principle of knowledge of the past, could be useful here. This means one must 'read the world in order to prove the books', using Foucault's formula,[287] as much as reading the books in order to show the truth of the world. But the relationship becomes increasingly ambiguous. Budé, who, as we said, had taken up the essence of philological knowledge to feed his Gallicanism, was nevertheless to maintain the possibility of superiority of a 'figurative' meaning over a 'literal' meaning. The figurative meaning, certainly not intended to express a real truth, nevertheless reflects a 'meaning of history' or philosophy of the present time, which is no longer entirely inscribed upon things themselves. The literal meaning is no longer, as had been the case with medieval exegesis, synonymous with the historical meaning; quite the contrary. The great problem of modernity lies just in this gap. Very soon, this meaning of history was no longer to have any tangible counterpart but itself:[288] the world had to be interpreted, and 'history' was to become political science.

Memory and the knowledge of the past were, in a structure of Christian time, to become the principle of recognition of the present and the indication of the future. Biblical exegesis had as its basis of the truth the divine hypothesis, simultaneously given and to be disclosed, to which any statement of 'literal' truth referred. The literal, 'historical' meaning was thus the end point of a hermeneutic act in which the 'future' (the new Testament) was the – divine – indication of the 'past' (the Old Testament). It never existed as such; as such it had no meaning. Through the philological revolution, we are now faced with a 'historical meaning' which is at the very root of all knowledge of truth and at the same time refers only to itself. The hermeneutic act no longer posits a future as primary interpretative principle: the future was henceforth to be only the projection of a truth furnished to us by knowledge of the past. It remains to develop these pieces of evidence that illustrate the truth secured by this new science of politics, and this was, in our view, to be the task of the 'historical school of Roman law'.

What philology had introduced was a historical study of documents, in particular legal ones; but now that knowledge of the past had attained the status of a new political science, a history of law and institutions was to develop where henceforth it was to be legal practices and institutions that were to be the evidence for a historical truth, the truth of the world. Alciade[289] seeks to posit links between a 'history of institutions' and 'the most certain of philosophies', in so doing take the philological method of text explanation as the only rational method. The legal reading can only be a literal documentary critique, so that Alciade rejects the old semantics according to which 'words mean, things are meant',[290] and the *general meaning of the text henceforth refers only to the general meaning of history*, with which nothing can interfere. The understanding of present time results from the understanding of past time that one recognises legal practice and institutions to have. The history of the origin, the foundation myth, thus becomes the problem of the origin of law, which is to indicate to us the secret nature of our world.

Du Rivail[291] takes up the Greek historiographical tradition of a history of constitutional forms, but does so within a future that no longer has much to do with Greek historiographical culture as we have already long seen it. Du Rivail's constitutional history is derived from an approach that takes as its question the origins of law (the law of the Roman kings; the law of the people, in plebiscite; the law called democratic; the law of empire), which alone can allow us access to our hidden identity and, by faithfully taking up the philological tradition, put the question of its origin in terms of 'usage'. What a history of institutions indicates to us is the truth of our present world in what is specific about it, a specificity that indicates authentic and hidden characters. 'Customary law' henceforth comes to occupy a fundamental place, since it enables the identification – by negative definitions – of a specific political regime (feudalism) whose legal forms are the traces of a hidden truth, a truth which also allows us to start to penetrate the truth of our own world.[292]

Philology made possible a history of law and institutions, yet did not bring out this hermeneutics of Christian religious thought known as the 'hidden meaning'. Undoubtedly these legal records indicate to us a truth about ourselves, but they are only the *index* of this truth, which is not reducible to them. What they indicate is an intention, a subjective will, which proves itself openly through these legal forms. The question of usage, which remained problematic in Valla, is here resolved through the historical truth which is that of the will of individuals. It thus becomes important in searching for usages to retrace their 'spirit', to show what they really *correspond* to. This path too Christianity took, as we have seen for Purgatory. Psychologism now becomes the means of access to hidden historical truth: truth is human, entirely human, and historical truth is the intimate will of individuals. Thus Budé, and Alciade along with Erasmus, by contrast with Valla, assert that the truth of a written record does not lie only in the terms constituting it, but is also to be sought in the *spirit* of what is at its *origin*. The philosophy of history and the intention of its actors are one and the same thing: from the letter we move to the 'spirit of the text', certainly, but no longer as this was done in the doctrine of the four meanings. The science of politics, the origin and destiny of the world, all this became the object of history. Roman law and its history were to be the material on the basis of which the truth of our own time, the 'meaning of history', could be proved. Le Douaren revealed the 'true Roman law'; Hotman, whose reformed sympathies were well known, proved the corruption of canon law and civil law through what he called 'Romanism'[293]; Cujas was incomparable in the application of philological knowledge, but also palaeographical in respect of manuscripts or printed versions of Roman legal texts.

New arrangements in the Western system of knowledge could be set up, and were certainly illustrated by Baudouin when he said that philosophy required knowledge of 'natural law', philology that of the meanings and derivations of words, and finally history that of the 'origin' of law. History, which cannot dispense with the philology through which it identifies the origin, the authentic word, came to place in foremost position a very old distinction: between the account and thus the interpretation of political events on the one hand, and the search for information on the other. Historical truth, no longer something revealed, was to be secured by discovering true events. An account had to be true if based on true documents. These new patterns of knowledge traced a new dividing line between observation of phenomena and truth. For instance, the interpretative knowledge of archives became the specialised knowledge of antiquaries (assisted by philology), who accordingly had to be capable of establishing the truth of 'events' and came to be closely associated with the legal method of identifying and classifying documents. The historian, for his part, no longer confined himself to the truth of mere events but considered the truth and destiny of the world, thanks to the concepts of cause and origin[294] (at the risk of appearing a 'liar', as was eventually to be the case with 'Pyrrhonism', the doubting of historical truth and proof). This is a very old dividing line which, as we have seen, was at the very root of medieval exegesis, between a literal meaning and an allegorical meaning.[295] We also meet with it in a legal pattern seeking to articulate the 'meaning of a rule' and the 'truth of the situation' to which the rule is said to be supposed to apply. This dividing line is always in motion, reflecting the articulation between *a reality one can manage to make observable and the truth that it indicates.*

This truth of history is called universal, and its mode of proof is definitively of a philological nature: 'the latest and most recent account of past events is generally the least trustworthy', says Baudouin, stressing the importance of primary sources, 'first-hand' documents. Its characteristic is a legal one: 'I am to prefer *witnesses* who *describe*[296] what they have taken part in to these indirect witnesses who are "hearsay", whose testimony is never accepted by lawyers', as Baudouin again says. This traditional position emerged from the theologico-juridical pattern that accorded the primacy to testimony, but and this is fundamental, took its distance from the kind of testimony known as 'tradition'. The philologist and the antiquary are the lawyers' very close collaborators in authenticating these written records, the available originals, which will become so many pieces of evidence for great historical frescoes unfolding all along the continuous thread of time, with a starting point and an end point, the cause of which (i.e. explanation/understanding) lies in this famous original point.

It is, moreover, interesting here to note a comparison drawn, by Baudouin but not only by him, between a historical account that touches on the meaning of the world's destiny and the legal truth inscribed within a system: both should identify a precedent. This latter is a record, and not hidden, of a truth. However, though not hidden, this record is not easily identifiable. Just as the allegorical meaning allowed the correct interpretation of an entirely human reality, of a true event, so the 'historical meaning' was henceforth to prevail in the interpretation of the 'true facts'. It is this historical meaning (very soon to be a 'philosophy of history' or 'philosophy of law', two expressions one day to be synonyms) that was to allow what was important to be distinguished from what is not, just as a spirit of the laws was to enable what is important to be hierarchalised and distinguished from what is less so.[297] This is the way to understand Baudouin's saying, obscure to say the least[298]: 'Roman law could not be correctly interpreted were we not capable of distinguishing between fact and law, that is, between what has an interest and what has legal authority'.

As being beforehand an archivist, advocate and antiquary, Jean du Tillet could hope to become one of the most gifted 'historians' of his time. The very delicate legal question he had one day to answer was the constitutional problem raised by the death of Henry II (1559). Had the legitimate heir, only fifteen years old, reached his age of majority, or was it instead needful to wait a further ten years? In answer, du Tillet made a 'feudal custom' prevail over 'Roman law',[299] thus denying that the age of majority was determined by Roman constitutions (twenty-five) and referring to an ordinance of Charles V of 1374 setting the age of reason at fifteen. Why this choice between two types of legislation? It was a consequence of a doctrine we have just mentioned, relating to the quality of written testimony. The truth of an event, the sole material on the basis of which a historical truth could be extracted, was established first of all by the 'direct' witness. All this testimony was just what was gathered in the public archives,[300] as the written proofs of a truth the authenticity of which was to be attested by philologists and antiquaries.

That legitimacy may be asserted by proving a written truth is not an innovation, as we have seen. What is more so, on the other hand, is the fact that henceforth this purely human written truth is to be the sign of a universal truth. The antiquary comes along to disclose ceaselessly the new pieces of proof of this universal truth, for instance that of the legitimacy of the French crown and its origins, from its derivation until the present time, that is, the '*tradition*'. We have also seen that philology, the knowledge that defines authenticity from origins, had undermined the Christian concept of tradition, which had become the favoured target of Reformation historical research. The problem was how to reconstruct the first ages of a process that extended until our day, to describe the changes[301] that had occurred, and explain them in order to justify or condemn a present situation. This historical truth was based on a truth secured on the basis of testimony which itself had to be defined. What witnesses, what 'faith' to attach to testimony from 'tradition', that is from doctrine not written by the original authors, thereby raising the question of the value to attach to secondary sources. What faith, in other words, was one to place in history?

The precedent became the manifest record, recognisable by all, of the non-hidden truth of history; the history of law and the history of institutions became the principle of this knowledge of truth. A 'historical' continuity (causal chronology) became productive of meaning. Dumoulin for example created this meaning by positing a direct relationship between a French law, a French monarchy and the Gallican church (one faith, one law, one king). Through philology – a knowledge of things at their origin and the usage that had been at the basis of examples and comparisons (which were more than just words and were already the index of a historical truth) – for the jurist, text interpretation was done starting from a prior meaning the truth of which was attested by precedents, the consequence but *at the same time* the principle of this prior sense, since the precedents were 'true facts' in themselves.[302] This prior meaning was, however, that whereby the identities and differences were to be newly discovered, where a tradition was henceforth to allow identification of a difference, the special nature of the present time.

Foucault sought to see this period as the moment of radical change in Western culture, when 'the whole episteme of Western culture was changed in its fundamental pattern'.[303] What seems certain at any rate and indicates to us this reorganisation of rational knowledge is that truth finds its manifestation and its sign in clear and distinct perception and that 'it is for words to reflect this if they can; they no longer have a right to be the mark of it … Language withdraws from among beings to enter its age of transparency and neutrality.'[304] This was henceforth what the distinction between antiquarian and historian was to express; the first supplied the evidence that the second was to translate if he could. If there is something new in the classical age for historical knowledge, it was not, as one reads almost everywhere, that the method finally became rational, heralding modernity, but its status. History is the philosophy of the world, and it was therein that it heralded modernity. Thus we do not share the conviction that Mabillon was the revolutionary of historical method, and we shall even say, with no polemical spirit, that he invented nothing, even though he was very revelatory of his time.

Mabillon's task was to prove the truth of events of the past using the necessary tool, since the acquisition of philology: the original. Nothing very revolutionary about this: the original qualifies the authority of a written record which, as we have seen, corresponds to a definition of testimony. Thus to the Christian tradition that assessed the authority of a text from the qualification of the witness (public authorities like Pope, emperor, prince, bishop etc.), philology had opposed criticism of the text, to which the authority of the witness became subject; we were thus able to say that the concept of origin was opposed to the Christian 'tradition'. Mabillon took up this philological heritage; he certainly does not reject the authority of a text on the basis of the authority of the witness, but the latter is subjected to the conclusions deriving from criticism of the text. In the search for truth, moreover, Mabillon seeks every records, whatever it be (medals, monuments etc.), here again not innovative, but typical of a culture based on writing; numismatics (the great age of which was the seventeenth century), like archaeology or palaeography (though the latter was not yet very developed), were already widely-used disciplines. Nor did Mabillon supply anything as far as the historical account itself is concerned; for a long time now the historical account in the chronicles had been condemned on the grounds that it did not distinguish between the true event and the legendary or romantic event. The most decisive thing is not, in our view, in Mabillon himself and his genius, but more in his time: the modern States became these forms of power henceforth imposed, thereby positing the State archives as the raw material for any statement of political truth. But the *mode of proof*, understood as the evidence on the basis of which a truth could be stated, did not itself undergo any great novelty: legal knowledge and method predominated more than ever.

Diplomatics, rather than appearing as 'the end of the separation between the professions of historian and antiquary',[305] in our opinion underlines the distinction. The diplomatist's material was what could take on legal value, these records which, with no possible dispute – if there was to be any dispute it would be on the basis of clear, rational principles – have the advantage of expressing a true event. The diplomatist, whose fundamental task is to authenticate an act by demonstrating that it emanated from such and such an authority, comes back to the alliance that the philologist and the jurist had been able to cement, like them entering into the search for 'sources' (or authentication, and thus authority, of an act through the concept of origin). He developed the philological legal method by working out a systematic order using the technique of the dictionary, where the definition of one word refers to the definition of other words. Here certainly we meet the table, the classification of writs, the reorganisation of libraries etc.; all techniques of classifying, but of a form of knowledge that is not new. This is why we feel it is preferable to say that before this time we see not a new way of *telling* history (now expecting something different from it), but of *making* it. The historian is the specialist in this science which is politics; he develops the meaning that legitimates the nascent State on the basis of records favouring in particular what may be called 'public law'. The antiquary (like the diplomatist), works on the truth of events, the truth of texts, the qualifications of the records.

Although we shall certainly find points of correspondence between these two activities, there was however to be an enormous difference that would very soon constitute a great problem for the historian (explaining, we think, his very late combination with the antiquary); we are speaking of the problem of proof. Proof of the historical meaning, the 'historical truth', will never have the same impact (and we shall soon return to this point) as the reasoning whereby (through numismatics, archaeology, palaeography, grammatical exegesis etc.) we prove, say, the existence of this or that personage or event. Science can separate from history, since one can never *conclusively* prove the truth or falsehood of the 'historical meaning'. The paradox is that, despite everything, this historical meaning is worked out on the basis of all those records which, at least so we believe, are above all suspicion as regards their existence and their mode of proof (their truth). It is certainly in this gap that the questions of modernity emerge, and we can perhaps dwell a little more on the distinction between antiquarians and historians.

It was approximately at the end of the seventeenth century that 'learned societies' proclaimed their interest more in what travel could teach them than in the emendatio of texts, and at the same time that 'literary texts' came to appear as less essential than coins, statues, vases or

miscellaneous inscriptions. These literary scholars thus shared the conviction that a direct witness, or a document contemporary with the event
attested, were worth a hundred times more than derived testimony (from
'hearsay', or coming directly from an 'original authority'). They indicated
thereby their concern over the nature of the interpretation of the evidence
adopted and maintained the philological tradition through the principle
of the search for the origin (in the legal sense of the term, that is, as a
manifestation of a reality that indicated a truth).

It is traditional to distinguish the antiquarian from the historian by
arguing that the historian writes on the basis of an order that is of a
chronological nature whereas the antiquarian uses a principle of a systematic nature. This chronological order explains the specific nature of the
historian's discourse, and this is the second great difference from the
antiquary, of being a causal discourse (the historian 'explains' a situation). The antiquary, for his part, far from explaining the world, contents
himself with gathering as many records as possible, which constitute his
'object'. However, this differentiation is acceptable only insofar as we are
capable of explaining how, firstly, the historian's plot 'arises' and through
whom, and secondly how the antiquarian's object is 'given'. If we cannot
answer this question, then the distinction has to be abandoned. And
indeed we have not yet found a satisfactory answer to this question. The
distinction between the historian and the antiquarian could also tell us
something else, not located at the level of method. Momigliano,[306] for
instance, cites Cainden, first professor of history at Cambridge, 1627, for
whom a professor 'should read a civil history and therein make such
observations as might be useful and profitable for the younger students of
the University, to direct and instruct them in the knowledge and use of
history, antiquity and time past'.

16

Direct observation and testimony of nature

What this demarcation line chiefly indicates, we think, is that a 'political' history does not feed from the same sources nor produce the same proofs as a history that aims to be only 'knowledge of things of the past'. When history of Greece or Rome was taught, it was to supply material reflections of a political or moral nature or to help in understanding texts (in an essentially stylistic perspective), but the truth of this traditional testimony was not questioned. It was not yet thought possible to write a history of Rome that would be preferable to, say, Tacitus. The antiquarian and the historian had, as their sole material, contemporary witnesses. We must insist on this marked taste of learned societies for this non-textual 'evidence', since, if such evidence was henceforth to the fore, that is because the accepted conception of proof of historical truth was withering. The religious controversy was certainly not entirely absent; once it had acquired the contribution from philology, there came the great moment of doubt of historical truth, 'Pyrrhonism'.

Bollandists and Maurists, for instance, concentrated all their efforts in the distinction between reasonable doubt and unreasonable doubt in history. Theologians, philologists, historians, once again turned to jurists, whose knowledge related specifically to the evaluation of testimony, to ask them for a definition of proof, of the characteristics of 'evidence', and thus a definition of historical truth. This was clearly asking too much of jurists, whose knowledge consists solely in the recognition of signs understood as a manifestation of truth, but not in the act instituting these signs.[307] Momigliano states that this was a time when many books on history were appearing, taking their distance from the rhetoric of the Renaissance in order to concentrate almost exclusively on the method of interpretation and of criticism of sources.[308]

The proof of truth undergoes a shift, consequent upon the way the effort was henceforth made to know (to interpret) nature. This is what the marked taste for coins, statues and ruins, i.e. all those records that are not texts (inscriptions being perceived not as texts or text fragments but as mere traces, of the same nature as an ancient monument), tells us. These non-textual traces are now regarded as proof superior to textual records, though they still make use of the application of philological legal knowledge. Nor did the Pyrrhonists fail to say that marble and bronze could lie, that all these traces could have been falsified,[309] or worse, that they might perhaps be *interpreted diversely*. The certainty that there could be a 'single right answer' to the question of what a past was now disappeared. Philologists and jurists could beaver away proving the authenticity of the records, that was their traditional baggage: but their science was not enough to establish the 'good faith' of testimony.[310] At the end of the seventeenth century, the archaeological proofs were perceived as more fundamental than literary ones, being simultaneously the symbol and the proof of what had happened; this was also the great age of numismatics.

Hence there was a shift in the mode of proof of truth coming from a new interpretation of nature, let us say. This primary importance henceforth attaching to numismatics, to archaeology, reflected the desire to interpret nature differently; if it was preferable to cite a medal rather than a text, an author, that is because the medal saves a detour – through the interpreter – and *testifies directly*. The new status of *'direct' observation* of knowledge of nature (new direct testimony) is found again with knowledge of the past;[311] other cognitive principles generated corresponding interpretive principles.

In order properly to understand this new mode of reading nature that locates the concept of 'direct observation' at the core of speculation, we shall take two excursus. For the first, let us introduce, albeit in brief, two seventeenth-century theologians. We shall then better understand the new links established among theology, history and law as to the conception of truth and its mode of proof. Richard Simon,[312] whose essential work was to come only a few years after Baruch de Spinoza's *Tractatus theologico-politicus*, reused, as Spinoza had done, all the heritage of philology in his desire to prove the immutability of the biblical revelation, with the aim of securing 'exact historical knowledge'. Theology always has as its object a historical reality, and it is therefore on the method of knowing the past that it must draw for its investigating procedures and its rules, its critique of evidence and its method of observing nature. Historicism, that is, the conviction that interpretations 'have a history', was to be born from this attempt by Simon.

It was not Port Royal with its logic and scholasticism that interested Simon, but Protestant criticism. To Protestants, he objected that in order to justify the least one of their dogmas the whole Bible did not suffice, so that it was necessary to refer to the tradition. But the 'tradition' was also to mean something other than the immutability of a truth; it was to become the *continuity* of a truth. Historicism and continuity are the two terms that summarise Simon's work: the two concepts that are to take account of differences in exegesis over time, showing that there is no Christian generation that has not furnished 'its quota of thought to the heritage it believed it was transmitting with the greatest integrity'.[313] This continuous change, according to Simon, in the transmission of a tradition is the necessary condition if one is to have any hold on consciences. The *expression* of the truth is historical, but this historicism clearly does not mean relativism, since truth is not historical. Such different hermeneutics as the literal exegesis of Antioch and the allegorical one of Alexandria, the hermeneutics of the first Fathers and scholastic dogmatics, responded, for Simon, to different needs for consciences and hence to no less differing applications of Scripture. But all these different, or even contradictory, applications had the same, absolutely unshakeable, point of support.

This historical manifestation of truth is reflected in Simon's systematics of philological science and legal science.[314] The 'literal meaning' tends to prevail over the 'allegorical meaning': Simon further accepts the idea that it is needful to expound Scripture by the ordinary rules of human language (a knowledge of Greek and Hebrew being indispensable), and that it is equally necessary to have a good knowledge of the usages, 'the history in force' at the time the Holy Books were written, and the 'character' of the authors.[315] Archaeology, numismatics and geography were also highly recommended.[316]

Undoubtedly philology, with its 'sense of origin', its technique of derivation and its definition of the present truth, was embarking on the road to a history of truth; yet this truth remained unique, crystallised in a single definition. The problem was to state a sole truth on the basis of different records, different histories (a hypothesis absolutely unacceptable, as we know, to Bossuet). It was for words to speak this truth if they could; and all histories are attempts, begun ever anew, to say it well. This was henceforth the problem that for Simon tradition was to pose. The truth must be known, and the tradition may sometimes express *errors* (again the influence of philology). For instance, Galileo's exegetic hypothesis 'on the passages of Scripture seeming to indicate the immobility of the earth' that the theologians of the Holy Office had condemned as formally heretical made a breach in the system of theological truths as then accepted.[317] It was exegetic dogmatism that made an ancient, unchangeable tradition out of any opinion whatever; the authority of theology, said Simon, could be upheld only if new principles enabled a rational distinction to be drawn between the right tradition and a wrong one. These new, philologico-juridical principles were to allow access to the historical expression (in each 'epoch') of truth.

Against dogmatism, the fundamental evidence constituted by the '*material state*' of the Holy Books had to be reaffirmed; the obscurer a text, the more chance it was ancient (and therefore close to the truth), just as among several genealogical data it was always the least intelligible reading that had to be taken.[318] The philological position, taking explicitly as its target interpretation through mystery, and redefining the obscurity of a text as a strictly semantic difficulty that philological research is able to resolve, is reaffirmed. For instance, the third book of the critical history has as first section a very long passage on the obscurities in the Bible, traced back to the inherent difficulties of the Hebrew language in particular, where, a fundamental point for Christian thought, there is a confusion of tenses and moods in a conjugation (the notion of past is not distinguished from the idea of future). Finally, Simon's search for the right dogma was to be flanked, good philologist that he was, by research into the origin of the Holy Books to show the multiplicity of their sources.

This philologico-juridical method pursued on the basis of grammatical literalism could clearly not rule out all allegorising interpretations. To a hermeneutics of hidden meaning, where words were only an envelope covering a deeper, hidden, truth, Simon preferred a hermeneutics where the meaning was elaborated through a strict philology. Dogmatic theology and speculative metaphysics became foreign to the exegesis, which was nothing but strict philology and grammatical method. For this reason, *all proofs no longer had equal value*, with some even *not proving anything at all any more*. A new dividing line was thus to be drawn between what could be the object of rational, probative demonstration (such as exegesis) and on the contrary what could not be shown rationally (such as dogmatic theology or speculative metaphysics). Using Foucault's terms again, this new dividing line resulted from an episteme that no longer posited a resemblance between words and the things they stand for, between records and the meaning they indicate. The link between the observable and the analysis, the sign and the sense, was no longer of the same nature.

'I challenge you with all your subtlety to conclude that comets have been the cause or the sign of the disasters that followed their appearance. Thus the testimony of historians is reduced to proving solely that comets did appear and disorders in the world did indeed ensue; which is very far from proving that one of those two things was the cause or portent of the other, unless one wish it to be permitted for a woman who never puts her head out of the window in the rue Saint Honoré without seeing carriages pass to imagine that she is the cause of their passage, or at least that she must when she appears at her window be a presage for the whole neighbourhood that carriages will soon pass.'[319] Bayle's essay in judicial astronomy had as its primary aim a critique of the principal authority for the *proof* of truth and had as its start and end point the Calvinist polemical tradition[320] between the Edict of Nantes and its revocation. The fundamental thesis was to show that the system of proof thanks to which the

Catholic church established the truth and set up its authority proved nothing.[321] The comet, that sign, is not the explanation for human phenomena. Historians are not well founded in saying that the causes of terrestrial ravages are the comets; knowledge about comets does not relate to 'things the province of historians'.[322]

If the tradition has always sought to give an account of the celestial phenomenon of comets on the basis of non-probative testimony, then it is that whole tradition that should be rejected. What the comet indicates is not what the tradition has always taught: the link between observation of a phenomenon and analysis of the phenomenon is not of the order of the *mysterious*[323] (thus entailing application of an allegorical meaning). Still further, if observation of a phenomenon does not lead to its correct analysis, this is quite simply because *that observation has not been correct,* that it is hard to distinguish between the signs that indicate something and those that indicate nothing.[324] This point is quite essential, even if today we have some trouble understanding what it reflected at the time in knowledge of the world. To seek to understand better what was at stake, we shall now take our second excursus through a number of legal practices that sought in a particular way to show the truth of the sublunary world by establishing the link between a phenomenon and its analysis. We shall talk of sorcery,[325] stressing in particular the cultural disarray that passage from one mode of knowledge of nature to another can cause.

Mandrou[326] has hypothesised a crisis in consciences in seeking to understand the epidemics of persecution of practices of satanic magic. The hypothesis is seductive. The descriptions of sabbaths describing the mass said *backwards* and recognition of an authority *symmetrical* to that exercised by the priest in his parish point to the fear aroused by the inability henceforth found to put forward a broad system for explaining the world rationally, for interpreting nature. One order falls apart, another reading is heralded, redefining the concept of nature. It was the educated public that appreciated the relevance of the proof of the existence of Satan's empire and his grip on the world. That this proof was administered by jurists does not mean that they wished to give themselves a 'good part and good conscience in the face of the enemy par excellence, Satan',[327] but this once again teaches us something about the nature of legal knowledge: it is to show the truth, rationally, on the basis of all the signs that a specific episteme has been able to institute. What trials for sorcery indicate is nothing other than a crisis in the order of knowledge.

This proof of witchcraft was in fact obtained by noting the concordance between the terms defined by the first theoreticians of satanism and the 'observations' made during the interrogation and torture of the accused. The truth, in other words, is always the outcome of the reading of a book containing it, to which one ascends by relying on the characteristic signs that surround us. The sign is always that which indicates something hidden, yet here the sign, the object of observation, is identified with the confession. This is the first point. The second point is that this confession relates to a whole set of traditional types of knowledge that magistrates, *physicians* and theologians all condemned because that knowledge, relating to natural factors, led to curing. These disturbing people in fact possessed the secrets of nature, and their knowledge ('power') could not rationally be explained by physicians, the new representatives of a new knowledge. But those involved did not themselves know how to explain how they knew, no more than they knew how to explain what they knew. The witch trial is in fact the proof that some did not know how to justify – rationally – their knowledge, which was after all thoroughly rational since it led to cures!

There is, then, indeed a secret of nature – which is its rational order – to which, however, human knowledge is not allowed access. The proof of possession is, then, the inability rationally to explain a knowledge of nature or to prove a supernatural power, which comes to the same thing; and it is not irrelevant that physicians were to the fore in the matter, since what was henceforth to be announced through them was a different view of nature,[328] a different hermeneutics. The criterion of sight, for instance, rendered suspect from the idea of various hallucinatory and satanic visions, was replaced by touch and smell, in other words sources of *contact*, 'the guarantee and immediacy of the evidence'.[329] Just as words are no longer anything but language, no longer including a secret, observation henceforth produces only a surface effect: contact indicates meaning.[330] The change is perceptible: if sight became suspect, *it was the very concept of testimony that was becoming problematic*, and the criteria of truth that were being affected.

From the early seventeenth century, the issue is the breakdown of society and the world, proved by new interpretations of Scripture, or new cosmic phenomena (and we have seen Bayle's response to the truth indicated by comets) or even biblical mathematics (the Scotsman Napier of Merchiston invented logarithms in order to be able to calculate the number of the Antichrist faster). The meaning of the world dissipates; belief in the 'world of darkness' takes on increasing force. The kingdom of God, the world of light, still furnishes its truth directly through observable signs one must know how to interpret, but this truth to be interpreted is no longer the same, any more than the signs that point to it. To seek to recognise this truth is to bring in an indirect proof, the 'world of darkness', which cannot be based on a coherent system of signs and requires a confession.

This methodological distinction in mode of proof, direct or indirect, expressed by these worlds of light and darkness, in our view reflects the change coming about in the knowledge of nature. This world of darkness is in fact the postulate that is to permit an unheard-of thing: the proof of a hidden truth being put forward without at the same time the system of signs pointing to it being defined. This is why we only have confessions. We have throughout our considerations noted that a rational thought was established through the articulation of a hermeneutics and a semiology; here, all we have left is a hermeneutics consisting in presupposing a system (and we have all the treatises of demonology) that is demonstrated by torture. But the problem of witchcraft ought not to be reduced to torture alone, since by itself it explained nothing. Undoubtedly it permitted a downright holocaust, particularly between 1600 and 1650.[331] But in England, for instance, where torture did not appear, the epistemological shift still generated the phenomenon of witchcraft.[332] Two worlds cohabited: the visible one proved by spontaneous testimony, directly, and the invisible one proved by indirect testimony, wrenched forth.

The visible world is the signs one knows how to interpret; the world of darkness indicates that the signs can no longer be interpreted, that anything and everything can be claimed to point to any truth whatever. This distinction reflects a crisis in consciousness, because the world of knowledge is becoming shaky: witchcraft is the confession of the impossibility of developing a science that institutes signs. The ordinary proofs are not accepted, since they do not allow the existence of the kingdom of darkness to be proven;[333] they prove nothing. In the absence of indices underlining a piece of 'evidence' (a cauldron full of human limbs, a written pact with the devil), which tended to be rare, one was content with proof by presumption (a wart, a point on the body incapable of feeling pain, etc.) which, of course, proved strictly nothing[334] without the confession. The phenomenon of witchcraft explicitly stated that the world of knowledge of nature had to be rebuilt; that another hermeneutics had still to be sketched out.

The only awareness there was of these phenomena is indicated by the theoretical distinction necessitated between proofs that actually proved a truth of nature and those that proved nothing of the sort. The proof of witchcraft indicated a mistrust of the *old* mode of proof, instead declaring the 'ordinary' proof. The rejection of witchcraft corresponded to the possibility of putting forward a mode of proof differing from the old one, since denunciation of the proof of witchcraft established a mode of proof that came to indicate another concept of nature and hence a new way of looking at it.

As the new knowledge of nature came to be established, magical beliefs started to collapse. Thus torture disappeared. It is clearly important to stress that it was not the abolition of torture that supressed magical beliefs, but the disappearance of magical beliefs as a principle of knowledge of the world that made torture disappear. If now we find jurists on both sides, this is once again for the reason we have already indicated, namely that legal knowledge is the rational knowledge that makes the *instituted* signs speak.[335] It is certainly true that legal knowledge took part in the overall form of knowledge defining a society; but this institutive knowledge cannot be summarised as legal epistemology alone. The lawyer-philologists of the fifteenth century, like many scholars of the time, were not sensitive to this question of witchcraft: the proof of truth was established through rational modes of reasoning. A century later, the situation had shifted, as a conception of nature divested of biblical fundamentalism began to emerge. Now we are within reach of modernity.

It was at this point that we intended to terminate our study. Our considerations in the first part of this work compelled us to enquire into certain types of knowledge, and in so doing we have been induced to move away from the modern period. However, it is not yet time to finish, since our conclusions could not be but very partial. It is true that, following what we have said throughout this whole second part, modernity cannot be interpreted (epistemology) without some minimal sketch of a 'pre' modernity. We do not believe too much in the notion of an epistemological 'break', even if it is quite clear to all that the way we today prove the existence of microorganisms, particles or whatever calls for a conception of nature without much relationship with that of medieval thought. Nonetheless, these vanished forms of knowledge continue despite everything to make their influence felt, which is why we have sought to reflect that effect in the term 'shift'.

When 'philology' came along to undermine theology at the root, it did so on the basis of cognitive principles that emerged from theology; in the critique, thus, something remains of that science (and one might perhaps wonder whether it may not be the essential part; think of the philologist's concept of 'origin') and substantially influences this different way of looking that was to be born from the development of 'philological' science. Quite similarly, when astronomical knowledge, as we shall see, took up the interpretive principles derived from philology in order to posit hypotheses as to the notion of nature, a different type of knowledge undoubtedly came to apply, yet in its very conception it must have undergone the influence of the science it supplanted. In these *false continuities and false breaks*, and where there is in our view a sense in talking of Christian civilisation, one figure seems to bestride the ages: the jurist. His work is always to reconstitute the truth of something that happened, on the basis of every type of record, written or spoken evidence. His instrument, proof, is a translation of the way we know nature: the jurist's interpretation and argumentation thus come to apply that science, which characterises a society and institutes the signs one must know how to interpret. With this prospect we may underline, but very briefly by way of preliminary conclusion, a few features that point towards the commencement of modernity.

17

Sign, sense, proof

The seventeenth and eighteenth centuries do not in any way constitute some sort of homogeneous bloc within which rationality was uninterruptedly growing. The two periods, if not opposite to each other, were at any rate very distinct. Cassirer has sought to express this difference in a nutshell: the seventeenth century was typified by the spirit of system, the eighteenth by the systematic spirit. In a spirit of system, truth is obtained only when reason manages to grasp the certainty that derives from the derivation of a knowledge that is itself derived. A fundamental certainty, an original truth, is posited, and by the method of proof and inference, very rigorously, the total chain of knowledge is linked up. It is not possible to isolate any link whatever of this chain, since it is not explicable in itself. The only explanation possible is provided through *derivation*, which takes place following strict deduction whereby every link could be explained by tracing it back to its 'origin' (and here we find an influence of philological knowledge). It is just this deductive principle and technique of proof that will very soon be disputed under the overwhelming influence of the method used in natural science.

Cassirer[336] has thus been able to show that the Newtonian model was the one that gave the best account of the question of truth as posed for the eighteenth century. Newton does not apply the method of strict deduction, but opts for the analytical method. He does not construct a model by positing principles (general concepts, axioms), on the basis of which, by abstract inference, he sketches the outlines of more special knowledge which we may henceforth call 'factual'. Newton's approach is exactly the opposite. His 'phenomena' are the 'data' of experience, his principles the result of his investigations.[337] the question we had arrived at from our thoughts on truth on history reappears in the same terms for (experimental) scientific truth.

The movement of thought has not to be from concepts or axioms towards phenomena, but conversely. Observation is supposed to be the source for the scientific datum. Rational principles and laws of nature are the objects of investigation. Just as should be the case for the 'true event' which is at the root of the historical truth, the 'meaning of history' ('historical philosophy', 'philosophy of law') is itself also the object of investigation. For both disciplines we have one and the same problem. It might perhaps be useful here to take a very quick look at the methodological conflict that lasted from Copernicus to Galileo, in order clearly to bring out this point of the link between an event, a 'phenomenon', and its meaning.

In writing 'on the revolutions of the celestial orbs', Copernicus had two major concerns. Firstly, mathematicians had 'hitherto remained in such uncertainty as to the movements of the sun and the moon that they have been able neither to observe nor prove the invariable length of the year ... Then when the need is to establish the movements of these two bodies and the five wandering bodies, they do not start from the same principles nor the same hypotheses ... If the hypotheses they have adopted were not deceptive suppositions, all the consequences deduced from them would without doubt be verified.'[338] Thus, both the concept of observation (the literal meaning, one might say in a different context) and the cognitive procedure, the hypothesis (the historical meaning, one might say), have to be rethought. When Copernicus made the results of his work known, the thoughts they suggested turned round whether this new theory *gave a good account of the phenomena*, that is, allowed precise knowledge of the movements of the heavenly bodies, and their calculation. The evaluation thus did not relate to the *reality* of these hypotheses, which were asked only to *save the phenomena*. Thus Ptolemy, who proceeded by analytical and inductive methods (discussing the phenomena and, following his discussions, suggesting hypotheses, in other words, proceeding from phenomena to causes) could be replaced if for these phenomena one suggested *other causes* that save the appearances still better. This was the way Copernicus was received. It was thought that with the new causes he was suggesting he saved the phenomena more exactly or more conveniently than did Ptolemy's causes. It was thought that Ptolemy and his successors could never have regarded their hypotheses as things of nature: 'whether things be or be not really made as they have imagined them, as long as their suppositions succeeded in saving appearances, they leave this other consideration to the philosopher of nature, and scarcely concern themselves with it'.[339]

In other words, from false premises one imagines that it is nevertheless possible to derive a true conclusion, or that different causes may produce identical effects.

Note that we again find that this approach among the theologians. Recall medieval exegesis: if words have a meaning it is because they cover a hidden truth, that which is contained in the Scriptures. Observation of the world must thus be effected inductively; phenomena (celestial or

sublunary) are pointers to a deeper truth. If, for instance, Luther declared
war on the Copernican hypotheses, that was not because he had an
irrational mind but because, by regarding the hypotheses of Copernicus
as expressing the things of nature, one arrived at a contradiction of
Scripture. This act was indeed irrational, since as we have said Scripture
contained the truth of the world. These hypotheses could thus only
pretend to save appearances, to express rationally a phenomenon the
truth of which could not claim to be of the order of pure hypothesis.[340]
And Melanchthon, like the others, was convinced that Copernicus had
conceived his hypotheses only with an eye to 'saving the phenomena'.

This is why, as we have seen, it was said that from a false premise a true
conclusion could be drawn. This argument could not be accepted for very
long, but questioning it again meant dealing frontally with the problem of
the truth of hypothesis in astronomy and thus of its compatibility with
Scripture. Tycho Brahé,[341] a Protestant, rejected Ptolemy's hypotheses
(in the name of the 'first principles of the art') and Copernicus's (in the
name of 'the authority of Holy Writ'), and said that 'astronomical
hypotheses ought not only to save the phenomena' they should, further,
agree both with the principles of the peripatetic philosophy and with the
texts of Scripture, since they express not only fictions, but *realities*'.[342]
Tycho Brahé, as far as the second part of the sentence is concerned, was
taking up, very 'traditionally', we are tempted to say, even though a
Protestant, the principle of interpretation of Scripture that posits that
events described in the Bible are *true* and therefore that any hypothesis on
the 'nature of things' obviously has to be in conformity with the texts of
Scripture.

The particular point here, and a very important one, was that this 'true
event' ('phenomenon') was not sublunary,[343] and the famous astronomer
was not unaware that extending this exegesis to the 'great book of heaven'
was a novelty. As being in contradiction with Scripture, the hypotheses of
Copernicus were rejected; they could not claim to tell us the truth. The
change was considerable, and was to be accepted by Kepler too.[344]
Hypotheses had to be in conformity with the nature of things and had to
accept the authority of the sacred texts. These hypotheses had accordingly to be able to interpret the signs surrounding us, certainly; but if the
interpretative method was that of biblical exegesis, as it to some extent has
to be because the hypothesis had to be 'in conformity with Holy Writ',
then these hypotheses were of a theological nature. The 'literal meaning',
in medieval exegesis, was worked out using, through, the 'allegorical
meaning'; it attested to a divine truth.

Kepler wished to convince people of the truth of his conclusions; for a
syllogism to be able legitimately to lead to a true conclusion, he said, it was
necessary for the premises (hypotheses) to be true. So much for the

question of false premises. There remained the problem raised by different premises that nevertheless led to identical conclusions.[345] This equivalence, said Kepler, could be only a partial equivalence, deriving from something that the hypotheses have in common. So a truth does exist. As for the 'literal meaning', it was through the *'realistic'* method that Kepler was to reveal it.[346] For Kepler, astronomy had to be founded in true hypotheses (which in our view once again reflects the extension of medieval exegesis to the interpretation of the sky, the 'great book' of heaven), not in contradiction with the truth contained in the Scriptures (here again we find the link between a 'literal meaning' and an 'allegorical' meaning expressed through the extension of sublunary physics to celestial physics).

If Galileo in an initial stage remained a Ptolemaist (the phenomenon induces the hypothesis), when he embraced the Copernican system[347] he did so in the same spirit as had inspired him when he held to Ptolemy's system. First, propositions had to be in conformity with the nature of things and established by reasons of physics; second, these truths had quite obviously to be in conformity with Scripture. Cardinal Bellarmino[348] said: 'if there were a sure proof that the sun were at the centre of the world, the Earth in the third heaven, that it were not the sun that turns round the Earth but the Earth round the sun, then one would have to proceed with great circumspection in expounding Scripture. But that such a demonstration exists I shall not believe as long as it has not been shown to me. It is one thing to *show that appearances can be saved by supposing* [our emphasis] that the sun is at the centre of the world and that the Earth is in the sky, another to *show* [our emphasis] that in truth the sun is at the centre of the world.'

Our cardinal was recalling that the truth incorporated in Scripture remained a divine truth that we must seek to wait upon, to induce, on the basis of the signs the divine truth institutes and points us towards, but he stressed in so doing that the 'literal meaning' by itself could never attain this truth, still less contradict it rationally, 'in truth'. We are still in a 'hermeneutics of hidden meaning'. This demonstration can never be supplied by Galileo, says Duhem, and it is vitally important to say why: 'those who hold the *course of error* [our emphasis] can have on their side neither reason nor any valid experience; on the contrary, with the *course of truth* [our emphasis], everything must harmonise and agree'.[349] The commonly accepted systems that cannot claim to give an account of appearances must be abandoned as being false. On the contrary, the system that agrees very well with appearances *may* be true. Accordingly, what is proof?

By pointing the way that leads to truth, a proof indicates what is conceivable as truth. Galileo was to conceive the proof of a hypothesis on

the model of the demonstration by reductio ad absurdum used in geo-
metry:[350] the experience, by convicting a system of error, confers certainty
on the opposite system. Yet proving the error of a system does not
necessarily imply the truth of the one opposed to it. That phenomena
ceased to be saved by Ptolemy's system leads to regarding his system as
false, but does not logically imply the truth of Copernicus's system.[351]

Galileo, for whom the assuredly true (as agreeing with the celestial
phenomena) Copernican hypotheses had necessarily to be in agreement
with Holy Writ, was asked by Cardinal Barberini, the future Urban VIII,
to prove that God was not able to order the world in another way 'such
that all the phenomena manifested in the heavens, everything we teach
concerning the movements of the heavenly bodies, their order, their
position, their distance, their arrangement, might nevertheless be
saved'.[352] This means that the confirmation from experience, however
numerous and exact they may be supposed to be, could never transform
a hypothesis into a certainty, because *the same facts of experience* would
inevitably contradict any other hypothesis that might be imagined'.[353]
Duhem's critique here is profound in pointing clearly to the fundamental
question raised by all knowledge of truth, which medieval exegesis had
sought to answer by suspending the 'literal meaning' (the 'real event'; the
'phenomenon', the 'fact of experience', one would say in other areas of
knowledge) to the allegorical meaning. Just as a 'historical fact' is nothing
without its 'historical meaning', a 'fact of experience' in physics is nothing
without the hypothesis (physical theory) that engenders it and the truth or
falsity of which it comes along to prove.

Observation of the world is always of an order of knowledge underlying
it, and the last question always refers to this. At the end of his work,
Duhem suggested that the assertion by such as Copernicus, Kepler or
Galileo that astronomy should take as its hypotheses propositions whose
truth was established by physics combined two very distinct propositions.
The first, which might mean that the hypotheses of astronomy were
judgement on the nature of the heavenly bodies and on their *real* movements, was 'false and harmful'.[354] The second, 'by requiring that the
hypotheses of astronomy be in accord with the teachings of physics
required that the theory of heavenly motions rest on foundations capable
of supporting equally the theory of motions we observe here below'.[355]
This second proposition, which Pierre Duhem regards as well founded,
was to legitimate the extension of sublunary physics to celestial physics: a
'same dynamics must, in a single set of mathematical formulae, represent
the motions of the heavenly bodies, the oscillations of the ocean, the fall
of heavy bodies; they thought they were renewing Aristotle, but they were
preparing Newton'.[356] We have definitively entered modernity.

To the question that all rational knowledge answers, what is one to observe, what does an observation indicate, Newton replied that it was from the phenomenon that one must start, that it was through the phenomenon that we could ascend to the principle. This approach, which led to Newton's cosmological formula about universal attraction, was the end point of what Kepler and Galileo had begun: observation is at the root of the laws of nature. 'The mind' must henceforth abandon itself to the abundance of phenomena, and unceasingly support itself upon them. There is a *logic of phenomena*, which will henceforth be called 'facts'. Another hermeneutics can be set up. Here we have the ambition of analytical thought: to conquer the real, to reduce the multiplicity of natural phenomena to a single law.

This definition of 'observation' institutes the foundations of dynamics, that is, a theory of nature that reorganises the relationship between hermeneutics and semiology. The phenomena of nature can be recognised by being uniform events, 'non-divided totalities'.[357] Observation grasps only the *surface of events* (just as words are not more than surfaces that are read, no longer enclosing anything hidden); explanation of the event is to consist in specifying the *conditions* for it to happen and in exactly analysing the way it depends on those conditions. Here is the role for analysis, which is to posit a *uniform* presentation of the event, which will accordingly be regarded as a 'given', homogeneous through the perception we have of it and the observation we make of it. Its specific nature will result from its constitutive elements. Through the understanding of the 'reason', observation of the world leads to the eternal verities, the rational causes of which are material and human. The allegorical meaning that helped penetration of the mystery was at the root of reading of signs here below, defining the 'literal meaning' by a hermeneutics of the 'hidden meaning'. Henceforth the 'unknown' supplements the mysterious, the reading of signs rejects an allegorical meaning and takes up the philological heritage of grammatical literalism; the 'facts' take part in knowledge of the laws of nature in the same way as 'words' make up a phrase and give it a meaning. Thus, it is thought, by acquiring all these factual truths, one might accede to the truths of the laws of nature (just as an accumulation of true events cannot do other than lead to historical truth).

In this way, throughout the seventeenth century we find this conviction that the time had come for nature to reveal all its secrets, to throw light on to all areas of darkness. Undoubtedly this new episteme was to develop in opposition to theology, 'the mother of the sciences', but this shift once again owed much to the forms of knowledge grouped under the term philology. When the grammatical literalism of philology posited the principle of derivation for etymology – by opposition to exposition – it presupposed a sense that was only at the 'surface' of words, the explanation of which consisted in circumscribing it as a phenomenon (concepts of 'origin' and 'usage'). Legal knowledge proved the truth of texts on the basis of this theory, using all the rational methods that this theory supplied or suggested.

What now disappeared were the Scriptures as the foundation of *all* truth, the astronomical theories, as we have just seen, not being strangers to this. But through this influence of astronomy it was a philological tradition that was being continued (Galileo boasted his philology) and was indeed manifested in an opposition to theology and to the hermeneutics of the hidden meaning. First, just as with philology, a text appeared as a 'mosaic' of words and phrases; a true science of nature[358] had to do with the 'mosaic' of a history of the creation (once again calling upon the concept of origin). Then, for the philology that sought to induce the historical truth of all these particular traces that words and phrases are (the new literal meaning), the sciences of nature (here following Galileo, not Descartes)[359] were similarly to induce the truth of the world from all these special traces that 'facts' are. Finally, like philology, which knows no final truth but provisional origins, Galileo's physics did not intend to venture beyond the description of natural phenomena, and this empiricism posits the phenomenon as relative and susceptible of further analysis. The truth of nature, but also the truth of history, rest equally upon 'facts' ('true events') and *are both* suspended from the state of knowledge of these; as soon as these increase (as we advance into the 'unknown'), it is the truth that shifts.

Perhaps there are reminiscences of medieval philosophy in Descartes's philosophy; for him the certainty, like the stability, of all knowledge rested on fundamental principles, whereas all 'factual' knowledge was of the order of the uncertain and the unstable. Indeed, for Descartes, the appearance of things was meaningful only in allowing us to gain access to something hidden from us, to posit a link between what we are empirically given and the concepts, which carry 'the proof of their truth *in themselves*'.[360] Descartes makes the 'literal' observation take second place to a non-apparent, abstract meaning, just as medieval philosophy made the allegorical meaning (or the mystical, i.e. mysterious one) predominate over the literal meaning[361] which, we have said, corresponded to something hidden. Astronomy ended by leading to the positing of an inverse relationship between the signs we observe and the truths they express. Observation henceforth becomes not a mere hypothesis but a truth, which the fact (reality) points to, from which, then, a truth is *deduced*. The principle is not primary but derived, and it is the 'fact' that is immediate, 'given'. It is, to use philological terminology, 'original', and legal knowledge was to develop its reading in the same way as the knowledge of nature.

The principle is derived. No principle is certain by itself; every principle receives its truth only from the '*usage*' made of it, and this consists only in the aid the principle supplies in understanding the multiplicity of phenomena we are given and in the questions they raise through the perspective they offer. Just as for our sorcerers, we might be tempted to say, everything is potentially a sign around us; but the difference is that now we have the code that enables the distinction to be drawn between what is important and what is not, on the one hand the concept of experience, which on the other hand gives us access to a rational law of the world. Answers are found to questions without answers appeasing the fears expressed by the chase after magical knowledge.

The problem of historical truth and nature now being clearly put, the definition of proof could finally emerge: it was to be what an observation would confirm by experience; it was deduced from the 'facts'. That 'analytical' philosophy of law was, moreover, to be based fairly faithfully on this conception of nature and this method of knowing it. The law was always to be deduced from the 'case', which was to emerge at the same time as the legal principle allowing it to recognise among the multiplicity of events those usefully contributing to elaborating the decision ('evidence'), that is, to know the law. We are now in a hermeneutic circle. The political history of Britain, of the monarchy, by contrast to that of the continent, did not lead to this assimilation of the law and the king, in other words to this idea of the code supposed to set out the principles. Accordingly, these principles could result only from the whole set of decisions continually handed down, engendering a rather different argumentation, or rhetoric, from what we find where a 'code' is given *a priori*. But the knowledge that allows things to be known and recognised is similar in the continental and the insular tradition.

The other consequence of this method is that it reinterprets the continuous line of time. The present will henceforth draw its truth from the experience which, if it indicates a truth, must be identically repeatable: the prediction and the past become the verification of a present truth. The future is always this time that contains a truth, except that now it no longer announces but confirms, which means that the present time must be sufficient unto itself in respect of the statement of truth. But as soon as it finds application in physics, this structure of time posits a methodological principle that is heavy with consequences. When, starting from what 'certain' observations give us, we claim to anticipate other cases we have not directly observed, we are implicitly stating a law of uniformity of nature.[362] Without this postulate that allows us to state that the laws known today will apply in the same way in future, there would be no theoretical possibility of justifying conclusions regarding the future derived from experience gained in the past. 'Scientific prediction does not imply the syllogistically necessary conclusions of formal logic', Cassirer concludes;[363] for him this prediction was nevertheless a conclusion, valid and essential, by analogy.[364] The assumption is not purely logical in nature but biological and social, and we naturally find it in legal science too, for instance: there is an assumption of *uniformity of social experience*, whether collective or individual. The whole of 'case law' is solidly grounded on this iron law. And this law allows us a new creativity through the procedure of analogical inference, in order to set up a legal *'continuity'*.

'Observation' is, then, at the root of truth: by observation we obtain equally the truth of nature and the truth of reasoning. The basis of all knowledge is, more than ever, the 'true fact', the 'true event'. Diderot, in his 'De l'interprétation de la nature', sought to give priority not to the abstract sciences (mathematics) but to the sciences of facts. Here eighteenth century philosophy approached the problems of the truth of nature and the truth of history as a *single problem*.

Our work has once again sought to confine itself to research in what we have called the premodernity of Western rationality. We do not wish here to embark on contemporary epistemology and hermeneutics. The most important thing for us was to try to redraw a number of certainties that we still in part have. Thus we may say that the 'historical meaning', and here Thomas Kuhn will supply support, like a 'physical law' can no longer claim to refer to anything other than itself, since it can be fed only by 'facts' which are always *supports for prior statements*. This is, moreover, what analytical philosophy was not yet perceiving, even though philological research was already pointing to the problem (we would today talk of the 'hermeneutic circle', as we have said). Bayle is not a Cartesian; he does not reject the factual as such, on the contrary. According to him, the accumulation of well-established 'facts' is the fundamental basis of all knowledge. He is thoroughly 'positivist'. Just like Thomas Kuhn, resorting at the end of this century ('Second Thoughts on Paradigm')[365] to the jurists; method in order to get out of the methodological crises we have just identified in the natural sciences, so Bayle, to construct his fact, takes the same course as followed by jurists when they take trouble to show, from a reading of reality, what is true and what is false.

We still do not have the principle that is to enable us to take possession of the real world. We have seen that Bayle indeed believes in the 'truth of facts', but it is the very concept of observation that is the problem. Thus the comet, he would say (and we understand his choice) does not indicate the signs tradition sought to see in it. Like Galileo, who sought to prove the truth of his system by proving the falsity of the system opposed to it, Bayle has tried to show that the problem of the 'truth of facts' had to pass through the discovery of error (philological tradition takes its tribute). But we fall back into the fundamental flaw noted for the new astronomical theory. If observation has to pass through a cognitive process that locates errors, then 'meaning' is prior. A fact can never be what one starts from (terminus a quo), only what one moves towards (terminus ad quem). This knowledge that institutes the signs can clearly not be prior to the knowledge that identifies them. All these little things, all these details even, which are to constitute the proof (evidence) showing that a fact is true, can be recognised as such only because we have a code that offers a prior mode of interpretation.

We may say here that Bayle's attempt cannot succeed. What was it? It was the opposite of Bossuet ('Discours sur l'histoire universelle'), for whom all truth was biblical, for whom any 'true fact' had to be mentioned in Scripture ('literal meaning') or tradition. Bayle denounced the vicious circle constituted by adducing tradition as the foundation for the truth of facts where at the same time the content, like the value, of the tradition was *contained in* the true facts mentioned. The criticism was not well founded, since Bayle adopted a conception of the 'literal meaning' that had come not from the exegetic but the philological conception; then the circle indeed becomes vicious. But if Bayle, had put himself in an exegetic perspective, the problem would have become that of the 'hidden' meaning. Bayle, fed on philology, and against the Catholic church, was thus to posit error as the foundation of the truth of facts. But showing the error of an argument, as in Galilian astronomy, does not have the immediate, direct consequence of proving that this argument that has shown an error is an argument that tells the truth. Bayle is a philologist and not an exegete in his historical criticism; he was thus certainly able to prove that a number of things said to be true are false, but he was always to have the problem that arises with philology as soon as it becomes a *method of history*: proving the false indicates nothing as to the true.

As we have said, modernity sought to solve this problem by the idea of a 'historical meaning' (already in Montesquieu and the 'Esprit des lois'[366]). And appealing to jurists would serve no purpose since, as we now know, legal reasoning comes along to prove a statement, positively or negatively, nothing more. Legal knowledge is inseparable from a hermeneutics: it makes signs talk but does not institute them. Legal proofs are proofs recognised as such. Demonological proofs were done on the basis of valid reasoning, but from an *observation* of nature which was itself not 'rational'. Lawyers did not create 'the world of darkness'; they came along to demonstrate a truth in which the whole world believed, which expresses the difficulty they found in recognising the laws of nature. Thus everything and anything could claim to be the proof of a buried, hidden truth.[367]

The concept of observation, developed by astronomy, can equally prove the errors of what were accepted as proofs of the truth of nature. All that is henceforth accepted are the truths capable of intrinsic justification, which means not in need of transcendent revelation, in other words, sure and evident in themselves. Accordingly, by definition, on this perception of nature the proof of the devil was ruled out. One more point regarding legal proof. Coming along to support or contradict a given supposition, it may, like philology, prove that a proposition is false in order directly to prove that the opposite proposition is true, because argumentation operates on the basis of antinomic propositions. The Church justified its possessions and its powers by the donation of Constantine: proving that the Donation is a fake means at the same time proving that the Church is wrong and thus that Valla is right in saying, as the truth, that the Church has no legitimacy, no right, over Naples for instance. Philologically, one creates truth, a creation that is indeed valid for historical method, and this proof is a proof of falsity. It must not be made to say less than it does: they are words, nothing else, and one may thus be right by showing that the other is wrong. But it should not be made to say more than it does either; the law cannot claim to take refuge in pure convention. More than in many fields of knowledge, it must always *claim* to be capable, if possible with certainty, of establishing the truth.

18

Conclusion

Ginzburg's famous article 'Signes, traces, pistes'[1] seems to us to make an excellent base for starting our concluding thoughts. Among its many virtues, this essay excellently locates the unavoidable share of strictly philosophical considerations that all attempts at knowledge of the past raise. This work may, moreover, be presented as an exciting essay in the philosophy of knowledge, even if its *form* remains chiefly a traditional historian's work, we might say an account.

We know how Ginzburg begins his 'text': by recalling the 'Morelli method' thanks to which we shall henceforth – or at least so it is believed – be able to recognise an authentic painting from a fake or a copy. This sets the guiding line, the plot, which will lead us through five successive places.

The first speaks to us of the secret or hidden things that testify to a truth we have to discover. The paradigm of the *index* is posed; the specific locus is the end of the nineteenth century, where hidden meaning came into contact with psychoanalysis which, according to Freud himself, as cited by Ginzburg, 'customarily [divines], from neglected or unnoticed features, from the dregs of observation, secret or hidden things'. Here Freud feels himself close to Morelli, who intends to discover the principle of the distinction between authentic and fake on the basis of 'all those little gestures that escape us by inadvertence'. The chief cognitive principle here is the identification of the intimate core of the personality (artistic in the case of recognising paintings) from elements outwith conscious control. Sometimes infinitesimal *traces* allow us to apprehend a deeper reality, be they called symptoms (Freud) or pictorial signs (Morelli), which relate to a model from medical semiology, 'the discipline permitting diagnosis of diseases beyond direct observation, on the basis of superficial symptoms the layman sometimes regards as insignificant'.[2] However, says Ginzburg, though this paradigm of the index, based on semiotics, began to prevail in the area of the human sciences between 1870 and 1880, it nevertheless had much older roots, to talk about which he brings us to a second point.

We are now in a place where time no longer has any grip: 'for millennia, man was a hunter'. The paradigm of the index is articulated around another hidden truth that Ginzburg believes in, that of the 'nature of man'. If during his 'endless moving about' man learned to reconstruct the types and movements of invisible prey on the basis of prints left on the ground and the like, then man enriched a knowledge 'of cynegetic type, characterised by the capacity to arrive, from apparently negligible empirical data, at a complex reality that is not directly experienced'.[3] Though it is located in a universe where time is no longer counted, we can easily recognise this time where inductive knowledge, a principle prior to the experimental act, comes to dominate in the order of knowledge: it is Newtonian time. But let us for a moment leave aside the epistemological aspect of the approach and follow the author on his journey this side of time. That the cynegetic paradigm is undoubtedly a specific heritage of humanity is given impressive proof by 'the Mesopotamian divinatory texts written from the third millennium BC' onwards. In this second place, we come to the first philosophical principle of knowledge proposed by Ginzburg. The index paradigm, according to the science within which it will develop, constructs temporal categories on the basis of which an argument of rational nature may be employed. If an index paradigm is indeed used to decide an action to be taken in the future, we have a science of divinatory type. If the paradigm is employed as a principle of action for the present, we have a medical semiotics. If, finally, the paradigm is employed as a principle for knowing the past, we have legal knowledge.

Knowledge of cynegetic type is primary, the very principle of the human specie's knowledge: it organises the rational approach to knowledge by breaking down the object 'time' into a 'before', an 'after' and a 'now'. Once this philosophical principle has been acquired, we can gain access to a third, non-historical, place where we learn to know things: specifically, the place of the categories of knowledge. At bottom, everything that has dominated the first pages of Ginzburg's text we have presented so far is the philosopher's concern, 'what is knowing?; with a very specific objective, that of transmission of a truth. This third place is that of methodological reflection, and though this place excludes the historical dimension, it remains easy for the reader to reincorporate it. What is this about? It is about thinking about those types of knowledge that organise an 'indirect, indicial, conjectural' knowledge.[4] The index paradigm is at the very root of medical and historical knowledge; these two types of knowledge are indirect and conjectural. 'Indirect': this is not obvious when it comes to considering medical knowledge rather than historical; we shall return to the point, which Ginzburg leaves perhaps too much out of consideration. They are 'conjectural' because the cognitive strategies of physician and historian remain 'intrinsically individualising'.[5] But let us not deceive ourselves. Ginzburg is not offering us, say, an introduction to epistemology of medical discourse but, as we have said, is concerned with the *transmission* of types of knowledge, which has the effect of leading him to posit in his text a profound break in the order of knowledge starting with the *status* of writing. For knowledge of cynegetic type was presented to us by him as a type of knowledge fed principally by smells, tastes and sounds, and if that was the case it was because the very nature of the human species so commanded. But writing is a type of knowledge without smell, taste or sound. What has to do with voice or gesture is held to have no relationship with writing, which is characterised by the absence of any reference to the perceptible, by a 'dematerialisation of the text'. Suffice it to think of the decisive role played by 'the intonation of the voice in oral literature, or by calligraphy in poetry, to understand that the concept of text we have so far adopted is bound up with a cultural choice of considerable importance'.[6] Philology is thereby proclaimed to be 'atypical'.[7]

This break pointed out by Ginzburg allows him to set out a second philosophical principle which brings us to a fifth place (we shall come back to the fourth in a moment), taking up again the distinction between nature and culture. Analysis of tracks or of the heavenly bodies is accordingly a different thing from analysis of painting, writing or discourse,[8] yet without the cognitive principle supposed to be at the root of this difference being explained to us, or even stated. Nor does the methodological consideration that takes us to the fourth place help us any further in understanding this distinction. For this place is just the one where the author enquires after the scientific *practices* that find a start to an explanation in this 'antianthropomorphic' status of writing that no longer takes account of anything but the reproducible characters of text. The transmission of knowledge henceforth depends on its capacity to be *reproduced*. Starting from a consideration of Galileo, Ginzburg tells us that 'for the philosopher of nature, as for the philologist, the text is like a deep, *invisible* entity that has to be reconstituted behind the perceptible data'.[9] Pursuing the cynegetic hypothesis as he had defined it, the author argues by assuming a perceptible world from which one induces a profound truth, and he maintains this hypothesis whatever the object considered, enabling him to conceive the text as this profound, invisible entity 'that has to be reconstituted'. He thus produces, on the basis of this fundamental hypothesis, the concept of *causality*, citing for it Mancini, a physician contemporary with Galileo and famous like him, who took the diagnostic signs by 'placing his ear on chests shaken by rhonchi, by smelling faeces and tasting urine'. What, then, was this physician's great originality? That he wrote a book about the art of identifying paintings, that is, *recognising fakes.* So here we have someone who knew things by smells, but also knew how to recognise them by a special look, the clinical gaze, at the same time laying the basis of connoisseurship. Here, Ginzburg tells us, there is 'more than a coincidence'. We are very willing to believe this, but what is it?

Ginzburg offers us an answer not by, for instance, analysing the forms and principles of knowledge at the time of Galileo and Mancini, but by making a move through time doing what we have (following Veyne) called a retrodiction. This takes the form of an alternative. The index paradigm in cynegetic knowledge stressed a whole set of special features, details, that shared, we might say, in knowledge of the individual. Writing for its part is supposed to have introduced knowledge intended to be capable of *faithful* reproduction, supposed to have brought the concept of text to a purging of features regarded as inappropriate, in order to secure knowledge of the general. Here the author speaks: 'the more individual features were regarded as relevant, the more the possibility of rigorous scientific knowledge crumbled'.[10] Hence the alternative: 'either sacrifice knowledge of the individual factor to generalisation ... or seek to develop ... a different paradigm, based on the scientific knowledge ... of the individual'.[11] The retrodictive principle is given: 'the first path was blazed by the science of nature, followed fairly recently by the alleged human sciences'.[12]

The point of knowledge is thus seen as being to incorporate knowledge of semiological type into a tradition that was proposing to turn its back on it – and this thesis is demonstrated to us by 'what happened' in the eighteenth and nineteenth centuries. 'Around the middle of the nineteenth century, we see an alternative emerging: the anatomical model on the one hand and the semiotic one on the other',[13] and the human sciences ended by adopting the indicial paradigm of semiotics to the detriment of this knowledge that sought to be total. Why? Ginzburg posits a link, by way of conclusion, between ability and knowledge. At the time of Mancini 'we can see the emergence of an increasingly marked trend towards ramified qualitative control over society by State power, using a concept of the individual similarly founded on minimal, involuntary features'.[14]

Once again, this text has the enormous merit for us of properly locating the problem posed by all knowledge that tackles the idea of the past: truth, even historical truth, *is not in the manuscripts*, but always has to be made.[15] However, between our viewpoint and Ginzburg's broad view there is one absolutely fundamental difference, relating to the status of the record that writing is. For Ginzburg, we have seen that the philologist is seen as conceiving the text as a 'profound, invisible entity' that has to be 'reconstituted'. We instead feel able to say that philology, in order to oppose the 'marvellous' as a *principle productive of meaning*, posited the principle of grammatical literalism, which meant that the text became a *surface*, a visible entity that it sufficed to observe.[16] Writing was, *ante litteram*, a 'phenomenon' and this is why, in our view, philology interested Galileo: from the phenomenon, something hidden was induced. For this reason, we do not think that Ginzburg's semiological hypothesis can be posited in these terms.

If we still share with Ginzburg, and many others, this hypothesis, we do so in relation to the question of meaning. For grammatical literalism was a method of rationally extracting meaning from the records that writing is. Which means, and this should not be forgotten, however banal it may be, that *meaning is not in the text itself,* but in the method that constructs it. Accordingly, and this is a second objection to Ginzburg's text, philology is in no way 'atypical' in the range of disciplines of the indicium. Philology is instead at the very heart of that history of Western Christian rationality that was so keen to unravel the true from the false. This rationality, which we have once again called Western and Christian, corresponds to the movement of thought that creates truth from writings, and we have on the basis of medieval exegesis been able to see that the enigma of meaning could not be resolved by the testimony of written records alone. This was, moreover, confirmed despite itself by the philological hypothesis, and even at the very time it was setting up to dispute it.

It is, then, Ginzburg's whole plot framework that we have to abandon. To give fuel to our dispute, let us come back to the 'non-coincidence' he mentioned in connection with Mancini. Mancini wrote a book with its most innovatory section devoted to identifying paintings, and thus to distinguishing the genuine from the false, even though, as Ginzburg tells us, Mancini was (first) a physician. We know how the problem is located: by the distinction between nature and culture, by the opposition between a knowledge that aims to be total and a knowledge that proceeds by induction (on the basis of elements of indicia). However much we may recognise that the forms of Western knowledge have often oscillated between the claim to total, systematic knowledge and a claim to a knowledge of systemic type, a distinction which is nothing but a pointer to considerations of an epistemological nature, the distinction between nature and culture does not to us seem very useful here. We would have to be told rather more about medical knowledge at the time (Foucault did this work in his book on 'the birth of the clinic'), just as we should be told a little more about this knowledge that proceeds on the basis of the distinction between genuine and false.

We know, moreover, that those first centuries of the second Christian millennium were all concerned with tracking down the fakes swamping libraries, notaries' offices and miscellaneous archival depositories. And, by the way, saying that there is a presumption here that '*does not apply to written texts*' and that there is an irreducible difference between a painting by Raphael and one of its copies would be deceiving oneself. The mark of a particular personality had long been sought in written texts, and was, moreover, a fundamental assumption that the philological method was careful not to throw out. Here we have specifically an old characteristic of Christian thought (remember Bede and his remarks on deducing character from physical features); and Chenu[17] recalled some aspects of Abelard's method that highlighted:

(1) the author's style as being 'original' (by its grammar, imagery, conceptualisation or whatever;

(2) the author's personality (intentio auctoris), on the basis of many 'apparent obscurities' on the *surface* of the text;

(3) the intentio, which might, Chenu tells us, go so far as to void the statement of its positive value.

With the domination of written culture, the second millennium may, and this is what we have tried to do, be defined as the new dividing line between the sacred and the profane, and consequently as that which opens up entirely new practices in subjectivity. In stating the truth, the 'objective' and the 'subjective' set up a new relationship that we have sought to describe in terms of what we have called the theologico-juridical episteme. In Ginzburg's text, and this is our third criticism, there is one big lack: law, and hence dogmatic knowledge. How, for example, can one not mention the legal practices that establish truth in this world, in talking about an 'authentic document' (even if the document in question is a painting)? The paradox of Ginzburg's text is that the jurist, though running through it from one end to another, is never mentioned.[18] What unites all the diversities the author discusses is nothing other than legal knowledge. That is why, indeed, it is possible to posit a relationship between Morelli's method of indicia and Arthur Conan Doyle's Sherlock Holmes: the art-lover is, Ginzburg tells us, comparable to 'the detective discovering the author of the crime – (or the painting, we might be tempted to say) – by basing himself on indications that most people overlook'.[19]

The presence of this legal knowledge points to something absolutely fundamental. Citing Wind, Ginzburg indicates that 'some critics of Morelli have found it strange that personality was to be sought where personal effort is least intense', but immediately adds that modern psychology would undoubtedly agree with him, being interested in those little gestures that inadvertently escape us and 'are much more revealing of our character'.[20] Here we might again bring in Freud as cited by Ginzburg: 'I find Morelli's method very closely related to the medical technique of psychoanalysis. It too customarily divines, from neglected or unobserved features, from the dregs of observation, *secret or hidden things*'.[21] We have come to it. Rational thought seeks to set up meaning on the basis of traces that point to something hidden. Here we again find our medieval exegesis and its hermeneutics of the hidden meaning. The point is indeed to start from signs and find through them a buried truth, say from purely personal features that escape their possessor's notice, that he is unaware of.

This knowledge in fact seeks to identify a subjectivity on the basis of factors beyond conscious control. What is being organised, then, in other words? An episteme: let us keep this term as Faucault used it, to describe the relationship set up between a knowledge that institutes signs and allows them to identify (semiology) and a knowledge that interprets them (hermeneutics). This is what we have met with throughout our reflections on Western Christian rational thought. But here too we see only false breaks and false continuities; through this articulation of a semiology and a hermeneutics, shifts come about, perceptible in terms of the act of knowing oneself. The reason why legal knowledge was absolutely un-avoidable is because it was the knowledge that engaged, and still does, in discovering the traces of events that cannot be directly brought about by the observer (such as reconstituting a past situation or conversation).

This point should enable us to avoid one very big error that Ginzburg, and this is our fourth criticism, seems as far as we can see not to avoid. Understanding is not an interpretation of signs, traces, indicia, through the immediate reality of which 'we manage to attain something of man (or reality) of other times'.[22] If we can attain something through the act of understanding, it is the man *of today*; and that is not too bad at all.[23] Putting it in the words of Alessandro Pizzorno, to interpret is to lay the foundation, the refoundation and the critique of a certain collective identity.[24] In this excursus through what is called 'past', all we are doing is identifying – or at least trying to – a feature that belongs to our present. Ginzburg's so imaginative text may in this connection be given differing readings. It may seem like the sketch for a vast fresco of an epistemological nature by a philosopher-historian (though we reject the term, since we find it hard to imagine a historian who is not a philosopher by definition, however much he may deny it), or, more directly, it may look like an introduction to some thinking about the exercise of power in modern States,[25] and this reading would, then, he the specific sign of contemporary power practices. This second reading may, of course, find among many possible empirical illustrations the practices of criminal law.

The theoretical problem we are facing today in stating pieces of explanation of our present is indeed that of the relation between an element extracted from a process called observation, which is never a datum but always a construct, which is certainly another banality we think one always does well to recall, and the philosophising hypothesis, by which we mean the proposition regarded as expressing a truth, the proof of which is supposed to be given by the constructed element of 'reality'. In order for this theoretical problem to be given a rational answer, it is certainly necessary for the concept of 'cause' to be reconsidered, that is, for new definitions to be offered regarding 'explanation' and 'understanding'. This is the line Pizzorno pursues in the article we have cited.

This philosopher-sociologist is interested in all the little mechanisms we activate in seeking to understand a particular situation, which leads him to describe the interpretive act on the basis of which we understand, or seek to understand, things. In the first place, the sasine of reality, to use a Scots lawyer's term, is always a construct, as Pizzorno says in putting forward the concept of 'reidentification'. We know any social event whatever, we project an explanatory hypothesis onto it, which, say, proves in the last analysis to explain nothing at all, or then we have to regard the event as a 'senseless' act. We must then redefine the actor's identity in order to maintain rationality in explaining the phenomenon. The first thing to stress, then, is that, in the act of explaining and understanding any social phenomenon whatever, the 'social subject' is not the subject's actual being ('identity'), and secondly, and this is entirely fundamental, that the *meaning* of the action cannot be reconstructed by an observer referring *purely to the precedents and consequences* of an act. In other words, this causality that takes shape in a linear, realistic structure of time must appear as suspect. Still in connection with the relationship with the real world and the hypothesis of the construct, one must bear in mind[26] that an event is comprehensible only within a 'history' (without it being necessary for me to invoke some unobservable entity like 'mental state') and that there is no *unique* identification (we are in the order of the construct). For it is the *interests the observer brings to bear* in his observation that govern the selection process.[27]

Now that our construct is set up, what does Pizzorno show us? On the one hand, that 'explaining' is the act that comes about when cognitive instrumentalisation has proved *inadequate*. On the other, that understanding consists in gathering the *motives* for an action by another subject, that is, what we imagine has to be present as 'cognitive component of a decision-making process about which we can say nothing other than what we deduce from what emerges from his action',[28] since its content is not made to be communicated. There is nothing obvious about the act of giving an account of a subject's *action*; it is explained by reidentification of a subject 'by relocating it in a belief context that only a specific theory is capable of reconstructing'.[29] This very well shows, we feel, and we cannot repeat it enough, that *all interpretation of the past is always only done on the basis of our interpretive community, so that all 'history' is never testimony about a past but testimony about a present.*

Interpreting is being capable of saying something different and more about a particular action than the subject of the action could; it is a 'second rationality', but certainly not superior. For this, the historicist hypothesis of all hermeneutics, far from being a 'lazy philosophical conclusion',[30] is an unavoidable postulate that has no other claim than to say, as Croce did long before us,[31] that 'reality and life are only history, and nothing but history', that is to say, according to us, *that form of knowledge* without which no society could establish its own truth-values but which, though it always speaks in the name of a past, points only to the identity (its traces) of the interpreting community. Here, in our view, lies the special interest of what is called history, the interpretation of the present via a detour through a 'past' which, when it was 'real', was something quite different for the actors living through it.

These records, identified because interpretation is done in the name of knowledge of a past, are what a society knows at a present time and recognises as true, and this changes in no way if one says that this knowledge rests on 'true events', if by this one means that this truth binds the interpretive act of an interpreting community. This cognitive act does not bind the interpreter; it is one of the tools with which a community seeks to define its own identity. Let us take an example. Furet, with his proposal for 'quantitative history',[32] seems to us to be interesting from this viewpoint. This history would consist in *procedures for treating* quantitative 'historical' data: problems which, he tells us, have to deal with 'the technology of research' in the social sciences and with a 'retrospective economics' by economists, who elaborate particular data using which we may understand, which is to say manage, the economy of our present time. One can arrive at this cognitive equipment by constituting the 'historical fact' as 'time series of homogeneous, comparable units', so as to be able to 'measure developments over given intervals of time'.[33] The object is to arrive at a genuine historical science, since serial history is supposed to allow the 'unlikely event' of positive history to be replaced by 'the regular repetition of data selected and constructed in terms of their comparability'.[34]

Here we are plumb in the middle of a *'constructivist'* methodology where the *'event'* gives way to the *'series'* and the construction of the historical datum is in terms of a *probabilist analysis*. Whoever says methodology says definition of the working materials (theory of 'sources'), that is to say, the actual definition of what helped to constitute what is called truth, by the compulsory detour of setting up a definition of reality. Furet thus proposes, in order to replace an 'unreachable external scenario of the fact by an internal approach to the fact',[35] that the event no longer be selected because it marks the heartbeats of a history whose 'meaning' has been defined beforehand but is henceforth 'a phenomenon chosen, and perhaps constructed, in terms of its repetitiveness and therefore comparable over a unit of time'.[36] This means, then, that there is no longer any datum other than that indicated by the 'prior meaning' deduced from the cognitive hypothesis. Furet tells us that this method is an authentic advance for historical research, since the historian is going to have to 'renounce his epistemological naivety (and) construct his research object'.

Quoting the Arab proverb that 'sons resemble their times more than their fathers', we would be tempted to say here that any change in the cognitive equipment always looks like decisive progress by comparison with the mode of knowledge of a previous time, and the term 'advance' to understand and explain this phenomenon is undoubtedly largely pseudo-explanatory. As far as the 'construction of the research object' is concerned, by definition every historian has always had to perform this act, and if Furet was once able to doubt this, it is because he himself had great 'epistemological naivety'. What is true is that this constructive act no longer follows the same methodological principles, which is another matter.

The task of serial history is to constitute its material for analysis (and we can recognise in this act the act that one day created the 'archive'), and Furet very logically keeps the consistency of his constructivist choice: sources do not define the problem, but on the contrary the problems define the sources, and this operation heralds a revolution: time, that is, the conception the historian has of it and the representation he gives of it, is to be transformed. It is true, or at least we too believe so, that the method by which we claim to know the past, until today at any rate, incorporates something called the 'fact' into an account, which is a *continuous form* of recognition of reality whereby truth propositions are stated, whereas serial history on the contrary is going to have to describe continuities on the basis of the *discontinuous*: by the 'analytic decomposition' of what is perceived as reality, by recomposing rhythms that no longer have to match the 'realist' perception of time.

This essay, intelligent, innovative and tempting as it is, leaves us, let us face it, rather indifferent about what it is intended *explicitly* to show, namely that historical method is in a phase of unparalleled revolution; we are indifferent because we have long seen that any act of knowledge turning towards the past always needed the treasures of creative imagination, and has also been able to arouse whole areas of new knowledge, and if this form of history were one day to come to prevail it could never – though this would be a remarkable compliment – be at a higher level than its predecessors. What by contrast interests us greatly in this text and certainly does not leave us indifferent are the new interpretive premises that a society adopts to tell itself about itself in the present time. What does this thinking of Furet's *implicitly* indicate to us, we mean as a trace that is neither visible nor hidden? It indicates a number of pieces of cognitive equipment that a society gives itself in order to define its truth principles. It does not speak to us of the past, but of the present, which remains a riddle[37] that we want to understand, which compels us to create a past. The movement is always the same even if, once again, in this creative act one always has to base oneself on a phenomenon that one *proves true*. We do not want to insist too much on this; everyone will have recognised in the very principle of this method the weight technology has in our everyday life, and it does not much matter in the context of this discussion whether this is a good thing or a bad thing. The computer is the expression of these *new forms of knowledge*, 'a remarkable theoretical constraint', according to Furet.[38]

There are new forms of knowledge in it indeed, which have already, along with so many others, as de Certeau[39] stressed in connection with the computer, produced new effects on the conception we have hitherto had of the notion of *text*, with the 'constitution of *new archives* conserved on punched tape'.[40] The foremost methodological point is that there is no signifier except in terms of a series, not in relation to some 'reality'. All that becomes an object of research here is what is formally constructed before programming and, for de Certeau, contemporary analysis upsets procedures bound up with symbolic analysis that consisted in '*recognising a hidden meaning*'.[41] This analysis, says de Certeau, consists in constructing models ('set up decisionally') to replace the study of the actual phenomena by that of an object *constituted by its definition*, in setting the *limits* of the signifiability of this model.

What, then, do the cognitive practices of historians of today, at any rate those engaged in this 'something' that Furet has called serial history, have to tell us? They highlight the 'limits of the signifiability of these models or these languages', for instance by multiplying or transforming the systems constituted (physical, literary, biological etc. models). This is a renewal of the cognitive equipment of our society, and what the work of historians in particular points us to is the discursive statements that our society is capable of accepting and of rejecting, its possibilities, in other words, of proof and of truth. We say a renewal, since we share de Certeau's viewpoint, seeing in this cognitive process of the limit what 'yesterday' appeared in the mode of a 'past relative to an epistemology of the origin or of the end'.[42] There is, then, a continuity in our form of knowledge, but also undoubtedly a break, since these new forms of knowledge grouped under the heading of information technology and symbolised by the computer set new prohibitions by definition, as expressed by the two hypotheses we brought up in connection with Furet's thoughts on the act of recognition and the demonstration of the truth. We may illustrate our ideas by citing some research by de Certeau. By what Furet calls series and model, a new distinction is drawn in the historian's practices of knowledge between the *construction* of research objects (and 'units of understanding'[43]) and the *accumulation* of 'data' (to use the customary term, which does not lack savour in its ambiguity), which will allow a specific *exploitation*: 'the old interpretation becomes ... the highlighting of *differences* by comparison with these models'.[44]

Traditionally, we enunciated our truth propositions by a coherent and substantive understanding which sought to be comprehensive, on the basis of various indicia or traces revealed by a semiology and translated by a hermeneutics. The cognitive act thus proceeded in part by an inductive movement. The new method is based upon formal comprehensiveness set up decisionally: 'it moves towards the differences revealed by the logical combination of series'.[45] It therefore still plays upon limits, but 'does not start from a "rarity" (traces of the past) to arrive at a synthesis' – which in any case remains a pointer to an interpreting community – but from a formalisation, which is the new pointer to an interpreting community, which 'leads to residues ... and thence to a past that is the product of labour'.[46] What, then, is meaning? The new historical knowledge tells us: it is that which measures the differences ('one time things were not like today'), which have become a *result* when there was a question. Producing meaning is, then, producing *meaningful* negation: knowledge develops, is renewed, through interpretive modes capable of manufacturing 'relevant differences that allow one to "extract" greater rigour in programming and its systematic exploitation'.[47]

Everything is grist here too for the historian's mill[48]: the biographical detail, the fall in wages, 'all these forms of exception, symbolised by the importance of the name put forward in history',[49] which are the renewal of the relevant differences between the explanatory systems and that 'something' that is supposed to give an account of the mystery of our present. Finally, rebaptising 'fact' as a 'something' is not inevitably an advance of intelligence in understanding the present. The conception of document also becomes transformed,[50] even if here as elsewhere it is also appropriate to speak of false breaks. For after all, one might say, is not computing chiefly the technique that one day managed to elaborate what is called legal science in its conception of depositing and of filing, in its function in other words of storing, rediscovering and spreading knowledge? In the very action of the compiler as we have defined it, ought we not similarly to find an identity with this action of the informatician taking pieces of text here to link them with bits of text there so as to construct another text, by simple compilation? Yet it seems accepted that data-processing, which 'consumes', 'produces', 'stores' and 'distributes' writing in considerable quantities, brings a break with the traditional procedure of writing and above all of *reading*, of which the dissolution of the notion of author, or at any rate the difficulty we have today in protecting him legally, is perhaps a first indication.[51] To this indication another is added, which is for us the approach of contemporary philosophical hermeneutics in its close links with phenomenology (Heidegger, H. G. Gadamer, P. Ricoeur), in offering a systematic critique of the illusion of objectivity on the basis of the determination of an author's intention.[52] P. Ricoeur spoke, in order to emphasise this approach, of a 'semantic autonomy',[53] where the idea of 'intent' 'is both fulfilled and abolished by the text, which is no longer the voice of someone present, the *text is mute*'.[54]

By this approach, the interpretive act, like the questions it raises, will be thought of not as a problem generated by a sort of incommunicability of the mental experience of an author, but instead generated by the very nature of the 'verbal intent' of the text. Henceforth the interpretive act will be intended to be inscribed within a purely semantic space, absolutely not a psychological one. Here, by the way, we come back to the proposition put forward by Pizzorno, which we took up[55] in relation to the interpretive act, translated by Ricoeur as a hermeneutics of 'textual plurivocity', where the meaning of a text must not be sought, let us say, 'behind the text', but instead 'in front of it', in a movement that elaborates meaning through references, which goes from what is written towards what it deals with. This is certainly, in our view, the great issue that a historicist hermeneutics has to face 'today'.

How is this problem to be approached?

To use the language of computing, the texts we read are no longer anything more than texts about texts, and should not therefore appear any longer as texts about 'testimony' (of which we have attempted an epistemological sketch), recording their historical meaning in connection with the 'event'. Thus, just as the old perception of the text could claim to herald a 'historicist' hermeneutics, so the new concept would seem to condemn that sort of method. Yet we do not believe that this will remain insurmountable. The fact is that this new constructivist language can evidently not do without thought about the transmission of knowledge, which is even its sacred principle, and thus cannot avoid the problems bound up with any dogmatic activity, which we have unfortunately had to neglect overmuch in this study. It is following this constraint, this work on dogmatics, that the historicist hermeneutics will reappear, obviously with new issues. For in fact the very latest work in the area well shows in its method of integration and assimilation that dogmatics is still working at describing the poiesis contained in any act of enunciation of the meaning of a written record, or 'texture' to keep a more computer-like terminology, is still working, putting it differently, on the unavoidable share of creative invention contained in every interpretive act, which very specifically constitutes the record on the basis of which a historicist hermeneutics is developed. Here is where the distance is established between what indicates and that whereby we recognise what is indicated, the episteme of a particular society.

It is in this gap, and these will be our closing words, that the concept of author was born, that hermeneutic key developed between the sixteenth and nineteenth centuries that constituted the new concept of the 'meaning' of a 'text'. The author, in fact, is 'the one who denounces or announces the text by retro-reference to the one who has written it';[56] he is *function of the text*, which does not mean that one should never seek 'the author's intention' but that it should always be conceived of as a hermeneutic key, which compels us to apply this distance, in terms of which we have sought to describe premodern Christian Western rationality, between a semiology and a hermeneutics; a distance in which our model of truth is established.

Notes to Part I

1 G. Canguilhem, *Etudes d'histoire et de philosophie des sciences*. Librairie philosophique, Vrin, Cinquième édition augmentée, second tirage, 1989, p. 297.
2 Without here wishing to open up a philosophical controversy, we shall do no more than point out that some results of Canquilhem's work, in particular the third part of the work cited above, 'Investigations', seem to us to be singularly close to what none other than Jacques Ellul arrive at on the basis of his work on technology, in particular: 'La technique ou l'enjeu du siécle', Première édition Armand Colin, 1954; 'Le systéme technicien', Paris Calman-Lévy, 1977.
3 G. Cornu, *Vocabulaire juridique*, Association H. Capitant, PUF, 1987, 'Analogie'.
4 F. Gény, *Sciences et Technique en droit privé positif*, 1922, I; esp. p. 158ff.
5 *Recherches interdisciplinaires du Collége de France*, Vol. I, *Aspects historiques 'Analogie et Connaissance'* sous la direction de A. Lichnerowicz, F. Perroux, G. Cadoffre, Introduction p. 5.
6 Ibid.
7 E.g. C. Ménard, 'L'analogie de l'équilibre économique exclut-elle l'histoire?', in *Analogie et Connaissance, Recherches Interdisciplinaires du Collége de France*, op. cit., p. 208.
8 Thus Kepler, cited by D. Walker in 'Kepler's musical theories and analogy' in Analogie et Connaissance, o. cit., p. 65f., who shows belief in an analogical structure of the universe and of history: 'the movements of the heavens are nothing other than a perpetual symphony (rational, not vocal) which moves, through dissonances, through as it were certain suspensions or cadential formulae (through which men imitate the natural dissonances) towards definite, prescribed cadences, each chord being made up of six terms (as it were six voices), and by these marks (cadences) it divides an distinguishes the immensity of time; so that it is no longer astonishing that Man, the ape of his Creator, should finally have invented this way of singing in several parts, unknown to the Ancients'. We shall return to this question at length in the closing section.
9 G. Marty and P. Raynaud, *Introduction générale á l'étude du droit*, 2nd ed. Sirey, 1972, p. 230ff.
10 G. Marty and P. Raynaud, op. cit., p. 234

11 G. Cornu, Vocabulaire juridique, op. cit., 'Analogie'.

12 Ibid.

13 In this connection, see M. Troper *La séparation des pouvoirs et l'histoire constituionnelle française*, LGDJ, Paris, 1980.

14 J. Carbonnier, *Droit Civil, 1, Introduction, les Personnes*, PUF, 14th ed. 1982, pp. 185ff. Arises, a contrario, the traditional conception of legal interpretation.

15 J. Carbonnier, o. cit., p. 190.

16 See M. Troper, *La séparation des pouvoirs et l'histoire constituionnelle français,* op. cit.

17 See the report by L. Legaz Lacambra, 'Le raisonnement par analogie comme méthode d'interprétation et d'application du droit dans les différents systèmes nationaux', Tenth Congress of the Associaton of Comparative Law, p. 73ff.

18 N. Bobbio, L'analogia nella logica del diritto, Torino, 1938.

19 N. Bobbio, o. cit., p. 81.

20 The methodological problems of this approach are obviously numerous, and we shall repeatedly have occasions to come back to some of them. Let us emphasise merely that on this approach, history is a discourse which tells the truth; the distinction between empirical sciences and social sciences is accepted on a positive basis like the one the Vienna circle was able to define.

21 This pre-theoretical aspect of the acceptance of 'properties common to two objects' is not explicit in Bobbio. For instance: 'resemblance is a concept of relations: resemblance means relation between two or more objects *said to be similar* our emphasis; two objects are said to be similar when they have something in common', N. Bobbio, op. cit., p. 88.

22 N. Bobbio, op. cit., p. 93.

23 'Deductive or inductive.' This is perhaps not all that obvious, and would merit some clarification, it being understood that in the natural sciences, for instance, analogy is accepted as an inductive inference.

24 'The war of x against y is an evil; the war of y against z is an evil. the war of x against z is an evil. Implication: war against neighbours is an evil', N. Bobbio, op. cit., p. 94.

25 The author continues: 'all this is proved by previous cases in case law, where a particular situation provided for by the legislature is not adopted very exactly, but as a model situation to be extended to all similar cases' (op. cit., p. 95). On this notion of 'creative imitation' in the act of pronouncing justice, see P. Nerhot, 'The notion of narrative coherence in legal interpretation' in *Law, Interpretation and Reality*, ed. P. Nerhot, Reidel, 1989.

26 Mary B. Hesse, *Models and Analogies in Science*, University of Notre-Dame Press, Notre-Dame, Indiana, 1970; Mary Hesse thus presents the logical model, the mathematical model, the theoretical model, the imaginary model and the analogical model, the last being defined as the three-dimensional physical representation of an object or a system. 'In this category we find the planets, electrical circuits considered from the viewpoint of acoustic models, some mechanical models and graphs. All these models have in common

that they are *representations based on isomorphism between the laws governing the two processes considered'* (p. 8).

27 N. Bobbio, op. sit., p. 96.
28 Ibid.
29 N. Bobbio, op. cit., p. 97
30 E.g.: *Bird*   *Fish*
              wings   fins
              lungs   gills
              feathers   scales.
31 M. Hesse, op. cit., p 82ff.
32 N. Bobbio, op. cit., p. 101.
33 N. Bobbio, op. cit., p. 102, our emphasis. It is interesting to note the gradual shifts in the object aimed at: these definitions intended to define analogical inference turn into a definition of what law itself is.
34 Ibid. Our observation in the foregoing note is still more plainly illustrated here. Through these definitions, what is in fact happening is preparing the ground for the theory known as that of 'lacunae' in law.
35 N. Bobbio, op. cit., p. 104.
36 Ibid.
37 Ibid.
38 N. Bobbio, ibid., our emphasis. We shall meet with this question of observation again in the last section, when we come to consider philology and astrology.
39 See e.g. C. Bicchieri, op. cit., p. 14, for this type of opposition and analogical inference.
40 C. Bicchieri gives an example: the temperature of a gas (measured with a thermometer) is proportional to the average kinetic energy of the molecules making it up. This rule of correspondence brings into relation something *unobservable*, the kinetic energy of the molecules, with something observable, the temperature of the gas. The 'modellist' thesis of Mary Hesse consists in giving the notion of model an essential role in the construction of the theory; it is to guide the choice of formal structure (see C. Bicchieri, op. cit., p. 24/25ff.).
41 N. Bobbio, op. cit., p. 107.
42 Ibid.
43 Ibid.
44 N. Bobbio, op. cit., p. 108.
45 In any case, the idea of a search for the object of a law implies an interpretative act. It is only this that can bring into play the principle of resemblance, but Bobbio tells us nothing about this.
46 This would, then, be the general principle that determines resemblance in the analogical argument, but Bobbio does not tell us why, still less how, the idea of certainty emerges from this.
47 'Law is thought in movement, not an intent that has stopped' (op. cit., p. 115).
48 N. Bobbio, op. cit., p. 121.
49 N. Bobbio, op. cit., p. 132. He goes on to say 'this activity cannot be regarded as *creative* but as *interpretative*' (our emphasis).
50 N. Bobbio, op. cit., p. 78.
51 For example, G. Fassò, *Storia della filosofia del diritto*, Volume III.

Ottocento e Novecento, Il Mulino, 1970, p. 12ff.: 'Le Teorie della codificazione'.

52 The unity is of an organic type in a natural-law ideal formed through the whole past of a nation, but we also find the idea of a unity of logical type. Our attention was drawn to this by G. Fassò, op. cit., p. 71, citing Savigny in his *System des heutigen römischen Rechts*, p. 214; 'an operation which however leads to abandoning the historical plane to move instead on to the formal one, (Fassò) in a search for the 'intimate connection that binds all the institutions and all the rules of law together into one great unity' (Savigny).

53 This legal culture overdetermines the development of rationalist legal practices since the nineteenth century. Consider, for instance, German legal scholarship. Savigny, known as the founding father of the historical school in legal science, moved steadily towards formalist positions (see note 52); these positions come to be central in such an author as Puchta. He was, thus, the great disciple of that school: history is nothing else but 'history'; if all value reduces to 'history', then nothing else exists but historical law, which becomes the same thing as positive law. The historicism progressively disappears, to give way to systems of abstract concepts; the systematicity of law is henceforth understood as the logical chain of concepts (Puchta). From the search for historical knowledge of laws – which derives from the theory whereby law is history and the science of law is nothing but the history of law – the historical school thus comes to bring into being a legal science founded on a 'genealogy' of concepts. The way is opened to what is called 'pandectism', conceptual jurisprudence. The method consists in a formalism which seeks, and still does, we would say, to bring the whole of law into a logical system. Thus, Windscheid went on to prepare codification in Germany, though the movement of ideas he came from declared itself strictly opposed to any idea of codification.

54 G. Lazzaro, *L'interpretazione sistematica della legge*, Giappichelli, Turin, 1955. It seems that the first work in Italian devoted entirely to the argument of systematicity is the one by Donato Donati, 'Il problema delle lacune dell'ordinamento giuridico', published in 1910, and therefore not long after Italian political unity. For a more general bibliography, see R. Guastini 'Completezza e analogia', *Studi sulla teoria generale del diritto italiano nel primo novecento – Materiali per una storia della cultura giuridica*, 1976 (pp. 513–91).

55 Piano Mortari, *Il problema del 'interpretatio iuris' nei commentatori*, Annuali di storia del diritto, 1958, p. 78.

56 G. Lazzaro, op. cit., p. 17.

57 Op. cit., p. 18.

58 After posing the systematic argument in form and as to the substance, Lazzaro repeats, without much change, Bobbio's argument on analogy: for instance, Lazzaro's pages 45, 46 and 48 should be compared with what Bobbio called subjective and objective analogy.

59 The organicism of the nineteenth century is now giving way to the cellular biology of the 'origin' – the birth of law is thought to lead to the reproduction of law itself (drawing the explanation from cellular biology that the birth of the cell is part of the analogy of the

reproduction of the cell). For all this, see Maturana and Varela, and as far as law is concerned, Niklas Luhmann.

60 'In the first rank of intellectual tools, as it were the best synthesis of the work of abstraction that remains their common source, there is the Begriff of the German jurists, the role of which is a primary one in the area of legal thought.' F. Gény, *Science et Technique en droit privé positif. Nouvelle contribution à la critique de la méthode juridique*, vol. I, Second edition, p. 146.

61 F. Gény, op. cit., p. 156.

62 F. Gény, op. cit., p. 158. Our emphasis. This systematicity is to be explained by the 'need for unity inherent in the human spirit' (p. 160).

63 See p. 7 above.

64 F. Gény, op. cit., p. 154. The notion of a 'common' character remains undefined.

65 'in all this, all we have disclosed as a real principle of justification is analogy which, identified and clarified thanks to the schematic decomposition of things, legitimates for the mind, by way of "subsumption", an assimilation of the unknown to the known, the only peg our faculties of cognition can grasp' (p. 161); 'analogy ... inherent in the work of the mind' (p. 173); 'the procedure of scientific elaboration most commonly used in the constitution and interpretation of positive law is the simultaneously vague and fruitful procedure of all methodical investigation known as analogy ... It is this procedure that dominates ... in all law' (p. 179).

66 Fundamental dichotomies in Gény's method. See e.g. p. 97ff.

67 *Interpretazione della legge e degli atti giuridici (teoria generale e dogmatica)*, 2nd ed., Milan, Giuffrè. See also A. Plachy, *La Teoria dell'interpretazione. Genesis e storia della ermeneutica moderna*, Giuffrè 1974. This work stresses the new starts and breaks brought about by Betti in the herneneutic sphere, particularly his rejection of the idea of 'completeness' of the legal system in order to prefer talking of 'coherence', for which completeness would be more than an ideal. See e.g. p. 137ff. In this rejection, however, one should in our opinion see, more than a great conceptual rupture, the resumption of consideration of a theory that had become definitively established, the theory of lacunae in law, and its translation into a 'hermeneutic' approach.

68 'whether it comes from the notion of similar cases of analogical material – analogia legis – or is justified by the appeal to general principles of law – analogia iuris ...' (op. cit., p. 163).

69 Ibid.

70 Ibid.

71 E. Betti, op. cit., p. 164.

72 In order for legal analogy to be perfect so that the conclusion is certain, it is necessary for the resemblance between the case provided for in the provisions of law and the one not provided for to consist in the fact that, together, the cases have as common terms of reference the sufficient reason of the provision itself: ubi eadem ratio, ibi eadem iuris dispositio. The ratio legis is nothing but the sufficient reason for the law ...' (E. Betti, op. cit., p. 165). Here we

again find what Bobbio says on analogy, just as, p. 166, we find: 'the sufficient reason can be understood either as the reason for existence of the law or as the reason for its truth'. This is exactly what Bobbio says.

73 'Reasoning that gave no guarantee of certainty but is only probable would be useless argumentation for legal technique, which in its interpretive activity cannot in any way escape the fundamental presupposition on which the whole operation of law is based, the principle of certainty' (Bobbio, op. cit., p. 100).

74 For all this, once again see Bobbio, p. 108ff.

75 Bobbio's essay thus constitutes, in our view, a failure in his attempt to make analogy into 'rigorously logical' argumentation. We might, by the way, derive this finding of the failure of the author's very intentions where he considers that 'the reasons for existence' and for 'truth' of a norm are the *presuppositions* of any argument from analogy and that they are outside the argument itself.

76 E. Betti, op. cit., p. 169. Our emphasis.

77 We have, moreover, seen that Betti spoke of the legal system in terms of 'organic unity' and that reasoning from analogy consisted in the 'self-integration' of that order.

78 E. Betti, op. cit., p. 170.

79 Cf. Gény, above.

80 On all this see Patrick Nerhot, 'The law and its reality', in P. Nerhot (ed.), *Law, Interpretation and Reality. Essays in Epistemology, Hermeneutics and Jurisprudence*, Reidel Publishing Company, Dordrecht/Boston/Lancaster/Tokyo, 1990, pp. 50–70, 193–225.

81 E. Betti, op. cit., p. 91.

82 E. Betti, op. cit., pp. 93/94: let us say very briefly here, since we shall return to the point shortly, that he had a conception of historical methodology that is at least traditionalist. Moreover, if interpretation in legal science consists, and we use Betti's own words, which are extremely relevant, in an '*enquiry* into the interests at stake', how can this act be distinguished from interpretation in historical science?

83 Here Betti takes over a notion of Carnelutti's; E. Betti, op. cit., p. 94.

84 On this argument, see e.g. E. Betti, op. cit., p. 97.

85 E. Betti, op. cit., p. 99.

86 Betti distinguishes legal interpretation and description according to whether the act (the social action) to be interpreted is still devoid of any legal description. No doubt description is not a synonym for interpretation. However, the relationship the author assumes between these two terms is acceptable only if at the same time the notion of 'crude fact' is accepted. If it is not, the posited relationship has to be reconsidered. Let us note, moreover, that this relationship soon becomes obscure in Betti himself when he says: 'it is certainly incumbent on legal interpretation to choose, among the rules governing interpretation, those that best regulate the act to be interpreted; such a choice presupposes provisional, preliminary identification of the type of legal act to which the practical act corresponds ...' (E. Betti, op. cit., p. 100). This idea of 'provisional and preliminary identification' allows one to suppose that the relationship between interpretation and description is perhaps not

so simple as might *a priori* be thought.

87   P. Nerhot, op. cit., p. 195ff.
88   H. G. Gadamer, *Vérité et Méthode*, Seuil, 1976, p. 166ff.
89   P. Nerhot, op. cit., p. 40ff.
90   This understanding is not explicitly defined, but one may never-theless implicitly find the idea these authors have of it: real events which one narrates, which exist in themselves, which have to be discovered.
91   Bobbio and Betti, for instance, recognised the historical dimension of all law, but they did not derive any consequence from this for the hermeneutics they were developing; Betti even explicitly posited ahistoricism for the notion of judgement.
92   François Ewald, *L'Etat providence*, Grasset, 1986, p. 30: 'norma-tive practices, practices of constraint and social sanction probably, political practice certainly, and practice of rationality too'.
93   Ewald, for his part, says that 'the elements of recognition and identification of law are themselves historical'; F. Ewald, op. cit., p. 30.
94   F. Ewald, op. cit., p. 35.
95   Joachim Hruschka, *La comprensione dei testi giuridici* (Italian trans.), Edizioni Scientifiche Italiane, 1983.
96   On this argument, as one example among many others, see: 'Phenomenology, Structuralism, Hermeneutics and Legal Study: Applications of Contemporary Continental Thought to Legal Phe-nomena', Donald H. J. Hermann, *University of Miami Law Review*, Volume 36, May 1982, no. 3 (pp. 379–410).
97   J. Hruschka, op. cit., p. 51.
98   Ibid., p. 54.
99   Ibid., p. 57.
100 In history, the notion of document has been extended to the notion of 'trace', so as not to restrict historical objects to written docu-ments only. In this context, one might be surprised at the link we make between history and law, since here the notion of 'document' seems at first sight to refer exclusively to written things. Yet the distance is not very great. We are aware of the danger of reification (see below), and we shall see that the completion of an interpreta-tion, far from establishing the existence of a natural object, sets out the principle on the basis of which an object is recognised. This is why reducing law (or history) to a written document would be a gross error.
101 Paul Veyne, *Comment on écrit l'histoire, suivi de Faucault révolutionne l'histoire*, Seuil, 1978, p. 217ff.
102 Ibid., p. 219.
103 Ibid., p. 229.
104 An excellent illustration of this can be found in the marvellous article by A. Ross, Tû-Tû, *Harvard Law Review*, 1957 (pp. 812–25).
105 M. Foucault, *L'archéologie du savoir*, NRF Gallimard, 1969, p. 11: 'the order on the basis of which we do our thinking does not have the same mode of being as that of the ancients. For all our seeming to have the impression of an uninterrupted movement of European reason from the Renaissance to our days ... all this quasi-continuity

at the level of ideas and of topics is undoubtedly nothing but a surface effect.' M. Foucault, *Les mots et les choses, une archéologie des sciences humaines*, NRF Gallimard, 1966, p. 13.

106 A reconstruction which presupposes a starting point, a definite path and a termination. The problem is that this termination is always the outcome of a present meaning, just as the starting point is.

107 M. de Certeau, *L'Ecriture de l'histoire*, NRF Gallimard, 1975, p. 9.

108 M. Foucault, lectures given in Brazil, unpublished in French. 'La vérité et les formes juridiques', Première Conférence, p. 6: 'Legal practices – the way in which wrongs and responsibilities are arbitrated among men, the way in which in Western history one has conceived and defined the way in which men could be judged in terms of wrongs committed, the way in which particular individuals have had imposed on them reparation for some of their actions and punishment for others ... all these practices, regular but at the same time ceaselessly changing through history, seem to me to be one of the ways in which our society has defined types of subjectivity, forms of knowledge and, consequently, relations between man and truth.'

109 M. Foucault, 'L'histoire d'Oedipe', Deuxième Conférence, p. 33. The philosopher here raises the questions of the legal search for truth in archaic Greece (the technique of the 'ordeal' that we find again in the high Middle Ages) and shows that the whole Oedipus play is a way of 'shifting the statement of proof from a discourse of prophetic and prescriptive type to another discourse of a *retrospective order* [our emphasis], no longer the order of prophecy but that of witness' (p. 43).

110 There is certainly a need to be much more precise here, since it in fact seems that there was *simultaneously* a transformation of the old practices of ordeal and a rediscovery of enquiry.

111 Breach was a wrong against the State, against the law, against society, against sovereignty, against the sovereign, who would exact reparation. But justice did not come to belong solely to the sovereign, contrary to what Foucault thinks. More exactly, the sovereign is indeed an invention of the Middle Ages, but there is not just one form of sovereignty. Justice is the right of the Lord, who may be a lay person, an ecclesiastic, a corporate body etc., and the fact that the State of Justice (right of appeal) crowns the social edifice is one of the major issues in the political and social conflicts between King, Lords and Church.

112 The enquiry thus appears at first sight as a form of investigation bound up with new forms of justice: Inquisition, royal and princely justice. But it is also a specific practice of justice that gradually supplants the other ways of stating the right law, of knowing the truth (be it the judicial combat, the ordeal or the private accommodation). Perhaps it is the inquisitorial enquiry that is the model of everything.

113 Foucault extended his argument by showing that this judicial enquiry was to spread into a number of other social and economic areas as well as into other areas of knowledge. These types of

enquiry seek to establish truth on the basis of a number of pieces of evidence carefully gathered in such fields as geography, astronomy etc. We shall return to this question.

114 R. Mandrou, *Histoire de la pensée européenne, 3 – Des humanistes aux hommes de science. XVIème, XVIIème siècles*, Points Seuil, 1973, p. 15. The Church's authority came gradually to be disputed (fourteenth and fifteenth centuries); the Church universities were increasingly royal foundations, law came increasingly to be an issue between Prince and Church, canonists and civilists, Church courts and others, etc. But the model of the enquiry was ultimately to prevail in all jurisdictions of whatever type.

115 Even though the clergy cannot be totally recognised in and identified with the monarchical apparatus; quite the contrary.

116 Alchemy, for instance, 'which constitutes essentially a corpus of procedures in the sense of tests' (M. Foucault, op. cit.).

117 See also P. Ricoeur, *Temps et Récit, III, Le Temps Raconté*, Seuil, 1985, especially pages 12, 172, 204.

118 G. Bourdé, H. Martin, 'Les écoles historiques', *Points Histoire*, Seuil, 1983, p. 82.

119 Ibid., p. 92ff.

120 Ibid., p. 108.

121 Here we ought certainly to ask ourselves carefully about the more specific function in the enquiry of the *nature* of the proof. Before the modern period, the enquiry was not the sole essential element in order to prove. In other words, is it really necessary to confuse interrogation and collection of testimony with establishment of the truth? Are not torture, the Question, extorted truths? We have to come up to the century of the Enlightenment in order to come closer to the emergence of the modern system of proof (search for the material evidence of a crime), plainly bound up with creation of the modern police (let us recall here only the very fine text by Carlo Ginzburg, *Le débat*, November 1980, pp. 3–44, number 6) and the passage of society from status to contract. Summarising, then, it is perhaps hazardous to see the enquiry as a procedure which *from the outset* gives a rational truth. We shall return to this point.

122 M. de Certeau, op. cit., p. 98.

123 Ibid.

124 Ibid.

125 'The historical operation consists in cutting up the datum in accordance with a present law that distinguished it from its "other" (past), in taking one's distance from a given situation and thereby marking in discourse the actual change that has allowed this distancing' (M. de Certeau, op. cit., p. 100).

126 For M. de Certeau, history was our myth; if our hypothesis – that history was first of all a necessary category for the statement of modern law – has some relevance, then these legal forms on the basis of which social images are expressed have to be regarded as a fundamental dimension of the myth of modern society, and the present celebrations of the 'revolution', of 'rights', of 'equality', cannot really shake this hypothesis. Law would be a fundamental dimension of the modern myth, because here the 'thinkable' and

the 'origin' are linked, in conformity with the way a society understands itself (cf. M. de Certeau).

127 M. de Certeau, op. cit., p. 46.

128 Ibid., p. 49.

129 R. Barthes, 'Le discours de l'histoire', *Social Science Information*, February 1967, p. 65ff.; 'L'effet de réel', *Communications*, April 1968, p. 84ff.

130 Ibid.

131 'Authenticate the reality'; which brings us to, for instance, the whole of contemporary technicism.

132 Cf. Note p.160

133 N. Bobbio, op. cit., p. 101.

134 On this point, see also B. Grassò, *Appunti sull'interpretazione giuridica*, Università degli studi di Camerino, 1974.

135 N. Bobbio, op. cit., p. 134.

136 Ibid.

137 Ibid.

138 Ibid.

139 Once again, this sort of criterion can never be acquired definitively; it is truly in constant becoming, recognised by signs hopefully constitutive of it which are, as it were, recognised after the event.

140 J. Esser, *Precomprensione e scelta del metodo nel processo di individuazione del diritto*, Ed., Scientifiche Italiane, Italian trans. by G. Zaccaria and S. Patti, 1983, I, Premessa, finalità del lavoro.

141 See J. Esser, op. cit., p. 136ff.

142 In this sense, A. Aarnio, *The rational as reasonable*, Reidel Publishing Company, 1987.

143 Cf. M. Foucault, *L'archéologie du savoir*, NRF Gallimard, 1969, p. 80ff.

144 In the sense Michel Foucault spoke of, that is, that strategic choices 'do not arise directly from a vision of the world or a predominance of interests proper to this or that speaking subject' (*Archéologie du savoir*, p. 96) or to this or that social group. The possibility of these 'strategic' choices is determined by the points of divergence in the interplay of concepts.

145 See G. Gavazzi, *Topica Giuridica*, Novissimo Digesto Italiano, XIX, Turin, 1973, p. 409–17.

146 G. Zaccaria, *Ermeneutica e Giurisprudenza: Saggio sulla metodologia di Josef Esser*, Milan, Giuffrè, 1984, p. 47.

147 According to Josef Esser, what has been subsumed is not the facts but the declaration that characteristics present in the normative fact are fully realised in the 'real' fact. On this approach, Esser shows the decisive part played by the judge's assessment in evaluating circumstances of fact (J. Esser, *Precomprensione e scelta del metodo*, op. cit.). This is exactly what Barthes said about historical facts as being primarily signifiers. He, moreover, considered that for any conceptual syllogistic preparation, one should trust in a specific parameter of application, which could be constructed only through a 'reasonable' weighting of the legal *consequences* of application. For Esser, then, the centre of the applicative process of law is the judicial assessment of the outcome or the legal consequences

bound up with reference to particular legal facts, along with discription of the factual circumstances. See G. Zaccaria, *Ermeneutica e Giurisprudenza*, op. cit., p. 56ff. For this 'consequentialist' argument, see also N. MacCormick, 'Le raisonnement juridique', *Archives Philosophie du droit*, vol. 33, 1988, pp. 99–112.

148 Paul Ricoeur notes that '"having been" raises a problem precisely to the extent that is not observable, be it the having been of the event or the having been of testimony. The pastness of an observation in the past is not itself observable, but recallable. It is in order to solve this riddle that we have developed the notion of representation or standing–in ... (which in turn means reduction to the Same, recognition of difference, analogising assessment)', P. Ricoeur, *Temps et Récit*, op. cit., p. 228.

149 P. 54ff. above.

150 For the hypothesis of narrative in general, in addition to the authors already cited, see Hayden V. White, *History and Theory, Studies in the Philosophy of History*, 1975, 'Historicism, History and the Figurative Imagination', pp. 46–67; F. R. Ankersmit, 'Narrative Logic, A Semantic Analogy of the Historian's Language', Martins Nijhoff Publishers, 1983; Teun A. Van Dijk, *Poetics*, North-Holland Publishing Company, 1976, pp. 287–338; William Dray, *Philosophical Quarterly*, Edinburgh Scottish Academy Press, 1954, 'Explanatory Narrative in History, pp. 15–27; Livia Polanyi, *Journal of Pragmatics* 6, North-Holland Publishing Company, 1982, 'Linguistics and Social Constraints on Storytelling', pp. 509–24. For the legal narrative, see esp. R. West, *New York University Law Review*, Vol. 60, May 1985, No. 2, 'Jurisprudence as narrative: an aesthetic analysis of modern legal theory', p. 145–211.

151 M. de Certeau, op. cit., p. 100: 'A group can express what it has before it only by redistributing its past.' The bare movement of time is the expression of western Christian rationality (see our Part II).

152 P. Bourdieu, *La force du droit, Actes de la recherche en sciences sociales*, September, 1986. On this point, see also P. Ricoeur, *Temps et Récit*, op. cit.

153 M. de Certeau, op. cit., p. 104ff.

154 On this point see also P. Veyne, *Comment on écrit l'histoire*, op. cit.

155 M. de Certeau, op. cit., p. 112.

156 Dworkin's last work, *Law's Empire*, is an outstanding example of this.

157 The rationality of the 'body of laws' and the systematicity of the 'body of laws'.

158 We are here taking over the ideas put out by P. Veyne in *Comment on écrit l'histoire*, op. cit., p. 97.

159 P. Veyne, op. cit., p. 78.

160 P. Bourdieu, *La force du droit*, op. cit., p. 16.

161 G. Zaccaria, *Ermeneutica e Giurisprudenza*, op. cit., p. 169.

162 See e.g. A. Giuliani, *Le raisonnement par analogie*, Tenth Congress of Association of Comparative Law, p. 81ff.

163 F. Ewald, *L'Etat providence*, op. cit.

164 We are not, on the other hand, certain that we can see, as he does, this rule of judgement as a category peculiar to social law, which on

that basis engenders a new positivity.

165 Authors are divided on whether analogy is *analogia legis* (such as Bobbio) or on the contrary *analogia iuris* (such as Lazzaro). If one takes legal provisions to be 'codification of a legal thought' to be brought into systematic relation, one will speak of *analogia legis*. If on the contrary one claims to be able to formulate legal thought on the basis of the idea of a 'system superior' to the positive order, then one will speak of *analogia iuris*. Since personally we find it hard to see any very sharp delimitation in the interpretive act between the legislative aspect and the judicial aspect, this difference is of no real interest to us.

166 H. G. Gadamer, *Vérité et Méthode*, op. cit., p. 120.

167 N. Bobbio, op. cit., p. 10.

168 Ibid., p. 29.

169 Ibid., p. 35.

170 Ibid., p. 48.

171 Ibid., p. 52. Our emphasis.

172 Under the impetus of monarchy's action against feudalism, and in order to develop trade and commerce still further.

173 M. Foucault, *Les mots et les choses*, op. cit., preface, XIII.

174 Ibid., pp. 40–1.

175 Ibid.

176 Ibid., p. 71, referring to Leibniz.

177 Ibid., p. 158.

178 P. Nerhot, op. cit.

179 M. Foucault, *L'Archéologie du savoir*, op. cit., p. 170.

180 The 'unwritten law' (common law) which is traditionally defined as a custom coming down from time immemorial is to be understood as nothing other than this hermeneutic principle whereby 'the law' is worked out, is stated, at a given time.

Notes to Part II

1 G. Monod, 'Du progrès des études historiques en France depuis le XVIème siècle', *Revue historique*, 1976, p. 287ff.

2 B. Guénée, *Politique et Histoire au Moyen-Age, Recueils d'articles sur l'histoire politique et l'historiographie médiévale (1956–1981)*, Publications de la Sorbonne, Série réimpressions no 2, Paris 1981, p. 205.

3 Marc Bloch, *Apologie pour l'histoire ou Métier d'historien*, préface G. Duby, 7ème édition, Armand Colin, 1974.

4 G. Monod, op. cit., p. 297.

5 Ibid., p. 298.

6 'Representation of events,' 'recounting in original fashion.'

7 B. Guénée, op. cit., a work whose immense erudition we appreciate.

8 Ibid., p. 224.

9 Ibid., p. 275.

10 Ibid.

11 Ibid., p. 297.

12 Ibid., p. 218.

13 Blandine Barret-Kriegel, *Jean Mabillon*, Presses Universitaires de France, 1988; *La défaite de l'érudition*, Presses Universitaires de France, 1988.

14 B. Barret-Kriegel, op. cit., p. 10.

15 Ibid., p. 20.

16 'The original feature and the peculiarity of scholarship was to have been from the outset dispersed, created within disciplines with different goals; of having been involved in debates, disputes and controversies originally alien to each other' (B. Barret-Kriegel, op. cit., p. 20ff). And again, 'Philology ... is enigmatic ...', p. 24ff.

17 B. Barret-Kriegel, op. cit., pp. 76ff, 80ff, 90–130.

18 Op. cit., p. 17.

19 Op. cit., p. 38.

20 Op. cit., p. 179.

21 'More than pure historical contemplation of the past, what scholarly effort did was supply the weapons for the massive production and dissemination of a religious culture ... Before *historians* [our emphasis] worked for the State, rediscovering and affirming legal acts, they had worked for the Church, finding and establishing sacred documents' (B. Barret-Kriegel, op. cit., p. 75).

22 B. Barret-Kriegel, op. cit., p. 76.

23 B. Barret-Kriegel, op. cit., p. 81 (our emphasis).

24 Op. cit., pp. 84 and 99.
25 Op. cit., p. 129.
26 Op. cit., p. 130, 'Publication and legitimation, the two original, dated characteristics that put on the civil law of the French monarchy this stamp ... of the search for establishment.'
27 B. Barret-Kriegel, op. cit., p. 135.
28 B. Barret-Kriegel, op. cit., p. 137.
29 I wish to thank my translator, Ian Frazer, for this exact formulation.
30 B. Guénée, *Politique et histoire au Moyen-Age. Recueils d'articles sur l'histoire politique et historiographique médiévale (1956–1981)*, op. cit., p. 243ff.
31 B. Barret-Kriegel, op. cit., p. 127.
32 B. Barret-Kriegel, op. cit., p. 137.
33 Op. cit., p. 136.
34 B. Barret-Kriegel, op. cit., p. 18.
35 Ibid.
36 Op. cit., p. 24: 'Philology ... is enigmatic. It has been imagined by poets, rhetoricians, prose writers ... How did art move to science? ... Why is it supposed to involve ... erudition and archaeology, in a word, the knowledge of history?'
37 Peter Goodrich, *Reading the Law – A Critical Introduction to Legal Method and Techniques*, Basil Blackwell, 1986. This author is rather too sketchy in saying 'the law is promulgated in books and found in books and it is, we will suggest, of the essence of legal power to take a written form' (p. 21).
38 P. Brown, 'Society and Supernatural, A Medieval Change'. *Daedalus, Journal of the American Academy of Arts and Sciences*, 104 (1975), p. 134.
39 P. Brown, op. cit., p. 137.
40 P. Brown, op. cit., p. 136.
41 P. Brown, op. cit., p. 137.
42 P. Brown, op. cit., p. 138.
43 P. Brown, op. cit., p. 139.
44 P. Brown refused to see a new consensus, speaking of authority, essentially that of writing. This is still a semiology, but was to give rise to other types of interpretation, a different hermeneutic.
45 M. Bloch cited by M. D. Chenu, *La théologie au XIIème siècle*, preface by E. Gilson, Librairie philosophique Vrin, Paris, 1978, p. 224.
46 J. Le Goff, *Pour un autre Moyen-Age: Temps, travail et culture en Occident, Dix-huit essays*, NRF Gallimard, 1977, p. 10.
47 J. Le Goff, *La naissance du purgatoire*, NRF, Gallimard, 1981, p. 183.
48 P. Chaunu, *Le temps des réformes, 1: La crise de la Chrétienté, 1250–1550*. Ed. Complexe, 1984, p. 37.
49 J. Le Goff, *La naissance du purgatoire*, op. cit., p. 228.
50 See J. Le Goff, op. cit., in particular pp. 11 and 19.
51 Ibid.
52 J. Le Goff, op. cit., p. 287.
53 J. Le Goff, ibid.
54 J. Le Goff, op. cit., p. 289.
55 J. Le Goff, op. cit., p. 290.
56 It was under Louis VII that the primary truths of Christianity were rethought. Jacques Le Goff reminds us, moreover, that 'purgatory

was born in the springtime of scholasticism, at that time of exceptional creativity' (op. cit., p. 228).

57 M. D. Chenu, *La théologie au XIIème siècle*, preface by E. Gilson, Librairie philosophique Vrin, Paris, 1976, p. 322.

58 Andrew of Saint-Victor, cited by M. D. Chenu, *La théologie au XIIème siècle*, op cit., p. 29.

59 M. D. Chenu, op. cit., p. 33.

60 Ibid., our emphasis.

61 M. D. Chenu gives us the example of Honorius of Autun for the details of this confusion between the scientific explanation of the cosmos and its religious meaning; op. cit., p. 58.

62 Op. cit., p. 309.

63 And, we believe, one must abandon the psychologism suggested by Jacques Le Goff: 'in his pastoral zeal, Gregory understood two examples of the collective psychology of the faithful', op. cit., p. 128.

64 The good, the bad and the in-betweens, corresponding to Heaven, Hell and Purgatory. On all this, in particular the mechanisms of correspondence, see J. L Goff, op. cit., p. 299f. Note also the success of the term 'status', designating both socioeconomic condition here below and the spiritual-legal status of individuals.

65 J. Le Goff, op. cit., p. 308. Citing Euclid, Alexander of Hales, the Parisian university teacher (Gloss on Peter Lombard's *sententiae*, thirteenth century) said: 'Proportionality is the similitude of proportions', ibid.

66 Recall that for Saint Augustine the 'foundation' of religion is Scripture.

67 We shall return to this point later on the basis of a text by C. Ginsburg. Let us here note merely that the Benedictine tradition, which already translated theological thought into legal terms, was an incomparable advance here. Benedict in his Rule prescribed over four hours daily reading the Bible and the Fathers to his flock; the Benedictine order was to produce such exegetes as Christian of Stablo (after 880), Rabanus (born around 776), Rupert of Deutz (after 1129). See *Dom Philibert Schmitz*, 'Histoire de l'Ordre de Saint-Benoît', Editions de Maredsons, 1942, 4 vols. In particular vol. 2, pp. 50f.; 106f.

68 P. Chaunu, *Le temps des réformes, 1: La crise de la Chrétienté*, op. cit., p. 102.

69 Henri de Lubac, *Exégèse Médiévale, Les quatre sens de l'Ecriture*, Aubier-Montaigne, 1961, 4 vols, vol. 1, p. 25.

70 Henri de Lubac, op. cit., p. 43.

71 Scripture always remains first in everything: all knowledge finds its ultimate explanation there. By way of example, H. de Lubac, op. cit., III, 'Regina artium' esp. pp. 75, 77, 82.

72 In the course of the twelfth century, the 'questions', as we know, began to proliferate and take on the character of heightened scientific curiosity. In their search for the 'Vera Scriturarum scientia', these 'dialecticians' sought to invert the order of certain factors. See esp., H. de Lubac, op. cit., pp. 104–9. The conflict was to see the victory of 'dialectics' and its 'questions', under the influence of Aristotle's philosophy.

73 Jerome, 'Qui quantum in verbis simplex videtur et facilis, tantum in
    majestate sensorum profundissimus est', cited by H. de Lubac, op.
    cit., p. 120 note 4.
74 M. D. Chenu, *La théologie au XIIème siècle*, op. cit., p. 172.
75 This symbolism was to feed anagogy, as we shall see with Dionysius.
76 H. de Lubac, op. cit., p. 122.
77 John the Scot, in H. de Lubac, op. cit., p. 122.
78 Hugh of Saint-Victor, cited by H. de Lubac, op. cit., p. 124.
79 H. de Lubac, op. cit., p. 134.
80 For all these developments, see H. de Lubac, op. cit., p. 139f.
81 Remigius of Auxerre, Abelard, Rupert of Deutz, Peter Lombard ...;
    see H. de Lubac, op. cit., p. 145.
82 Peter of Poitiers, Peter of Celle ... and even Peter Lombard in the
    explanation of certain psalms: H. de Lubac, op. cit., p. 153.
83 Adam of Perseigne, cited by H. de Lubac, op. cit., p. 154.
84 Op. cit., p. 169.
85 According to whether the 'moral' meaning comes immediately after
    the letter or 'body' of Scripture or whether it extends and presup-
    poses the allegorical meaning, we have either a Christian doctrine or
    one that need not have anything specifically Christian. It is only if the
    'moral' meaning follows the allegorical meaning *on the basis of the
    same history* that a specifically Christian doctrine can be affirmed,
    since it is only after the enunciation of the mystery and in relation to
    it that the 'moral' meaning comes to the spiritual explanation. If the
    moral meaning precedes the allegorical meaning, we shall then be
    facing a doctrine where the speculation is all human, nothing but
    human.
86 Cassian, cited by H. de Lubac, op. cit., p. 190.
87 These two meanings are to each other as the Old to the New
    Testament; more exactly they are the Old and the New Testaments.
    The New Testament emerges from the Old; it changes its letter into
    spirit.
88 See below, p. 130f.
89 K. Barth, *Dogmatique*, French transl. I, 2, 1 (99), cited in H. de
    Lubac, p. 309.
90 Cicero, cited by H. de Lubac, op. cit., p. 373.
91 Here we again find the figure of reasoning by analogy.
92 H. de Lubac, op. cit., p. 377.
93 Th. Preiss, 'The mystery of the imitation of Christ and of unity in
    Ignatius of Antioch', RHPR, 1938, pp. 223–4, cited by H. de Lubac,
    op. cit., p. 398: 'However strange the exegesis practised by the first
    Christian generations may seem to us today, it nevertheless differs
    from that practised in Hellenistic circles in its *sense of history* [our
    emphasis] ... In a world thoroughly strange to history, this exegesis,
    though fantastical in detail, specifically defended this historical
    meaning in whose name we often today treat it, with some misunder-
    standing that perhaps does not do much honour to our sense of
    history, as similar to a type of mythical thought.'
94 H. de Lubac, op. cit., p. 397.
95 Saint Augustine, cited by H. de Lubac, p. 399.
96 Tripartite division: historiae, moralia, mystica. Quadripartite divi-
    sion: historiae, tropologia (= moralia), allegoria, anagogia.

97 We shall return to this point; let us say now that Tropologia was to take up the Christian tradition of *exempla*. A continuity in the act of stating the law was to come about through this Christian hermeneutic, since here too we find the principles of the letter and the spirit and the linearity of time that allow a meaning to be conferred on the present on the basis of the idea of a sure past that, like a trace, points to our own truth.

98 In this sense, H. de Lubac, op. cit., p. 413.

99 Op cit., p. 417.

100 Origen, cited by H. de Lubac, op. cit., p. 417.

101 Clement of Alexandria, cited by H. de Lubac, ibid.

102 Saint Gregory of Nyssa, Preface to his commentary on the Song of Songs, cited by H. de Lubac, op. cit., p. 419.

103 M. Foucault, *Les mots et les choses*, op. cit., p. 73.

104 See M. D. Chenu, *La théologie au XIIème siècle*, op. cit., p. 172.

105 See the examples given by Chenu on metaphors relating to numbers, op. cit., p. 161.

106 M. D. Chenu, op. cit., p. 166.

107 M. D. Chenu, op. cit., p. 167. The sensible forms are linked among themselves by the relationship of likeness that Foucault noted in *Les mots et les choses*, inscribed upon the surface of things like 'signatures'.

108 M. D. Chenu, op. cit., pp. 176–7.

109 Ibid.

110 M. D. Chenu, op. cit., p. 182.

111 Antonia Gransden, *Historical Writing in England, c. 550 to c. 1307*, Routledge and Kegan Paul, London 1974, p. 27.

112 In this meaning, M. D. Chenu, op. cit., p. 191.

113 M. D. Chenu, op. cit., p. 202.

114 Bede, a virtuoso of computation, who accorded a considerable place in his method to chronology, wrote some thirty-five works, twenty being comments on Scripture, six on computation and the measurement of time, two on hagiography and finally two on what is traditionally regarded as history, and we for our part would term juridical. See e.g. A. Gransden, op. cit., p. 25f.

115 'Sometimes the Old Testament is Christianised, sometimes the New Judaised' (M. D. Chenu, op. cit., p. 219). It is through this procedure that the 'past' continues to be present, and we understand at the same time that this memory of the past is to be not only a 'historical' memory but, as M. D. Chenu tells us, outside this successive development in time, an '*archetypal*' *memory*, typical of the Christian age. Typology and theology were to be the method for constructing these types; they flourished in the twelfth century and were undoubtedly not without influence on the 'lay' conception of the legal rule.

116 The 'History of the Abbots of Wearmouth and Jarrow' is a chronological presentation of the abbey's archives, that is, legal documents or writs. The monks took extreme care to conserve their archives, since these documents established their rights and privileges. See A. Gransden, op. cit., p. 34ff.

117 Again we find this philosophy of the sign, and geography is its most immediate result. The traces on the ground are so many signs

enabling knowledge of the characteristics of a specific place that
helps to *prove 'properties'*.

118 This is clearly already a philosophy of time – Bede wrote a *De
Temporibus* and a *De Temporum Ratione* ('On the Reckoning of
Time') – drawn, as we have seen, from the Scriptures as well as
from the sophisticated practices of calculation (the computus).

119 B. Guénée reminds us that during the second half of the ninth
century the monks of Saint Germain-des-Prés had available, as was
the case until the eleventh century, only hagiographical sources;
this in no way embarrassed them, he tells us, in writing their
chronicles.

120 Arnaldo Momigliano, (French translation) *Problèmes d'historiographie ancienne et moderne*, Gallimard 1983. Polybius was introduced
to Italy twice: in 167 BC and around 1415 AD, when his manuscripts were probably at the Badia Fiesolana at San Domenico di
Fiesole, an abbey of the Benedictines of Florence and today the
seat of the European University Institute. A. Momigliano, op. cit.,
p. 200.

121 A. Momigliano, op. cit., p. 25.

122 We know on the contrary that in some civilisations the written
accounts of events were inspired by the figurative arts; thus,
Oriental historiography drew its origin from paintings and narrative reliefs. Medieval historical accounts likewise evoke contemporary painting and are in close relationship with a philosophy of the
sign; these accounts are often illustrated by illuminations.

123 The three major elements in Herodotus's enquiry were ethnogra-
phy, the search for constitutional history and military history; see
Momigliano, op. cit., p. 18.

124 A. Momigliano, op. cit., p. 84: 'We know the Romans' keenness to
follow Greek models in recalling precedents'. We would be
tempted to say here that biography continues to supply examples of
lives, both positive and negative.

125 A. Momigliano, op. cit., p. 172.

126 A. Momigliano, op. cit., p. 174.

127 There is influence of e.g. Judaeo-Hellenic historiography on Christian historiography through Philo; A. Momigliano, op. cit., p. 140.

128 A. Momigliano, op. cit., p. 134.

129 A. Momigliano, op. cit., p. 159.

130 Clearly, we are thinking of archives.

131 Momigliano points to the considerable gap that existed between
the creators of scientific chronology in the third century BC
(Eratosthenes) and the Christian canons; here chronology formed
part of a history of the world established on the basis of the Bible.
A. Momigliano, op. cit., pp. 36, 139.

132 Archaeology, numismatics, the study of inscriptions etc. were
progressively to develop (fourteenth century) as *proofs of hidden
truths*; see below.

133 M. D. Chenu, 'Conscience de l'Histoire et Théologie au XIIème
siècle', *Archives d'histoire doctrinale et littéraire du Moyen-Age*, année
1954, p. 109.

134 'Historiae est rerum gestarum narratio', Isadore, who takes this
formula from Latin commentators on Virgil: 'Historiae est narratio

dei gestum per quam eaguae in praeterito facta sunt, dinoscuntur', cited by M. D. Chenu, 'Conscience de l'histoire et théologie au XIIème siècle', op. cit., p. 110.

135 For all these developments, see M. D. Chenu, *La théologie au XIIème siècle*, op. cit., p. 66.

136 Coming back to this point one last time, here is the whole difference between the theology put forward by Bede and that put forward by Hugh. With the former, the 'meanings' were suggested by forms, colours, etc. without there being any need for the least causal historical connection. With Hugh, on the contrary, all allegorisation had to have as its basis the historia, a rational earthly account.

137 Cited by B. Guénée, *Histoire et culture historique dans l'Occident Médiéval*, Aubier Coll. historique, 1980, p. 34.

138 B. Guénée, *Politique et Histoire au Moyen-Age*, op. cit., p. 229.

139 B. Guénée, op. cit., p. 233.

140 B. Guénée, op. cit., p. 234.

141 Whereas epic, for instance, was more or less indifferent to chronology.

142 G. Arnaldi, 'Il notaio-cronista e le cronache cittadine in Italia, La storia dei diritto nel quadro delle scienze storiche', *Atti del primo congresso internazionale della società italiana di storia del diritto*, Florence 1966, pp. 293–309.

143 B. Guénée, *Histoire et culture historique dans l'Occident Médiéval*, op. cit., p. 34.

144 The 'precedent' well reflects this idea expressed by the term 'custom', that something from the past which is true binds us. But what must equally well be seen is that this argumentative procedure is above all a hermeneutic principle that expresses a structure of our thought. What P. Goodrich identifies in the nineteenth century (P. Goodrich, op. cit., pp. 70–1) is not the principle of precedent but the contemporary interpretive technique of the idea of the precedent (once the ideas of system and of systematicity became established in the order of Western knowledge). *The idea of precedent, on whatever side of the Channel one may be, is intrinsic to our principle of law, to the structure of our knowledge applied in the search for law.* The ordeal ignored this form of thought, even though ordeal was the knowledge that led to law; the case was the law. We wish further to point out the confusion Goodrich makes between custom 'custom refers to established patterns or order-maintenance and dispute-settlement within a given social group', and ordeal. Once again, this means overlooking the fact that 'custom' is a hermeneutic key that gives rise to a written provision (which will, moreover, be reutilised by philology) and not a culture (the creation of a particular polis) that has been swallowed up. The common law, in any case, appears under Henry II, at that great epoch we have sought to identify, just when Roman law 'reappeared', and was to be so useful for its vocabulary and its categories. 'Common law' is the result of an 'administrative triumph', to use the words of S.F.C. Milsom (*Historical Foundations of the Common Law*, Butterworths, London, 1969, p. 1). It is further extremely interesting to read A. Fraunce, *Shepherd's Logike* (1585) and all his

disquisitions on 'memory'. In particular see P. Goodrich, *Languages of Law – From Logics of Memory to Nomadic Masks*, Weidenfeld and Nicolson, London, 1990; a structure of our thought, let us say, expressed through Goodrich's pen as he works on Fraunce, when he states that 'the path of the law is precisely memory ... The most relevant and practical science of law will be a theory of memory' (p. 35).

145 This type of argument should not be understood as the expression of a particular legal genre ('custom') but on the contrary as the general structure of legal statement of truth in premodern Western rationality, which is, moreover, valid for present-day argumentative legal discourse.

146 History and 'history with a small h' start from the same ingredients. History with a small h meets History with a capital H: they are both made up of human, earthly, causal things that anyone whatever is able to experience.

147 'Libris authenticis, id est auctoritate plenis', Remigius of Auxerre, cited by B. Guénée, *Histoire et culture historique dans l'Occident Médiéval*, op. cit., p. 133. 'Homo autenticus autorisabilis, id est autoritatis cui debet credi', Huguccio of Pisa, cited by B. Guénée, ibid.

148 See e.g. the exegetic method advocated by Giovanni Nanni in B. Guénée, op. cit., p. 139 (1) one must unreservedly follow those whose very function was to write authentic, approved accounts; (2) no-one may reject history and annals whose official version has been conserved in libraries and public archives; (3) historians ought not to follow 'hearsay' except where it is not in disagreement with official history. Here we are already in the stage of constitution of nation States.

149 If a false act cannot become true, an apocryphal text can become authentic and worthy of faith: it is enough for it to be approved by an authority.

150 A. Momigliano, *Problèmes d'historiographie ancienne et moderne*, op. cit., p. 84; above, pp. 143 and 148.

151 For Salutati, the *scientia rerum gestarum* (knowledge of the past) constituted an essential dimension in the education of men, since this knowledge enabled one to know how to behave as a citizen in relationship with others, in public life and in private life. In this sense, see Walter Ullman, *Medieval Foundations of Renaissance Humanism*, Paul Elek, London 1977, p. 161.

152 See W. Ullmann, op. cit.

153 The account remains essentially the narration of 'memorable' events.

154 See e.g. Philibert Schmitz, *Histoire de l'Ordre de Saint Benoît*, Editions de Maredsons, 1942, 4 vols.

155 'This is a state of affairs which you will find in many places in England: the evidence has been destroyed by the violence of enemies, so that only the names of saints remain and their modern miracles, if any, William of Malmesbury, *Gesta Pontificum*, in R. Southern, *Aspects of the European Tradition of Historical Writing: 4. The sense of the past*, Transactions of the Royal Historical Society, Presidential Address, read 24 November 1972, p. 248.

156 This is exactly what the writings of Abbot Walfstan (Worcester) or the account of Saint Cuthbert (Durham) or again William of Malmesbury indicate.

157 R. W. Southern, op. cit., p. 252.

158 For this list see R. W. Southern, op. cit., p. 254.

159 Let us note briefly here, since it is not the objective of our study to draw comparisons between two *a priori* different expressions, that this idea of hidden meaning, inherent in the record that writing is, is rendered perfectly by the articulation between common law and legislation in the legal culture of the English-speaking world. 'Legislation is seen as a restatement or correction of common law and, more generally, that legislation is always seen in the context of an established body of law' (P. Goodrich, op. cit., p. 53). Leaving aside the end of the quote, which expresses a historically dated interpretive principle, we can see that in order to be stated, the idea of law presupposes something which is not written but which nonetheless contains the mystery of meaning.

160 'The general conception of the Church as realisation of the announced kingdom was most affected by reference to the old covenant, since this old covenant is the first stage, the preparation and prefigurement simultaneously, of the new. The synagogue was the pattern of the church; accordingly, the Church transfigures the synagogue. Here too, the typology operates in such a way that the Church seeks in its "past" a conduct upon which to model its "present".' M. D. Chenu, *La théologie au XIIème siècle*, op. cit., p. 215.

161 'In telling of the first times, as of the last times, Otto of Freising or Vincent of Beauvais based themselves on biblical texts; to understand the prophetic accounts of the Old Testament and hence pierce the mystery of the future, methods developed in the twelfth century by biblical criticism were used' (B. Guénée, *Histoire et culture historique*, op. cit., p. 20). 'There is no difference in type between knowledge of the past and prophecy. It is only that for past events the date is assured, whereas for prophecy it is uncertain.'

162 Marc Bloch, *Apologie pour l'histoire ou métier d'historien*, A. Colin, 7th ed., 1974, p. 20.

163 O. Cullmann, *Temps et histoire dans le christianisme primitif*, 1947, p. 35, cited by J. Le Goff, *Pour un autre Moyen Age*, op. cit., p. 49. For the Greeks the cosmos is eternal, and at the beginning there is chaos: God is only a demiurge. With Christianity comes the affirmation of the creation of a world which will always be distinct from the God that created it. The creation is a beginning, a creation that supplements time as the dimension of the created by time in opposition to eternity. The Christian metaphysic thus demands history.

164 K. Lowith, *Meaning in History*, Chicago 1949, cited by M. D. Chenu, *La théologie au XIIème siècle*, op. cit., p. 64 (quotation translated from French).

165 This same realism was to set him against Abelard, for whom the unity of the faith requires the identity of its content down through the ages – tempora variata sunt non fides – on the basis of the Nominalists' position of the logical identity of propositions stating

actions differing in time. For Hugh this meant the voiding of history and hence failure to recognise the primary, literal (historia) meaning of Scripture. We know that scholasticism was to move away from sacred history and that Thomas was to reject Hugh's dualism. For all this, see M. D. Chenu, op. cit., p. 60f.

166 There are increasingly numerous local accounts from abbeys that turned into general histories.

167 J. Le Goff, *La naissance du Purgatoire*, op. cit., p. 389.

168 B. Guénée, *Histoire et culture historique*, op. cit., p. 21.

169 J. Le Goff, *La naissance du Purgatoire*, op. cit., p. 307.

170 M. Foucault, *Les mots et les choses*, NRF Gallimard 1966, pp. 40–59.

171 P. Goodrich, in the two works cited, remains faithful to this great epistemological 'break' that Foucault proposed: in his first work, 'Reading the Law', but also in his second, 'Languages of Law' (in particular pp. 56 and 66ff). For our part, we have preferred to speak of false break and false continuity. In the fascinating passage on the Eucharist (in particular pp. 60ff), we can see very well that this reconstruction of Goodrich's can be explained only if previously, as we have sought to do, one were able to speak about the theologico-juridical matrix as the fundamental structure of knowledge. What Goodrich seems to wish to highlight in the sixteenth century is more an autonomisation of the *judicial function* ('a distinctive jurisprudential literature now emanated virtually exclusively from the Inns of Court, and its explicit object of study was no longer a branch of some other discipline – of theology, rhetoric or poetics – but rather a discrete concern with a specifically English legal method ...', p. 68) than an epistemological break (again, p. 69: 'the common law became in their texts a unitary discourse, a professional "*ecriture*" ...') A very interesting passage, though, in illustrating this idea of false break and false continuity, is the one on 'the polemical context' (p. 71ff), where we see, in a movement (begun by Continental philological criticism) of distancing of lay power from religious power and domination over it, the affirmation of what seems to be a systematic opposition to Medieval exegesis, a new legal hermeneutics. This illustrates our thesis perfectly. And if it is hard to speak of an epistemological break, this is because the knowledge that institutes signs and orders them is still largely determined by this theologico-juridical episteme. Once again, Fraunce is an excellent jumping-off point for evaluating this shift – if rational argumentation shifts into the concept of memory, it was necessary for a certain conception of time to have been born beforehand in the very order of our knowledge.

172 M. Foucault, op. cit., pp. 53–4.

173 M. D. Chenu reminds us of the influence that Jewish science was able to have in determining a 'literal' meaning of the Bible, of the works done by rabbis on a linguistic and historical approach (tenth century) and of the profit drawn therefrom in the twelfth by the Christian schools. M. D. Chenu, op. cit.

174 B. Guénée, *Histoire et culture historique*, op. cit., p. 188ff.

175 M. Foucault, op. cit., p. 44.

176 M. D. Chenu, *La théologie au XIIème siècle*, op. cit., IV, 'Grammaire et théologie', pp. 90–130.

177 Here we are referring to what was known as the 'dispute over universals'.

178 M. D. Chenu, op. cit., p. 99, in particular on the influence of the work of Boethius and on scholastic logic.

179 M. Foucault, op. cit., p. 56.

180 On the Pauline origin of the Christian allegory, see H. de Lubac, *Exégèse médiévale*, op. cit., part I, vol. II, p. 374f.

181 H. de Lubac, *Exégèse médiévale*, op. cit., part I, vol. II, p. 397.

182 Origen, cited by H. de Lubac, op. cit., p. 417.

183 Gregory of Nyssa, Preface to his commentary on the Song of Songs, cited by H. de Lubac, op. cit. (footnote 101).

184 Here we again find the new system of proving records belonging to a remote past of which there may no longer be any eyewitnesses.

185 Raoul Glaber, cited by H. de Lubac, op. cit., p. 468.

186 H. de Lubac, op. cit., p. 498.

187 Cited by H. de Lubac, op. cit., p. 54.

188 H. de Lubac insists on Greek allegory. Certainly the distinction between an ordinary meaning, purely apparent or not going beyond the truth of appearance, and a deep meaning, the only truly real one, was familiar to the Greeks; but this distinction does not yet supply a general definition of allegory. 'The appearance (or the "lie") Greek mythology speaks of does not correspond to the 'letter' or 'history' of Christian exegesis; the 'truth' of the former does not, even from an entirely formal point of view, correspond to the truth of the second' (H. de Lubac, op. cit., p. 517). Far from constituting the even approximate analogue of the Greek pairs one might think of treating them as reassembling, the Christian pairs constitute more of an antithesis to them.

189 Radically different from say, the Greek relationship; cf. our p. 185ff. on the notions of witnesses, oral culture, knowledge and understanding of the present and the idea of change.

190 H. de Lubac, op. cit., p. 523.

191 H. de Lubac, op. cit., p. 527. 'To move from history to allegory is certainly always to move to spiritual understanding: but that also therefore means converting to the faith ... In the strongest sense of each word, there is, in the perception of the unity of the two Testaments, a "fides veritatis"', p. 536.

192 Let us note that the distinction of form and content is a very old one, appearing within this biblical exegesis too, and receiving, as from the twelfth century, its technical consecration. The text is in fact gone over at three levels of understanding: ad litteram (linguistic analysis), ad sensum (meaning of the words) and ad sententiam (sense of the passage), and in profane works the distinction is drawn between the superficies verborum and the intima sententiarum.

193 'In the early seventeenth century, the period rightly or wrongly called Baroque, thought ceases to move within the element of resemblance' (M. Foucault, *Les mots et les choses*, op. cit., p. 65). Beforehand, the author said: 'The status of discontinuities is in

general hard for history to establish. And certainly still more so for the history of thought' (op. cit., p. 64).

194 F. Dagognet, *Le catalogue de la vie, Etude méthodologique sur la taxinomie*, PUF, 1970.

195 F. Dagognet, op. cit., p. 19.

196 The expression of a very fine semiotics, for the character is easy to see, it is on the surface. But it is a relevant sign: that is, this primary observation must express an ontological truth that follows from the plant's very name. Here we again find the movement from allegory to historical record in the Christian hermeneutics of Scripture. The record is certainly there, visible to the naked eye, yet it is allegory alone that can make it speak, that is, allows us truly to see. The record is hidden by Scripture, yet visible; the 'character' of our plant, for its part, is *not visible, but not hidden*.

197 F. Dagognet, op. cit., p. 36.

198 Ibid.

199 'Linnaeus believed in the existence of a directly perceptible signature that would point out the family for us.'

200 Our emphasis.

201 F. Dagognet, op. cit., p. 42.

202 Ibid.

203 F. Dagognet, op. cit , p. 53.

204 'He was to bring botany closer less to the exact sciences [sciences de l'ordre] ... than to chemistry' (F. Dagognet, op. cit., p. 53).

205 F. Dagognet, op. cit., p. 53.

206 'Tractatus de legibus et consuetudinibus regni Anglie' (Ramelph Ganvill). J.-Ph. Genêt mentions the case of Bracton, who sought to arrange English law by recopying the plan of the Institutes: J.-Ph. Genêt, 'Droit et histoire en Angleterre: La préhistoire de la révolution historique', *Annales de Bretagne et des Pays de l'Ouest (Anjou-Maine-Touraine)*, vol. 87, 1970, no.1, p. 321. We would very briefly emphasis that the twelfth century was every bit as essential in England as on the Continent, where the theologico-juridical culture was equally dominant. S. F. C. Milsom (op. cit., p. 13) also notes that 'The courts Christian were the earliest in England which would have looked to us like courts of law rather than meetings'. The same author says a little further on (op. cit., p. 15): 'it is an important element of the background to the process by which justice came to be centralised that the men who did it, the men who guided the common law in its first and greatest formative period, were largely ecclesiastics having some canonist learning, capable of thinking of the law as an intellectual system, and having some of the details of a mature system in mind'. Similarly and just as fundamentally, equity, which came into being in this period, is the pure expression of this Christian legal culture.

207 See S. F. C. Milsom op. cit., pp. 33–4.

208 Cf. our chapter 13 on allegory.

209 The 'writ' may be defined as 'a royal order which authorised a court to hear a case and instructed a sheriff to secure the attendance of the defendant' (S. F. C. Milsom, op. cit., p. 22). In the twelfth century, it was still no more than a description of appeals

normally received, which was progressively to become structured as a way of stating the law, recognising it, and was then to be perceived as 'precedents' that it would be hard to add anything to or subtract anything from. In this sense see S. F. C. Milsom, op. cit., p. 25.

210 Cf. p. 168ff. on the notion of 'precedent', on palaeographical, archivistic, etc. knowledge, on truth and text in general. Be it in the area of archival research, heraldic interpretation, topography and genealogy or the rise of philology, to all of which we shall return, it is impossible to do without thought about the legal method and about proof. For a first indication of this, see J.-Ph. Genêt and the many examples of English lawyers he presents from the years 1500–1600.

211 Except, of course, for mentioning that this perception is not foreign to the continental lawyers' one, forged to define not some 'English law' but their own law, by opposition. We shall return to this point soon; this legal theorisation is certainly linked with the publicists' forging the legal tool of a strong central state (the concept of the law in the king's person and hence of systematics through a single code).

212 For a more detailed study, see S. F. C. Milsom, op. cit., pp. 27–37.

213 Cited by J.-Ph. Genêt, *Droit et histoire en Angleterre*, op. cit., p. 326.

214 Let us recall what Momigliano said on the notion of truth in connection with the invitation by Sozomenes to Theodosius II to remove or add whatever he wanted to the history he was offering him.

215 This can also be established on the basis of particular knowledge of what we call politics. In this connection, see J. C. Holt, *Magna Carta*, CUP, 1965, p. 13.

216 J.-Ph. Genêt, op. cit., p. 329.

217 And we shall then speak of the 'regulatory' dimension of the statute.

218 The knowledge that is the condition for stating our law.

219 These are all elements that can bring us to the idea of law that was emerging during this period in the West. 'The Law', once again, is not something given to us. Still less so for this period! S. F. C. Milsom shares this idea, even if our responses, or rather our methodologies, greatly diverge, when for instance he says: 'The rise of equity is intelligible only if we remember the medieval familiarity with earthly institutions of conscience, and the medieval belief in absolute right'. Just as I have battled with the last pro-position, in particular in its certainty, so I find the first one welcome. I would further recall in this connection what I had to say at length regarding Purgatory. It was a whole idea of law that was being born then, of which we have no doubt kept something today, let us say its Christian core; a thing we have great difficulty in reactivating in its more strictly legal conception – and in its technical extension: 'Nothing in the history of English institutions is so obscure as the rise of those courts which are usually regarded as having exercised the residuary powers of the king ...', Milsom tells us (op. cit., p. 76).

220 Just as we have no epistemology special to English law, we shall have none for history as practised by English historians; it is in fact part of this theologico-juridical knowledge characteristic of the Christian West.
221 M. Foucault, *Les mots et les choses*, 'Don Quichotte', NRF Gallimard 1966, p. 63.
222 Ibid.
223 Op. cit., p. 64.
224 Ibid.
225 Wyclif, cited by P. Chaunu, op. cit., p. 263. We cannot within the scope of this study go into the various councils held between the two fundamental ones of Constance and Trent.
226 See P. Chaunu, op. cit., p. 260.
227 We believe P. Chaunu is wrong to feel he can speak of him as a 'historian'.
228 On all these points see also P. Chaunu, op. cit., p. 260ff. All medieval ecclesiology posited the principle of delegated justice on the basis of the miracle of the unbaptised infant that died and was resuscitated by the Virgin Mary so that, through the sign conferred by God on the church (baptism), the child could enter paradise. In other words, only the 'delegated' temporal power of priests could allow access to paradise.
229 It is perhaps rather venturesome to locate this reversal in the sixteenth and seventeenth centuries, under the impact of the 'natural sciences'.
230 On these developments in particular see Lorenzo Valla, 'Umanesimo e teologia, Salvatore I Camporeale, Instituto nazionale di study del Rinascimento', presentation by Eugenio Garin, Florence 1972.
231 S. Camporeale, L. Valla, 'Umanesimo e teologia', op. cit., p. 85ff.
232 Ibid.
233 The written learned language, Latin, was to be the object of very special attention by Valla, who accused the philosophers and theologians of scholasticism of not knowing Latin grammar well. He proposed to rework a number of fundamental texts – including the Vulgate – and to attempt a translation of Scripture more in line with the Hebrew and Greek original. This would, in other words, mean coming back to a single 'authentic' text of the Revelation, to make all biblical exegesis refer to it, and accepting the 'tradition' only on its basis – nothing less.
234 On all this, see the analysis by S. Camporeale, op. cit., pp. 152–3. For Pierre Duhem, the Decretum of 7 March 1277 was the remotest date of entry to the modern world, since it denounced the metaphysical abstraction at which scholasticism had arrived in interpreting the Bible, in order to reaffirm the 'truth of faith'. For us this still falls short, if by 'truth of the faith' Duhem intended to allude to a 'literal meaning' and thus to the exegesis to which this meaning gave rise, bound up with 'allegorical meaning'. Pierre Duhem, *Etudes sur Léonard de Vinci, Paris 1906–1913*, Vol. II, p. 411ff, cited by P. Chaunu, op. cit., p. 99ff. Scholasticism was thus denounced by the theologians, but also by those who were later to be called philologists.

235 On all this, P. Chenu, op. cit., p. 101ff.
236 The influence of Boethius on the rational thought of our period, the twelfth century, can be found most clearly in the link posited between logic and grammar. See P. Chenu, op. cit., and E. Gilson, *La philosophie du Moyen-Age. Des origines patristiques à la fin du XIVème siècle*, 2nd ed., 1962, esp. p. 138ff.
237 Valla took particular interest in the notion of 'person', criticising the acceptance Boethius had taken of it.
238 See S. Camporeale, L. Valla, op. cit., p. 176.
239 He was to try this out particularly in his translations of Herodotus and Thucydides – used by Manetti in 1457 for his critical-historical philology applied to biblical exegesis, cf. S. Camporeale, op. cit., p. 16 – as well as, certainly, for reasons we have already mentioned connected with the concept of history. But he also made translations of Latin texts, doing comparative studies between the two languages, an essential dimension of what was to be called 'philology'.
240 By which he explained the misundertandings between the Eastern and Western churches.
241 Tropology was, as we have seen, the figurative aspect that persons, things and events ('res') took on, thereby distinguished from littera, that is, the 'voces' of the account. The problem lay in the link between them. It was considered that the holy book, radically different from human books, was meaningful for its 'voces', but also for its 'res', since these res were loaded with spiritual meaning. Thus allegory was progressively to dissolve the literal tissue of Scripture.
242 Biblical exegesis, by affirming the authority of mystery and expanding the importance of the allegorical meaning, aroused an enormous growth in metaphorical knowledge, ending with conceiving of etymology as an 'expositio'; explaining the name of a man or a place was already *revealing the nature* of that man or place, announcing their destiny (bringing us back to our Christian hermeneutics of the hidden meaning and of the future anticipated through a reading of certain records). To open up the names to the light, 'the search brought up eponyms, found derivations and in particular constructed expositions for which it felt it was raising itself well above the level of grammar' (B. Guénée, *Histoire et culture historique dans l'Occident médiéval*, op. cit., p. 191). L. Valla's protest consisted in *reducing etymological explanation to the level of grammar alone*, to limiting it to derivations (concepts of origin, chronology) and rejecting expositions.
243 S. Camporeale, L. Valla, *Umanesimo e teologia*, op. cit., p. 232.
244 We shall here allow ourselves a brief criticism of P. Goodrich's work *Reading the Law*, op. cit. In defining the written law, the common law, the author offers a vast historical fresco that is certainly too rapid and schematic but would take too much time and space to deal with in detail here; what we do wish to stress is his anachronistic interpretation of the history of legal culture. Take, for instance, the passages on exegesis, which are numerous and frequent, in particular on p. 92ff. In a few lines, we move from the history of the church to the rabbinical tradition, from the Church

Fathers to a quote from Umberto Eco on medieval exegesis, a bit as if the very idea of 'text' was everywhere the same. That is far from being the case; quite the contrary. We would even say that if all these social phenomena are posed as 'categories', this is precisely because they express very definite and very distinct cultural periods. 'Exegesis' is not a particular interpretation invented once and for all. It is not always, and uniquely, a 'literal' method (in this sense too, see Goodrich, p. 54ff). We have instead seen that medieval exegesis was something completely different. The author develops out of exegesis a theory that is conceivable only in our century, that is, this period that has seen so many cultural earthquakes, in particular, and this is not the least of them, the one in the status of grammar so well analysed by Michel Foucault in *Les mots et les choses*. Since he does not grasp this idea of a break in modes of knowledge, Goodrich offers us very disputable forms of continuity (see p. 99ff), where the idea of the Corpus and the Glossators is expressed in the same terms as the idea of the Code Napoleon which is, moreover, put side by side with the Law of the Twelve Tables. We dispute this notion. It falls into the trap of naive nominalism: we find the word 'code' more or less everywhere in history, so it is the same thing we have; it also presupposes something that is always there, 'the law'; and finally, it remains blind to the interpretive method, leading to this confession of helplessness: 'the development of the common law is a complex and distinctive legal tradition based upon a system of custom and precedent rather than upon a code' (p. 102). In other words, the common law is opposed to code and the code is opposed to common law. This is a false definition, and tells us nothing about the law.

245 Accordingly, for Valla, the problem, before translating the Vulgate, was to establish the text of the Latin and Greek versions as well as possible.

246 S. Camporeale, op. cit., p. 293.

247 Studies dealing with this problem are numerous. We would recall that Abelard was the first to use the term 'theologia'; he did so to designate the *coherent, rational exposition* that Christian dogmatics of Scripture was to be, an exposition bringing out the deep meaning of the Bible. Collections of sententiae grouped into chapters around theses were debated, as were commentaries. The Summa came from collections of Sentences (initially intended as abbreviations), systematic works presenting a rational organisation of theological knowledge. On all these developments, see esp. P. Chaunu, op. cit., p. 105ff.

248 S. Camporeale, op. cit., p. 302.

249 A. Momigliano noted that the work of philology essentially dealt between the fourteenth and nineteenth centuries with Greek and Latin works. A. Momigliano, *Secondo contributo della storia degli studi classici. L'eredità della filologia antica e il metodo storico*, Edizioni di storia e letteratura, Rome, 1960, p. 463.

250 As we have already said, it is often the Christian dimension of time that brings the causal consideration of the links between events.

The account of an abbey's history is the starting point for a general history constructed in the same way (e.g. the account by Ordericus Vitalis in 1143, restored to us by P. Chenu, op. cit., p. 72). The sense of continuity was secured: since there is a sequence without return (in contrast with myth in antiquity), this sequence unfolds to cover the stages that are to be the signs of the *progress* of time (the six days of Genesis become the ages of man; likewise, time ante legem, sub lege, sub gracia). This temporal Messianism of permanence of the past already meant impregnation of the future, in order to interpret the present.

251 Language was opened completely to historical and social analysis, which became *its sole foundation*, and at the same time a break was created between Scripture (biblical exegesis) and theological speculation. At the same time, we may say that Hugh of Saint-Victor's endeavour had completely failed.

252 The classifications of grammarians – nouns, verbs, adjectives or adverbs – directly expressed the subjective and objective reality; here Valla retained only 'substance', 'action', 'quality'.

253 Here we recall certain exegetes like Gregory of Nyssa, p. 174ff above, for whom words were only secondary, a 'sacrum', not 'arcanum', containing the truth of the world.

254 This becomes precedent.

255 Donald R. Kelley, *Foundations of Modern Historical Scholarship. Language, Law and History in the French Renaissance*, Columbia University Press, New York London, 1970, p. 33.

256 Donald R. Kelley, op. cit., p. 39.

257 The Treatise of Lorenzo Valla on the Donation of Constantine. Text and translation into English, Christopher B. Coleman, New Haven, Yale University Press, 1922.

258 We shall concentrate our remarks on Lorenzo Valla, which is not to suggest that he was the great absolutely original scholar of his epoch. Great scholar he certainly was, but he belonged to a very diversified movement of thought (grammatical literalism and legalism, coupled with a semiotics: 'philology'). For instance, the criticism of the donation of Constantine had already been done, we are told by Christopher Coleman, some seven years earlier using the philological method by Nicholas of Cues, 'De Concordia catholica' (C. Coleman, op. cit., p. 3).

259 The Treatise of Lorenzo Valla, op. cit., p. 4.

260 Imperial prerogatives and political control of Italy, head of the clergy and hierarchically superior to the other patriarchs, owner of property in the West, the order of the Roman clergy to be higher than all other orders, and so forth.

261 Op. cit., pp. 65–7.

262 Numismatics being explicitly invoked: 'such as a piece of gold, silver or something', pp. 69 and 71.

263 Valla was later to argue on the basis of Varro in order to heighten an argument found in two other minor and therefore less authentic authors: p. 149ff.

264 'two thousand passages in the Decretum which forbid the acceptance ...' (p. 75).

265 'The Acts of the blessed Sylvester, chief priest, though we know not the name of him who wrote it ...' (p. 77).

266 'We know [the donation] to be read by many of the orthodox of the city of Rome and in accordance with ancient usage the churches follow this example' (p. 77). The tradition can be what it likes, Valla might say, but can claim no more; nothing prevents tradition from using this argument subsequently, at any other time. The truth of the past always rests on proof by a witness, which helps to determine the truth of the testimony.

267 Let us once more recall that the perfect compilation was a dream that every scholar cherished. The compilation, far from being a faithful copy, offered an opening for creation, either by construction where the compiler did not like certain passages, or by extenuating certain aspects of the text reproduced by recalling 'incidents', that is 'facts' regarded as important and contemporary with the main story. B. Guénée, *Histoire et culture historique dans l'Occident Médiéval*, op. cit., p. 212. The compiler could also not be content with one main story, and put several together in parallel. In one chapter he could add various paragraphs, but also, within a paragraph, add sentences, and within a sentence, words of a different origin. Even compilation was an interpretation, a construction of meaning.

268 Chronology was of course also to be invoked; see p. 137.

269 Op. cit., p. 81.

270 'Possessions of landed estates is good usage, landed estates of possessions is not' (p. 99).

271 Any word must be related to its cultural content in order to establish its definition. Valla gives many examples (pp. 106–20), sometimes with particularly biting humour (see p. 115).

272 Op. cit., p. 161.

273 The legitimacy of modern States was established from a battle of archives where jurists were more than ever great warmakers, 'demi-Gods', to use the term so dear to Georges Huppert, *Les Bourgeois Gentilhommes*, University of Chicago Press, 1977.

274 We have already touched on this question in our first part. Let us note a very fine example of this still current rational construction given by Pontien Polman (of the order of friars minor, doctor of theology, professor of ecclesiastical history): 'in the study of the evolution of doctrines, one should start not at their origin but at the period when they reached their full development, in order thereafter to go back to their starting point' (Pontien Polman, *L'élément historique dans la controverse religieuse du XVIème siècle*, Gembloux 1932, p. XI.) Pontien Polman rejects the philological conception leading to sound knowledge in order to reaffirm tradition; which is what can retrodictively give true meaning to the original doctrine. It is thus always by a retrodictive movement that the 'true meaning' is secured, by philology and tradition are two retrodictive possibilities.

275 By the early sixteenth century, the division between 'humanists' and theologians was complete.

276 Pontien Polman, op. cit., p. 45.

277 This he himself calls 'historical method', though this is undesirable on grounds of clarity.

278 A philological principle recogising access to truth only through a representation of the origin.

279 The Swiss reformers were thus to renew the definition of 'testimony': (1) Gather testimony in every corner of the earth to make its display of conduct truly universal. (2) 'Guaranteed authenticity', suspicion towards the tradition. (3) Ruling out of works by the Fathers (only 'first-hand' works could teach us anything true). (4) 'Original usages', a concept that enabled Zwingli and Decolampade to denounce all 'deviations'. On this see esp. Pontien Polman, op. cit., p. 62.

280 We would nevertheless stress that Calvin wished to see the Bible as the *complete* expression of the word of God, a *systematic* legal *code*. We have not insisted on this point, certainly fundamental for Western knowledge, but it seems quite clear to us here that something that scholasticism had stressed has been left over from the theologico-juridical episteme.

281 Bullinger, quoted by Pontien Polman, op. cit., p. 99.

282 For instance, Luther was not a 'historian of the Church' but more a historian (of one absolutely has to use the term) of dogma. Two central ideas guide this history: the decadence of the Roman Church, but conservation, despite this decadence, of the truth.

283 For all this, see Pontien Polman, op. cit., p. 153 and the criticism of the distinction between higher and lower officials 'unknown at the origin'.

284 Cited by Pontien Polman, op. cit., p. 166. This position is perhaps more polemic than philological, but it is true that the proof of the falsity of the Donation of Constantine furnished by Valla weighed heavily in this debate.

285 So that the truth of the 'plot' was thus to be established by grammatical method.

286 In this connection, see Donald R. Kelley, *Foundations of Modern Historical Scholarship*, op. cit., p. 67.

287 M. Foucault, *Les mots et les choses*, op. cit., p. 61.

288 Le Roy, jurist, philologist, and specialist in ancient Greece, entitled his great work – which has been celebrated as the first great treatise of the history of civilisation – 'Vicissitude ou variété des choses de l'univers'.

289 In this connection see Donald R. Kelley, *Foundations of Modern Historical Scholarship*, op. cit., p. 95.

290 Donald R. Kelley, op. cit., p. 96.

291 Cited by Donald R. Kelley, op. cit., p. 90.

292 e.g. Zasius and his research on the 'origins of fiefs' using the philological method. See Donald R. Kelley, op. cit., p. 91.

293 On all this, see Donald R. Kelley, op. cit., p. 105ff.

294 La Popelinière is a good illustration: 'to know history is not to have a memory of human facts and events, but to know the motives and true occasions of these facts and occurrences'. *L'histoire des histoires*, with *L'idée de l'histoire accomplie*, vol. I, 1599, reissued Fayard, 1989.

295 A dividing line that it was the goal of exegesis to efface.
296 The term is important: we do not, for instance, say 'who recount'.
297 A memorandum from Bertin to Louis XVI, cited by B. Barret-Kriegel, *Jean Mabillon*, op. cit., p. 244, reads: 'The object and nature of this part of your administration must be explained to Your Majesty. History is a science which our kings, since Francis I, have always regarded as very interesting for their government and whose progress they felt they ought to advance. It is a science having to do with that of legislation, since it supplies the legislator with the facts that may instruct him and the materials that may assist him. The public law of a State is nothing other than the history of the constitution combined with the principles of natural law that God has given to all societies.'
298 Cited by Donald R. Kelley, op. cit., p. 116.
299 It is, by the way, extremely interesting to note that what is called 'common law' was able to forge its concepts in opposition to a dominant legal corpus (the legal tradition of the Church), and that, assuming that 'the word follows speech', an assumption that intends to reduce written legal documents to a secondary source, a legal hermeneutics was developed (on the basis of 'non-writing' as a key), which was to give a meaning, undoubtedly entirely lay, to the various legal provisions existing at the time: 'Inscribed time out of mind in the collective memory of the legal profession, customary law is sanctioned, protected, transmitted through the ages and finally delivered by a tradition of the unwritten word' (P. Goodrich, Languages of Law, op. cit., p. 87). The 'unwritten word' fulfils the same hermeneutic function as the 'feudal custom' invoked by the French Crown. This is certainly a renewal of philological criticism, but still within a hermeneutic of the hidden meaning, as it had been conceived by the theologico-juridical episteme.
300 Let us recall that it was at this period, the sixteenth and seventeenth centuries, that 'State archives' appeared.
301 Thereby taking up a Greek conception of historical research.
302 This is also the way the relationship between allegorical meaning and the literal meaning was posed, but here the account does not have a Christian orientation.
303 M. Foucault, *Les mots et les choses*, op. cit., p. 60.
304 M. Foucault, op. cit., p. 70.
305 B. Barret-Kriegel, op. cit., p. 167.
306 A. Momigliano, 'Contributo alla storia degli studi classici', *Ancient History and the Antiquarium*, Edizioni di storia e letteratura, Roma, 1955, p. 76.
307 This is a very old misunderstanding, which can be understood very well from the importance that legal knowledge had in constituting the premodern rationality of the Christian West. Petrarch, whom we may regard as one of the fathers of textual criticism, was already crossing swords with jurists whose science was furnishing nothing to the state of knowledge: Sesto Prete, *Observation on the History of Textual Criticism in the Medieval and Renaissance Periods*, St John's University Press, Minnesota, 1969, p. 19.

308 A. Momigliano, op. cit., p. 81. H. Griffet, 'Traité des différentes
     sortes de preuves qui servent à établir la vérité de l'histoire', 1769,
     F. Bianchini 'Le figure dei fatti – La Istoria universale provata con
     monumenti e figurata con simboli degli antichi', 1697 (note that
     Bianchini was an astronomer).

309 We know the history of Father Haudouin who, starting from a
     numismatic study, found contradictions between the coins and
     certain texts. To understand this contradiction, he put forward the
     idea that *all* the old texts (except, perhaps, for Cicero, Virgil, etc.)
     had been conceived by a 'gang of Italians' towards the end of the
     fourteenth century.

310 The school of Christian Thomas was specialised in the debate on
     the notion of 'fides historica'; see the bibliography in Momigliano,
     op. cit., p. 83. Consideration of the 'good faith' of sources
     remained the best way to give an account of the biblical truth.

311 It is from observation of non-literary records that historical
     knowledge was to be augmented by the discovery of pre-Roman
     Italy, in particular the Etruscan civilisation (by a Scotsman in the
     seventeenth century).

312 R. Simon, 'Histoire critique du texte du Nouveau Testament, où
     l'on établit la vérité des Actes sur lesquels la Religion chrétienne est
     fondée', 1678.

313 Jean Steinmann, *Richard Simon et les origines de l'exégèse biblique*,
     Editions d'aujourd'hui, Paris 1960. See also 'Essai sur Richard
     Simon et la critique biblique au XVIIème siècle', Slatkine
     Reprints, Geneva, 1970.

314 Simon was to show his complete mastery of legal science
     particularly in his 'Factum' to give victory to the cause of the Jews
     of Metz, and his 'Factum' against the Benedictine monks of Fécamp,
     near Dieppe, in favour of the Prince of Neubourg. Procedure,
     canon law, rhetoric and exempla, proof and precedents: everything
     is there. From his Factum of Fécamp, Benedictines were to
     conserve a ferocious hatred of him.

315 Here we again find all the principles put forward by Lorenzo Valla.
     Richard Simon was to contest the decision of the Council of Trent
     declaring Saint Jerome's translation, the Vulgate, 'authentic'. He
     said that this version could not be authentic, if *by the term one meant
     the first original* of the Holy Books. Our rhetorician pursued his
     critique to the limit in stating that all books whatever of the Old and
     New Testaments had to be denied this title, since we no longer
     have the original manuscripts. The philological argument was
     followed by the legal argument: Simon proposed to regard these
     texts as a good piece of procedure, that is, an act deserving to be
     taken as 'authentic' in a legal debate, in terms of the knowledge
     whereby one proves the truth of what one is putting forward.

316 The consistory of Charenton in 1676 had instructed a number of
     pastors to translate the Bible. Among these were our rhetorician,
     who presented a plan applying the techniques of philology but also
     displaying the knowledge available thanks to geography.

317 'Essai sur Richard Simon et la critique biblique au XVIIéme
     siécle', op. cit., p. 98.

318 'Essai sur Richard Simon', *op. cit.*, p. 122.
319 P. Bayle, *Pensées diverses sur la Cométe*, Réédition par la Sociéte des textes français modernes, Paris, Librairie Nizet, 1984, p. 33.
320 Bayle, specifies the Scriptural basis (Jeremiah, 10:2) which grounds the desacralisation of natural phenomena upon the divine word.
321 The – legal – exercise of rhetoric and argumentation in this is quite remarkable; moreover, the strategy developed by philological science is always present.
322 'If the issue were about a Council of State ... a battle ... the historian's testimony might be decisive, for it might be that historians had combed the archives and the most secret records and drawn the truth of the facts from the purest wellsprings. But when it comes to the influence of the heavenly bodies, our good historians have no longer the capacity to be authoritative, no degree of knowledge their author has gained in the study of nature' (P. Bayle, op. cit., p. 34).
323 'The earth is at the centre of the universe, and all weighty bodies have a natural inclination to approach that centre ... How do we know that the earth is at the centre of the universe? ... It must necessarily be agreed that there is in the universe a very considerable motion about a common something, whether it be around the earth as the philosophers of the university will have it, or around the sun as do the Copernican sectarians, or in part around the sun and in part the earth as the followers of Tycho Brahé do, is of little matter to me for the moment' (P. Bayle, op. cit., p. 46). As we shall soon see, it was judicious of him to leave the question open.
324 'We are right to reject the superstitions of ancient pagans [we appreciate Bayle's statement referring the Catholic tradition back to the paganism of antiquity!], who imagine that the flight of a bird presaged the winning or losing of a battle ... If eclipses were portents of evils to come, God must have given us them for signs, or by causing us to know that these evils depend on eclipses as their natural causes ... God has done neither the one thing nor the other, and consequently eclipses are not signs' (P. Bayle, op. cit., pp. 148–9).
325 For a conspectus of torture and Roman law on the one hand and sorcery and canon law on the other, see esp. H. R. Trevor-Roper, *De la Réforme aux Lumières*, French transl., NRF Gallimard, 1972, pp. 135ff, 145ff. (= *idem, Religion, the Reformation and Social Change*, Macmillan, 2nd ed., 1972, pp. 117ff., 130ff.).
326 Robert Mandrou, *Des humanistes aux hommes de sciences, XVIéme–XVIIéme siécles*, Seuil, p. 114.
327 Robert Mandrou, op. cit., p. 114.
328 Michel de Certeau, *L'absent de l'histoire*, Repéres, Maison Mame, 1973, p. 23, notes a distinction between Paris and the provinces, but for our purposes this distinction is unimportant.
329 M. de Certeau, op. cit., p. 26.
330 One touches a body, tastes the humours it secretes. On all this, see esp. M. Foucault, *Naissance de la clinique, Une archéologie du regard médical*, PUF, 1963.

331 See H. R. Trevor-Roper, op. cit., p. 134 (= 117).

332 Similarly, H. R. Trevor-Roper, op. cit., pp. 161–2 (= 145f.).

333 For Jean Bodin, not one person guilty of witchcraft in a million would be punished were the procedure made subject to the ordinary laws.

334 H. R. Trevor-Roper, op. cit., p. 163, tells us of examples such as lowering one's eyes during the accusation (indicating fear, hence guilt), physical traits like age (showing ugliness, hence a malefic presence).

335 By instituting a whole set of procedures, brought together in the treatises. Let us further note that the alchemists, different champions of natural magic, declared themselves against the witchhunts.

336 Ernst Cassirer, *The Philosophy of Enlightenment*, translated by Fritz C. A. Koellin and James P. Pettegrove, Princeton University Press, 1952, p. 6.

337 'The true method of physics can never consist in proceeding from any arbitrary *a priori* starting-point, from a hypothesis, and in completely developing the logical conclusions implicit in it ... ' (E. Cassirer, op. cit., p. 8).

338 Nicolaus Copernicus, cited by P. Duhem, *Essai sur la notion de théorie physique. De Platon à Galilée*, 1908. Introduction Paul Brouzeng, Librarie philosophique Vrin, 1990, pp. 12–13.

339 Alessandro Piccolomini, *Théories des Planètes*, cited by P. Duhem, op. cit., p. 97. We would also recall a number of passages we have cited from Bayle's 'Pensées diverses sur la Comète'.

340 P. Duhem op. cit., p. 105, indicates that Melanchthon, Luther's faithful disciple, rejected the hypothesis of Copernicus for reasons drawn from Holy Writ, and that these reasons were to be taken up again some twenty-four years later against Galileo.

341 See Tycho Brahé;s work on the 1577 comet, written in 1578 and published in 1588; P. Huhem, op. cit., p. 114.

342 Cited by P. Duhem, op. cit., p. 116. Our emphasis.

343 P. Duhem, op. cit., p. 137 notes that during Antiquity and the Middle Ages physics contained two parts so distinct from each other as to be opposite: 'the physics of celestial, imperishable things, and the physics of sublunary things, subject to generation and corruption'.

344 Kepler, *Mysterium cosmographicum*, cited by P. Duhem, op. cit., p. 120: 'we must take care to say nothing that might be contrary to Holy Write'.

345 A reference to Hipparchus's theorem that 'allows the movement of the sun to be represented indifferently either by an excentric or by an epicycle rotating round a circle concentric with the Earth'. Cited by P. Duhem, op. cit., p. 123.

346 'Astronomy is a part of physics ... Astronomers should not be given absolute licence to feign anything whatsoever ... You must be able to give likely reasons for the hypotheses you claim to be the true causes of appearances. You must,therefore, seek the foundations of your astronomy in a higher science, that is, in physics or in metaphysics ...' in P. Duhem, op. cit., p. 124.

347 P. Duhem, op. cit., p. 126.

348 Letter to Foscarini. 12 April 1615, cited by P. Duhem, op. cit., p. 128.

349 Domenico Berti, *Copernico e le vicende del sistema copernicano in Italia nella seconda metà del secolo XVI e nella prima del secolo XVII*, Roma 1876, cited by P. Duhem, op. cit., p. 131. The holders of the 'course of error' must be seen as those who use the conquests of the philological method, and those of the 'course of truth' as the users of the heritage of medieval exegesis and theology.

350 P. Duhem, op. cit., p. 132.

351 'At the very time of Galileo, could not all observations that could be induced in favour of the Copernican system equally well be saved by Tycho Brahé's?', P. Duhem, op. cit., p. 133.

352 P. Duhem, op. cit., p. 143. As we have seen, this is the question of different premises that nevertheless lead to identical conclusions.

353 Ibid., our emphasis.

354 P. Duhem, op. cit., p. 139.

355 Ibid.

356 P. Duhem, op. cit., p. 140.

357 E. Cassirer, op. cit., p. 10.

358 The truth of nature has no longer to do with 'the creation' but with our capacity to decipher – rationally – the process of creation (concept of experience).

359 On this, see E. Cassirer, op. cit., p. 50ff; likewise, for the position of the Encyclopedists in general and d'Alembert in particular, p. 56ff.

360 E. Cassirer, op. cit., p. 55.

361 Even if by definition the very idea of mystery in Descartes has no longer much to do with this meaning.

362 E. Cassirer, op. cit., p. 66.

363 E. Cassirer, op. cit., p. 61.

364 Jurists will recognise this type of argumentation, where analogy comes to be an ordering principle (see Part I). A movement in time came about, seeing the past as setting up conclusions valid for the future and presupposing a uniformity of social experience.

365 But he should not, as he has done, ask jurists for more than they can give (we refer to the concluding part of his work), for the reason we have often pointed to: legal reasoning is the form of reasoning that seeks to *prove*. This means that something must be put forward, beforehand. A legal epistemology and hermeneutics are essential as *permitting the induction of certain forms of knowledge,* in part our own episteme on the basis of which we think, and recognise the truth of things; they retranslate and re-express in part our world order. This is what must be sought through legal knowledge, and this alone (but certainly nothing less).

366 Like Newton, he sought to reduce the multiplicity of laws to a few definite principles.

367 And this subsequently leads to a feeling of doubt vis-à-vis legal proof.

Notes to Conclusion

1 C. Ginzburg, 'Signes, traces, pistes', *Le débat,* novembre 1980, no 6, pp. 3–44.
2 C. Ginzburg, op. cit., p. 13.
3 Ibid.
4 c. Ginzburg, op. cit., p. 19.
5 'In this sense, the historian may be compared to the physician using monographic tables to analyse the specific illness of an individual patient' (C. Ginzburg, op. cit., p. 19).
6 C. Ginzburg, op. cit., p. 20.
7 Op. cit., p. 19.
8 Ginzburgh's system of hypotheses; it may seem contradictory to find discourse among this category.
9 C. Ginzburgh, op. cit., p. 20. Our emphasis.
10 C. Ginzburgh, op. cit., p. 27.
11 Ibid.
12 Ibid. There follows an analysis of Mancini contemplating the anatomy of a two-headed calf, 'with the attention he customarily paid to considering paintings', yet in order to derive from it not scientific knowledge of the individual but the *'common properties of the species'* calf.
13 C. Ginsburgh, op. cit., p. 34.
14 C. Ginsburgh, op. cit., p. 35.
15 See, for instance, E. Dardel, *L'Histoire, science du concret,* PUF, 1946, p. 31ff.
16 This is just why Galileo can be called a philologist.
17 M. D. Chenu, op. cit., p. 362ff.
18 'Morelli's books have unaccustomed features when compared with those of other art historians. They are sprinkled with illustrations of fingers and ears that constitute a scrupulous summary of those characteristic details that reflect the presence of a given artist, in the same way as a criminal betrays himself by his fingerprints. As soon as Morelli embarks on the study of an art gallery, it takes on the semblance of a museum of crime', (op. cit., p. 7).
19 C. Ginsburgh, op. cit., p. 7.
20 Op. cit., p. 18.
21 Op. cit. p. 10. Our emphasis.
22 H. I. Marrou, *De la connaissance historique,* Seuil, 1976, p. 79.
23 This is how one may understand those 'retrospective prophecies'

that can be produced by history, archaeology, geology, physical astronomy or palaeontology, that is, all those types of rational knowledge that have emerged from our theologico-juridical episteme.

24 A. Pizzorno, *Spiegazione come reidentificazione*, Rassegna italiana di sociologia, 1989, no 2, p. 184.

25 We have in mind the passage we cited on the 'ramified, qualitative' control exercised by the State over society on the basis of the specific concept of the individual.

26 See e.g. P. Nerhot (gen. ed.), *Law, Interpretation and Reality: Essays in Epistemology, Hermeneutics and Jurisprudence*: 'The Law and its Reality', p. 50ff.; 'Interpretation in legal Science', p. 139ff., Kluwer Academic Publishers, Dordrecht/Boston/London, 1990.

27 Putting forward a psychological intention, for instance 'the legislator's intention' amounts to asserting that there is only one *true signified.*

28 A. Pizzorno, op. cit., p. 177.

29 A. Pizzorno, op. cit., p. 178. It is indeed certain here that the theories on which one reifies are different from those present in institutions, which should on our view be considered in the way we consider a text.

30 H. I. Marrou, op. cit., p. 142.

31 B. Croce, *La storia come pensiero e come azione*, Ed. Laterza, 1978, p. 53.

32 *Faire de l'histoire-Nouveau problèmes*. Sous la direction de J. Le Goff, P. Nora, NRF Gallimard, 1974: F. Furet, 'Le quantitatif en histoire', p. 43ff.

33 F. Furet, op. cit., p. 43.

34 F. Furet, op. cit., p. 44.

35 This constitutes the first strong hypothesis of every constructivist approach.

36 F. Furet, op. cit., p. 46; this proclaims the second strong hypothesis of a constructivist approach.

37 Let us bear in mind the allusion to economists made by Furet himself here.

38 Op. cit., p. 48.

39 *Faire de l'histoire*, op. cit. : M. de Certeau, *L'opération historique*, p. 3ff.

40 M. de Certeau, op. cit., p. 23. Our emphasis.

41 Ibid. Our emphasis.

42 M. de Certeeau, op. cit., p. 23.

43 M. de Certeau, op. cit., p. 25.

44 Ibid.

45 M. de Certeau, op. cit., p. 26.

46 M. de Certeau, op. cit., p. 27.

47 Op. cit., p. 31; M. Serres, in his way, shares this position in noting that 'linear progress, or the classic series, once shaped the genealogy of the sciences ... they are today breaking apart ... everything is happening as if the main thing were an epistemology of the ultrastructure or its interstructures: edges, joints, membranes, connections, surroundings, regulations ...', in *Faire de l'histoire, Nouvelles*

approches, op. cit.: M. Serres, 'Les Sciences': p. 293.

48 Let us, for instance, recall R. Simon's ideas: 'and do not slumber while you are at this work [translating the Bible], for if you are not extremely vigilant, you will assuredly overlook many little parts without noticing. History does not ignore the slightest detail', (R. Simon, op. cit., p. 258).

49 M. de Certeau, op. cit., p. 32.

50 M. Serres, says in this connection: 'the possibility conditions of historical knowledge are no different from those of physical knowledge. Not in the subject, but in the object itself. The point in both cases is solid bodies bearing information in writing'. (M. Serres, op. cit., p. 294).

51 On this point, see esp. *La Naissance du texte, ensemble réuni par Louis Hay,* José Corti, 1989: B. Cerquignoli, 'Variantes d'auteur et variance de copiste', p. 105ff; E. Hicks, 'De l'individuel et du collectif dans les manuscrits', p. 122ff: he rediscovers what C. Ginzburg pointed to in connection with the interpretation of works of art in Morelli, namely that the subject of a *text* is identified on the basis of signs that escape the subject's senses and will ('insignificant details'); H. R. Jauss, 'Réception et production, le mythe des frères ennemis', p. 164ff.

52 H. Gadamer has shown as R. Palmer stresses, that the redefinitions of the truth of man, of being, of language, of history, consisted in a redefinition of the whole of the interpretive context, of what we have called the interpreting community. From this angle, philosophical hermeneutics is 'a set of critical thoughts on the phenomenon constituted by the act of understanding' (R. Palmer, 'Allegorical, philological and philosophical hermeneutics. Three modes of a complex heritage', pp. 15–37, in *Contemporary Literary Hermeneutics and Interpretation of Classical Texts,* Ottawa University Press, Ottawa, 1981).

53 P. Ricoeur, 'with writing, the verbal meaning of the text no longer coincides with the mental meaning or intention of the text', in 'Allegorical, philological and philosophical hermeneutics', op. cit., p. 41.

54 Ibid. Our emphasis. The author is certainly right to target the object of his criticism in these terms. Lawyers, by way of example, say in fact when confronting a question they have to solve through a legal provision: 'what does the law *tell* us?'

55 In so doing, moving away from the definitions given by P. Ricoeur of the terms 'explain' and 'understand'. 'Explain' is held to find its paradigmatic field in the natural sciences (P. Ricoeur, op. cit., p. 31) and 'understand', by contrast, in the human sciences. This dichotomy is simultaneously epistemological and ontological (according to Ricoeur we have two methods and two spheres of reality, nature and spirit, completely differentiated).

56 *Exégèse et Herméneutique, Ouvrage collectif,* Ed. du Seuil, 1978: P. Ricoeur, 'Du conflit à la convergence des méthodes en exégèse biblique', p. 292.

Index

Note: 'n.' after a page reference denotes the number of a note on that page.